GERALD & SHEILA
GOLDBERG
OF CORK

A Son's Perspective

David Goldberg

Published by Oak Tree Press, Cork T12 XY2N, Ireland.
www.oaktreepress.com / www.SuccessStore.com

Cover photo: John Goldberg.

Cover design: Kieran O'Connor Design.

A catalogue record for this book is available from the British Library.

ISBN 978-1-78119-594-9 Paperback
ISBN 978-1-78119-595-6 PDF
ISBN 978-1-78119-596-3 ePub
ISBN 978-1-78119-597-0 Kindle

This book was funded by Cork City Council through the Cork City Heritage and Biodiversity Publication Grant Scheme and is an action of the Cork City Heritage and Biodiversity Plan.

DEDICATION

Gerald and Sheila

זיכרונה צדיקים לברכה

Zichronam Tzaddikim Liv'racha

May all that was good in their lives endure always as a
blessing and as a continual influence for good.

CONTENTS

THANK YOU

This book could not have been written without the assistance of many people, and a few in particular.

My thanks to Prof. Barbara Abrahms (Boston), Edwin Alkin (Irish Jewish Museum), Frank Baily (ABODE), Claire Brazil (ABODE), Sue Burgess (Cuckfield Museum), Theresa Campagno (Lavanagh), Peggy Cashman, Rachel Churchill, Ita Daly, John and Jean Dillon (Tuairim), Prof. Hasia Diner (New York University), John S. Doyle, Fr. Sean Enright CSSR (Limerick), Nataly Eremina (Moscow), Dr. Nick Evans (Hull University), Gerilyn Fadden (Co-Operation Ireland), Dr. John Fitzgerald (University College Cork (UCC)), Prof. Michael Fitzgerald (TCD), Ruth, Anne and Maeve Fleischmann, Peter Fleming, Richard Forrest (Cork City Library), Barry Galvin, Rev. Dr. Norman Gamble, Sean W. Gannon, Peter Garry, William Geoghegan, Rabbi Alex Goldberg, Nancy Goldberg, Theo and Val Goldberg, Trudi Goldberg, Rabbi Andrew Goldstein, H.E. Marijus Gudynas (Lithuanian Ambassador to Ireland), Martin A. Harvey, Robin Hayes (Solicitor), Sylvia and Tom Hogan, Tess Hogan (Soroptimists), George Hook, Sandy Hotz, Michael Houlihan (former President, Law Society of Ireland), Indre Joffyte (Lithuania), Mortimer Kelliher, Dermot P. Kelly S.C., Rabbi David Kudan, Mary Leland, Conor Lenihan, David Lenten, Robert Lentin, Ronit Lentin, Debbie Levy, Harriet Long, John Martin (Irish Newspaper Archives), Don McCarthy B.L., Brian McGee (Cork City & County Archives Service), Helen McGonagle, Barbro McCutcheon, Angela Moore, Brendan Moriarty (Solicitor), Alan Navratil, Paula Newman, Jim and Anne Noonan, Ieva Nurimen (Lithuanian Embassy), David O'Brien (Limerick Civic Trust), Dr. Seamus Ó Catháin, Timothy O'Connor (UCC), Crónán Ó Doibhlin (UCC), Dermot O'Mahony, Dr. John O'Mahony S.C., Michael O'Mahony (former President, Law Society of Ireland), Mairead O'Sullivan (Librarian, Law Society of Ireland), Larry Poland, Matthew Potter (Limerick Museum), Stuart Rosenblatt, Mike Solomons, Yannay Spritzer, Anthony Twomey (Presentation Brothers College), Emer Twomey (UCC), Niamh Twomey (Cork City Council), Suzi Usiskin, Inga Vismantienė (Lithuania), and Dr. Natalie Wynn. Of course, my thanks to Brian O'Kane at Oak Tree Press for his careful final edits, and his patience and willingness to understand the problems I was trying resolve. And a special thanks to the Library at UCC for so much patience and assistance.

When I set out to write this book my first call was to Canada, to my cousin Paula Chabanais. Paula is the daughter of Sheila's brother Sidney. I asked her if she would come with me on this journey and edit the book.

There was no hesitation, and she has been with me all through. I could not have done it without all her gentle coaxing in this direction and that, keeping my writing tight and stopping me from careering off at mad tangents.

Gerald and Sheila at home on their 50th wedding anniversary,
August 8, 1987. (Photo: John Goldberg)

Thank you too, Paula, for the wonderful passage you wrote about Sheila. I know how much she and Gerald meant to you, and you to them. It has been as much a journey about love, as well as discovery.

I had to investigate the story of Limerick. It occupies one third of the manuscript and is quite an intense interlude but, because it formed so much of who and what Gerald was, I could not omit it. I have kept it as short as I can. But I found the whole story from Laban's leaving Lithuania to my visit to Colooney Street the most fascinating part of the book. It would not have been possible to write it without the enormously generous assistance given to me by Des Ryan, historian of Jewish Limerick. All of my visits to Limerick, to Colooney Street and the cemetery at Kilmurry, were guided by Des. My deepest thanks for so much kindness and for the friendship that has developed during the writing.

Lastly, to my dearest wife, Carla, who helped in so many ways. She read the manuscript many times, corrected my errors in grammar and spelling, and made so many useful suggestions which improved the book.

FAMILY TREES

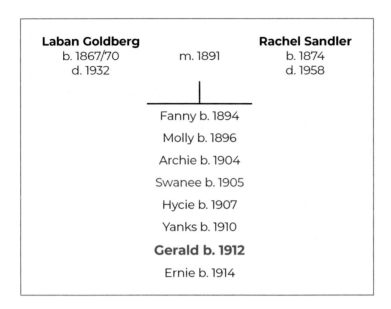

Laban Goldberg
b. 1867/70
d. 1932

m. 1891

Rachel Sandler
b. 1874
d. 1958

Fanny b. 1894

Molly b. 1896

Archie b. 1904

Swanee b. 1905

Hycie b. 1907

Yanks b. 1910

Gerald b. 1912

Ernie b. 1914

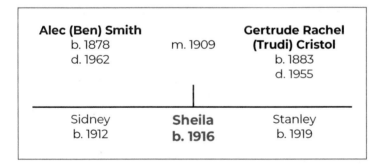

Alec (Ben) Smith
b. 1878
d. 1962

m. 1909

**Gertrude Rachel
(Trudi) Cristol**
b. 1883
d. 1955

Sidney
b. 1912

**Sheila
b. 1916**

Stanley
b. 1919

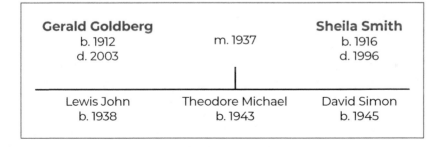

Gerald Goldberg
b. 1912
d. 2003

m. 1937

Sheila Smith
b. 1916
d. 1996

Lewis John
b. 1938

Theodore Michael
b. 1943

David Simon
b. 1945

PREFACE

In the late summer of 2020, I took part in a video about Jewish Cork, and also a Zoom meeting with people who came from Cork and are now dispersed all around the world. While my contributions were minor, the recollections this triggered of my father, Gerald, and my mother, Sheila, were overwhelming. I soon found myself surrounded by a trunk full of memories spread all around the floor of my living room. What was I going to do with them? My first impulse was to try to repack them, but they wouldn't fit. You know how hard it is to repack a suitcase? Then I discovered more memories that were not in the trunk. What could I – should I – do with them all?

They were my parents. I set out to record their public lives, to tell their story, neither as a eulogy nor as a detraction. Gerald and Sheila were important people in Cork, not only because they were the first Jewish Lord Mayor and Lady Mayoress, but because of the significant contributions they made to the city's cultural life over 40 years and more and how much the city and its people meant to them. I spent many months researching print and mixed media, archives, papers donated to University College Cork, and had numerous phone and Zoom calls with people in several countries who knew and remembered my parents. Gradually, information accumulated surrounding my father; information on Sheila was harder to find even though, it could be argued, her impact on the city, and its various cultural programs, was greater. Not only do all the projects she started continue today, but most are likely to continue long into the future.

Gerald and Sheila were two very different people who were married for nearly 60 years in a close, loving relationship, and who, at times, worked together but, at others, independently. My mission was to discover who they really were and what made them tick – and, perhaps, in the process, to discover something more about myself. Talking and writing about them demanded that I examine my own feelings; that has been the hardest part.

Gerald was a tall man, difficult and enigmatic, rather clumsy and unsteady on his feet, who buried himself in books and music. An Orthodox Jew, Gerald went through phases of being very religious and slightly less so, particularly as he got older. He prayed in the mornings, and sometimes, though not always, attended a Saturday morning service. He did insist that his three sons – John, Theo and I – went to services and that all High Holidays were observed. He could be tender, kind and generous but, conversely, he could be remote and cold. As children, we never knew in the morning which Gerald was coming downstairs and going into the office. Yet I looked for his heart and core all my life: we all did, I and my brothers,

John and Theo. But for so much of the time, he was not emotionally accessible. Whenever I tried to get through to him with an idea or an alternative, the suggestion was rejected. Equally, when he needed help, he would reject offers, regardless of his need. These feelings and reactions about Gerald are not only mine; I believe my brothers had similar experiences. Indeed, John and Gerald did not get along, and attempts to bring John into Gerald's legal practice were unsuccessful. Thank goodness for my mother, who was almost his complete opposite.

During the process of writing, I became interested in why Gerald was so detached despite, or because of, his brilliant mind. Why was he so brilliant, and also so difficult? I researched his whole career and family tree going back, as you will see, to his father, Louis (known as Laban, his Hebrew name), who came from Lithuania to Limerick about 1882-1883. Tracing Gerald through the life of his father took me into the whole realm of the dark period of immigration from Lithuania: the voyage to Ireland (**Chapter 3**), and the stories which Gerald told over and over again about the serious rows Laban had in the small community in Limerick (**Chapter 4**), and then the terrible events of the Limerick Pogrom in 1904 (**Chapter 5**).

There followed three more acts to this "Limerick" drama. In 1956, Gerald represented two Jehovah Witnesses in a case in Limerick (**Chapter 6**). In 1970, the Pogrom was inflamed again after an RTÉ documentary, as a result of which Gerald addressed a meeting of Tuairim in Limerick (**Chapter 7**). The final act was when the then Mayor of Limerick, Steve Coughlan, opened the Credit Union League Conference in 1975 (**Chapter 8**).

Jews have been telling stories about Lithuania for more than a century. After reading many papers on migration, I understand these do not always accord with what historians have revealed. Gerald considered everything that happened to his father in Limerick to be persecutory. When he took on cases and issues, I think Gerald treated all of them as projections on to his familial past. This is why there was such a fire in his head. It burned all his life and detonated from time to time when these issues were raised. Yet, he was never there, and the stories he told about Laban belong to what can be termed "cultural memory," rather than historical memory.   Sometimes, parts of a family history become embedded in the mind of a child who was neither present nor part of that history, yet they cannot get it out of their head; it lights a fire they cannot extinguish. In such fashion, I believe these events influenced and helped to shape Gerald's character. In addition, a persistent question arose: is there an autism disorder in the DNA of the family? Could this explain why Gerald was, at times, so closed and so brilliant?

Sheila Gerald on their 50th wedding anniversary.
(Photo: Goldberg Special Archive, UCC)

Trying to describe Gerald without including Sheila would give an incomplete picture. They grew together for more than 60 years; facing all the joys and tribulations that such a lengthy marriage brings: a remarkable relationship in every sense. Sheila was gracious, warm, loving, generous and dignified. She was practical, sensible, direct, had a remarkable sense of humor, incredible organizational skills, and as if this were not enough, she was an amazing cook.

Sheila did her best to keep Gerald on the straight path. She stopped him, if she could, from flights of fancy: no easy task. But she understood him, loved and cared for him. For her, he always came first. She was most supportive when he was depressed or rejected in some of his endeavors. She was always there for him, and for everyone else too. She was a woman with arms as long as love. Of the two, she was the one with her feet more firmly anchored. She was the real genius of the family. She inherited from her mother a great sense of the importance of family, of the warmth in love, and belonging. She cared for everyone.

She could handle Gerald well, and when he was being obdurate, remote or hard to live with she knew when and how to intervene. When Gerald went off after dinner, to read and listen to music alone, Sheila would detain me in the kitchen to have some fun which she called "craic." Her humor was great. I do not know anyone who did not love her. She was simply the best.

One final thought before I introduce them. Gerald had been accused many times of having a chip on his shoulder. His intellect could not respond until some years later he found a riposte by Bertolt Brecht who said: "I wear a brick on my shoulder to show the kind of house I come from." Gerald said his brick was painted in two colors, "blue and white because I am a Jew; and green and gold because I am an Irishman."

Gerald always asserted and defended his Jewishness and Irishness. He might have projected himself as Liberty leading the People, carrying two flags. This exposes the dichotomy he straddled all his life, navigating difference. I think it was difficult for Corkonians to understand him. He always wanted to be part of them, while at the same time remaining on the outside to maintain his identity. They respected and admired him as a lawyer; they accepted his generosity to the city, but also accepted how difficult he was to work with.

Gerald comes across as dominant, yet Sheila will also be heard in a much quieter and gentler voice.

This is the story of their lives, work and achievements as best I can tell it. It was a voyage of discovery, a tumultuous and fascinating journey which I pray has done them justice. It is about my parents, my own memories and those friends, and relations who have shared theirs with me.

PART ONE

Chapter 1

GERALD: EARLY DAYS

I am an Irishman, I am a Corkman, and as both I am a Jew.

Gerald Y. Goldberg, *Lost Soul of the World*

Legends are there to tell us what history has forgotten.

Elif Shafak, *The Island of Missing Trees*

J ust after he died in 2003, Gerald was described as a "Colossus" and a "towering giant of the legal world" (*Evening Echo,* January 1, 2004). But it was not until after his death that he was considered in such glowing terms. It took many years and devoted hours to reach that peak. Up to his early 60s, he progressed slowly and steadily through the ranks of his profession, establishing his reputation as a successful solicitor. In those early years I think he struggled a lot. I know he was a workaholic, and I saw how much he invested of himself in everything he did. He gave everything he had to all the causes and issues he took up. I watched that slow, steady ascent of the mountain of the law and success. I saw his successes and disappointments. Yes, there were failures too, but one is not possible without the other. No man is an island, nor is anyone perfect, and Gerald, for all his brilliance, struggled between good and bad, success and failure, winning and losing, rising and falling. He could never have made it without his beloved Sheila constantly at his side, propping him up when necessary. Gerald was difficult: no doubt about that. But he had an ability to rise to every challenge and perform.

Early Days

What was it like to be a child growing up in Cork in the second decade of the 20th century? Gerald was born on April 12, 1912. Most of Gerald's siblings were older, and were well integrated into Cork life. When my wife, Carla, a doctor, was screening children in a school in Co. Kilkenny in 1988 or 1989, she was taking a break in the staff-room when an elderly nun opened the door and asked, "Are you anything to the Goldbergs in Cork?" Carla said, "Yes, I'm Gerald Goldberg's daughter-in-law, married to his son, David." The nun said she hadn't known Gerald, as he was much younger, but that she had known the older brothers very well. "We all went around together. We used to go dancing and swimming. They were very good looking, and great fun, and we had a wonderful time."

The War of Independence

Gerald was one of many who lived through and experienced the violence of the 1916-1920 period. The Easter Rising occurred (April 24 to 29, 1916) when he was just four years old. Though the Rising failed militarily, the seeds were sown for the new republic which emerged after the negotiations of 1920-1921.

By the time he was 10, he had lived through violent riots in the streets of Cork City, and fighting on both sides. I don't know how many such scenes he actually witnessed but the general atmosphere at the time would have been tense and perhaps frightening to a small child. What I do know is that Gerald witnessed the burning of Cork in December 1920, which he recalled in *Notes towards an Autobiography* (Goldberg Special Archive, University College Cork). He wrote:

> After my brother and I went to bed, about 11.00 pm we heard the Crossley, and we went to the window and looked out. We saw uniformed men, Royal Irish Constabulary (RIC), forming a cordon across the street, turning people away. The city center was cordoned off.

Later they were awakened by their parents and told to dress. They heard explosions and saw Patrick Street on fire. The flames spread and buildings collapsed. They had to evacuate, as City Hall was also on fire. The family stood outside the house and watched the city burn. Gerald was very frightened and, when he got back into the house, he jumped into bed and covered his head with the covers.

Approximately 20 years later, Gerald remembered these events and wrote some stories for John, his eldest son. He wrote them on the top step of the stairs to his office while he waited for clients and in between reading legal texts. The stories were called *The Boy with the Magic Glass of Water*. There were several of these stories. Some were written down and others were not, but this is the only one I can remember.

> The fire of Cork was burning badly, and the Firemen were unable to put it out. Someone told them they should try the Boy with the Magic Glass of Water. They asked who he was, and they were sent to the place where the Boy lived. So, they found the house and knocked on the door. They said they had heard that there was a Boy who lived here who had a Magic Glass of Water, and they wondered if they could speak to the Boy. The resident said he would call him, and when the Boy appeared, he was asked if he really had a Magic Glass of Water, and could it put out a big fire. The Boy told them he had a Glass, and he could put out any fire. The Firemen begged him to come and help them extinguish the Great Fire of Cork. The Boy went with them and brought his Magic Glass. When they saw the huge fire, they were unsure if the Boy could put it out. But the Boy said he was definite he could. He took out his glass and he started to sprinkle water at the flames. The little spots of water exploded into huge torrents. They went up into the sky first and then they came

down with force on to the flames and the water started to put out the fire. Soon the Boy had complete control of it. Not long after the fire of Cork was quenched, thanks to the brilliant little Boy with his Magic Glass of Water.

City Hall burnt out, 1920. (Photo: Cork City & County Archives Service)

Early Influences

Gerald always said there were two major events that made a profound impression on him; both happened when he was very young. Tomás Mac Curtain was murdered on March 20, 1920, after being elected Lord Mayor only in January. The other memory was the death of Terence MacSwiney in Brixton Prison (October 25, 1920) after 74 days of hunger strike. As a child, he saw their bodies lying in state in the City Hall. "Everyone in our street went to the lying-in-state," he used to say. Gerald didn't want to go because he came from a family of *Kohanim* (the Priests) who are not permitted to visit a cemetery or be anywhere near a cadaver. He tried to explain this to his friends. Nonetheless, they viewed his hesitancy as showing a lack of "patriotism or cowardice. If you didn't go, you were guilty of both, so I went."

Tomas Mac Curtain's lying-in-state.
(Photo: Cork City & County Archives Service)

Terence McSwiney's funeral procession through Cork city.
(Photo: Cork City & County Archives Service)

Gerald spoke as if he was experiencing the event as a mature adult, but he was only eight. "Everyone had rosary beads except the Goldbergs, so we felt a little left out of it." He switched from the singular to the plural without saying who accompanied him. However, when he went to see Terence MacSwiney, he did not question whether to enter: he followed the crowd. "… quietly, blindly, sadly, and we approached the coffin standing on a bier in the great hall." Much later, as Lord Mayor, Gerald wrote a pamphlet on MacSwiney.

His older siblings seem to have been politically aware and involved at that time, his sisters Fanny and Molly had joined Cumann na mBan, had the uniforms and went out singing and collecting. Their father, Laban, was embarrassed by them and covered his face with his hands. But, in another version of the story, Gerald said that Laban did not know they were in the Cumann until a member of the community saw the girls on the street collecting money and reported them to him. He grounded them.

Despite the atmosphere of violence and aggression, there were lighter moments. As a young boy, Gerald experienced the Black and Tans. One evening when he was in town with his younger brother Ernie, returning home in the dark, they were stopped by a group of Black and Tans and were asked: "Where are you going, boys?" They said: "We are going home, sir." The officer asked them if they were Catholic or Protestant. They replied: "No, we're Jews, sir." They were terrified and their knees were knocking together. The officer told them to go home quickly, so they scuttled away. Another story Gerald told Anne Fleischmann was watching a Cork "shawlie" berating the Black and Tans in the street. She bawled out at them: "Bedad – the Boers put ye in khaki, the Germans put ye in tanks, but it took the Irish to put ye in cages."

Another major event was hearing Michael Collins speak. Gerald thought he had heard Collins speak four times. However, Collins only spoke twice in Cork. The first occasion was on March 12, 1922, and again on July 6, 1922, when Collins returned from London to Cork (Taylor, 1958). Gerald would have been 10 then.

The first address was described as a "monster address" (*Galway Observer*, March 18, 1922), when more than 50,000 people came to listen. It was delivered in the Grand Parade, so it would have been an easy walk for Gerald straight through Oliver Plunkett Street. Collins made a significant impression on him, and while Gerald couldn't recall the speech, he knew something profound was imparted. On reading the transcript of the speech, reproduced in Taylor (1958), it is an extremely powerful piece of oratory. Such events leave long-lasting impressions, and likely gave Gerald a strong sense of affinity with Cork and Ireland.

Home Life

The family's first house in Cork was in 21 Anglesea Street. Gerald said it was the house where James Joyce's father had lived. He loved that coincidence because he became a great Joycean later in life. Gerald was born there but brought up in 10 Parnell Place (it might have been known as Warren Place at the time), right in the middle of the city, between the two branches of the river, a few minutes' walk from Patrick Street. The roads were not tarmacadamed then and there was hardly any vehicular traffic. However, there were plenty of horse-drawn vehicles for passengers, and drays for deliveries of all kinds. Apart from the risk of being hurt by a horse and cart, it was safe for Gerald and his brothers to play on the street.

There were no accessible green areas, but it is likely they would have played ball with other kids around the area. In an unfinished short story, Gerald wrote about a man who had a cobbler's shop on the opposite side of Parnell Place. The story said that the "… street boasted of a football team" and the cobbler, Daddy O'Brien, was the manager of "Parnell Rovers AFC." As there was difficulty finding a full 11, it was not too difficult to get on the team. In the story, Gerald calls himself Yoel and says he was 13 when he first played for Parnell Rovers – where they played is not stated. Somewhere there was a playing field and entrance cost 6d for adults and 3d for children. None of them had any money. When they were not on the team and wanted to see the game, they begged men to take them in or they jumped the turnstiles. The games were on Sunday, otherwise he could not have gone. Equally, he should not be seen by any community member to be looking for charity. Such a breach would have been reported to Laban, who had quite a temper according to Esther Hesselberg, who knew him in Cork before she moved to Dublin. Apart from Parnell Rovers, there were games between the Dublin and Cork communities. I can remember Gerald once being in goal and diving very heavily on a ball, only to crack a rib.

Other street games they played were "last across," pitch and toss, Piggy, hurling and football. One game that I know Gerald played was called "gob stones." Gobs was played with five small white pebbles. You put a stone on the back of your hand and four on the ground. You threw the stone up into the air with a toss and, when it was in the air, you picked up as many of the stones on the ground as you could and caught the one in the air. Then you would put two stones on the back of your hand and the remainder on the ground. It became increasingly difficult as the number on the back of the hand increased. Gerald was very good at it. We played it when we were children.

When Gerald was very young, he suffered mastoiditis, and the infection resulted in the loss of hearing in his right ear. But he always said he could hear better with one ear than a man with two. Of course, this affected his balance, and often he was unsteady on his feet, stumbling, and falling, knocking things over. Many a vase went that way, and late in life several small tables. I don't think he associated his instability with his deafness, nor did we. But his sense of spatial awareness was definitely impaired.

The Synagogue, on South Terrace, Cork, in 2016 (since closed).

When he was growing up, Gerald's family observed an orthodox Jewish household, including all the rites and rituals. Gerald's father, Louis, known as Laban the Red, because of his red or blond hair, was a person who was able to lead services. Gerald said he had a beautiful tenor voice.

Gerald at the synagogue. His religion was an important part of his life –
"…he wore his Judaism on his sleeve." (Photos: Irish Jewish Museum)

Laban learned to *schochet* (that is, he was qualified to butcher animals, at least chickens). Of course, they kept a *kosher* house. Friday evening was kept for welcoming the Sabbath, and it would have been kept throughout Saturday until it expired at sundown. Laban would have made *Kiddush* and broken bread called the *Challah* which is baked for the Sabbath.

The children would have gone to the *Cheder* (religion class) possibly every day or a few days a week. They were all fully versed in the Hebrew bible (the *Torah*), the psalms, and daily prayers.

All his life, Gerald laid *Teffilin* every morning (putting on philacteries). These are little boxes which contain the *Shema*, the injunction that comes from Deuteronomy 6:8 and 11:18: "You shall bind them as a sign upon the hand, and they shall be frontlets between your eyes." I can remember so well his reciting the morning prayers with his arm bound in the leather strap and the other part on his forehead, while at the same time making breakfast. The toast often got burned!

He recalled to me his first day at *Cheder*; he would have been five years old. He was given an open book to hold, but could not make much sense of the pages. Then pennies started dropping down from over his head onto the book and a spoon of honey was put in his mouth. I have asked two Rabbis about this. They were acquainted with the honey which is associated with Ezekiel 3.3: "Then did I eat it; and it was in my mouth as honey for sweetness" (Jewish Publication Society, 1917). However, neither had ever heard of "pennies from heaven." It may have been a purely family custom, or one that they had brought from Akmian in Lithuania (**Chapter 3**).

Sol (Solomon), Gerald's uncle, told the same story of himself as a boy named Smerke (*The Jewish Chronicle*, 1928) He said that the only happy day of his childhood was when he was five years old and living in Lithuania, then part of Russia. His mother took him to *Cheder*. When two or three kopecs fell on the table, he was told they were thrown by an angel from heaven and that later, if he was good, the angel would throw him some more.

Gerald told me this story about how strict their adherence was to the Kosher laws. One day, when Gerald and Ernie were in town, they bought a packet of Rowntree's Wine Gums. When they got home, they offered their mother some, and she didn't know whether she could take one. She said she would have to take them and ask Laban when he came home. Gerald never learned if she had, in fact, asked Laban and, if so, what he had said, but they were allowed keep – and eat – the wine gums.

Gerald also recalled how during the meal on *Shabbat*, they sang songs for the occasion, followed by Grace after Meals. Then, in the kitchen, they sat on the floor in front of the fire, while Laban sat on a chair and talked to them about the *Parashat* (weekly portion of the *Torah*) to be read during the next Saturday morning service at synagogue. Gerald guessed that that was how Laban learned from Shimon, his father. But Shimon died when Laban can only have been about seven. Gerald explained that Laban read and translated several sentences of the text into Yiddish. Then he read from the commentary by the famous Rabbi Rashi. The children were encouraged to ask questions. Laban never asked them questions, because he didn't want to embarrass the child should he not know the answer.

Schooldays

When Gerald and his brothers, Yanks and Ernie, went out to play in the street, Rachel made them take off their shoes so that they would look the same as any other boy. Gerald said he had no difficulty growing up with Catholic boys and girls. He claimed that he did not learn English until he went to school, though he must have learned it in the street. He went to two primary schools: the first was Christ Church and then the Model National School.

Advertisements were placed in *The Jewish Chronicle* about 1924, offering places for boys in a new Jewish boarding school. The principal was Mr. Percy Cowen, who began tutoring in Hove, and then rented Ockenden Manor from the Burrell family, substantial landowners in Cuckfield, Sussex. Laban must have seen these ads and decided he wanted his two sons to have a Jewish education.

The school was located in a manor house on 30 acres of ground. Today, it is the luxurious Ockenden House Hotel and Spa. In March 2023, Carla and I were staying with Theo and Val in Guildford, which is about an hour away from Cuckfield. Val suggested that we should see this place as it was the school where Gerald and Ernie attended. Gerald had often spoken about it. But Val's account of how she and Theo found it in the 1990s is interesting. Theo and Val spent a weekend there, and entered through the side doors which are used today, opening onto a long low-ceilinged corridor. In the evening, when they sat down for dinner in the restaurant, Val noticed two huge double doors which she thought must have been the original entrance. The layout perplexed her, so she enquired, and the waiter went away and came back with a leaflet which said that it was a Jewish boarding school which commenced in 1924. She and Theo thought it was unlikely there was another Jewish boarding school in Sussex. So, when

Gerald made a visit in the late 1990s, they brought him to Ockenden Manor for lunch. He recognized the building immediately, became excited and showed them around explaining the use of the rooms in his time. Today, where there is a private dining room in a large dark wood-paneled room with a beautiful stucco ceiling, in Gerald's time this was the synagogue.

The private dining room at Ockenden House Hotel. It was the synagogue in 1924, when Gerald went to boarding school there with his brother Ernie.

There is a local museum in the town, which they visited. The curators were very excited to meet Gerald and hear about his time at Ockenden. Gerald was in his element and held court for a good hour. Val thought that he corresponded with the museum when he returned to Cork. It is probable that he did, but no correspondence is extant. However, the museum staff have been very helpful and made available a number of documents. The hotel also has a leaflet on the school which they gave me, and it specifically mentions Gerald.

In order to secure a lease on the property, Percy Cowen provided references to the Burrell family which "were hardly glowing," according to Roger Linn, who wrote about the school in *Sussex Living* magazine,

November 2011. The name of the school, Macaulay, is likely after the parliamentarian, Lord Thomas Babington Macaulay, who championed Jewish causes. It is the same name Cowen used for his school and crammer in Hove. The school was fitted with the new electric light system.

Macaulay House College (now Ockenden House Hotel and Spa), sketched by Frank Gusdorf. (Photo: Cuckfield Museum)

After the advertisements were placed, boys began to arrive, not just from England, or Cork, but from Germany, Austria, Australia, and South Africa. Fees were £36 per child per term, plus 9/- for toothpaste. Laban also had to pay for the ship and train fares from Cork to Paddington Station and then to Victoria for the train to Cuckfield. It all amounted to a tidy sum, though Laban could obviously afford it. The manor house was set on magnificent grounds, which Linn describes as:

> ... lush lawns, meadows and mature trees... the ground fell away to the playing fields of Cuckfield Cricket Club and pupils were treated to the stunning prospects of Sussex Weald and South Downs beyond.

But life at Macaulay was not so idyllic. Linn, and the hotel leaflet, tell us that Cowen was a tall imposing man who was both intimidating and a stern disciplinarian. Linn records all food had to be eaten, even the hated vegetables and breakfast kippers, regardless of how long the unfortunate boy had to stay at the table. "Beatings were common," Linn writes, "and a selection of riding whips were kept in a stand for this purpose." He continues:

> The school might not have been the Dotheboys Hall of Charles Dickens (in *Nicholas Nickelby*), but Dr. Gerald Goldberg – who went on to become Lord Mayor of Cork – and his brother were withdrawn by their parents because of the severity of the punishment regime.

Gerald told me how it all ended: when the school was celebrating Armistice Day, there was a German student who went to the headmaster and complained it would be inappropriate for him to salute the British dead, and he should be exempt. The headmaster agreed. When Gerald and Ernie heard this, they got the idea that they should also be exempt because of the British disturbances in Ireland. They too went to the headmaster and asked to be excused on the grounds that the British had murdered two Lords Mayor of Cork, Tomás Mac Curtain and Terence MacSwiney. Gerald said: "He [the headmaster] went through the bloody roof, and we got three lashes with the cane for suggesting such a thing" (Michael Carr, 2002). Ernie ran away. The beating may have been worse than Gerald remembered, for the discipline there seems to have been quite shocking. When the news reached Cork, Laban brought them home, and in 1926-1927 Gerald was enrolled in Presentation Brothers College, Cork (PBC). It is not hard to understand why, he said: "It was like a holiday camp compared with the other place." He sat the school and State examinations and passed.

When Gerald and Ernie were at the Macaulay House School, they were instructed to write home twice per week. One letter was copied from the blackboard; the other individually written, but censored. I found a postcard, now badly damaged from light, showing a class at the school. On it, Ernie wrote to his mother:

> My dear Mother, I am sending you a photo of the boys in the school, and I hope you like it. E. Goldberg.

Percy Cowen struggled to meet his bills. Even though girls were admitted in 1934, the school closed early in 1940 when Cowen and his wife ran away to Newquay, Cornwall. He was soon found and declared a bankrupt. When we visited in March 2023 and were having coffee in the lounge, the waitress said that there was supposedly a secret passage connecting the school with a pub, but she could not say if that was true.

When Gerald was finishing school in PBC, he expressed the desire to be a lawyer. He must have sent letters to some Cork solicitors seeking an apprenticeship, but no favorable replies were received. Finally, he approached Brother Connolly, the principal of PBC, to enlist his help. Connolly explained that he could write only one letter on Gerald's behalf. That letter went to Barry St. J. Galvin, a solicitor on the South Mall, and outlined that Connolly had a boy who had his heart set on law. It is likely he also mentioned that the student was Jewish. According to Gerald, Galvin had "been in the British Army during the War and had overwintered in Crimea." Galvin replied to Connolly that, without the latter's intervention, he would have found it difficult to accept a Jewish apprentice. Galvin went on to request Gerald's presence at his office, telling Connolly to "send the boy down at 3.00 pm" on a particular date. The meeting changed Gerald's life, and he never stopped extolling how wonderful his master had been. As he said, "the rest was history."

Gerald entered University College Cork (UCC) in 1930/1931 as a student of the Incorporated Law Society, which, at that time, required students to complete two years at university and two at the Society in Dublin. When he entered UCC, he joined both the Law Debating Society and the Philosophical Society. He said that he won a silver medal in the Law Debating Society and a gold medal in the Philosophical Society, but said that because he was a "jib" he could not be awarded the medals. By "jib," he meant a first year. In my time at college, and also in UCC, first year students were known as "freshers." No one could confirm the term "jib." I also asked the Librarian of UCC, John Fitzgerald, if there was any reason why Gerald would not have been given the medals; he said there was no such rule or reason.

Gerald remembered standing up to speak at the Philosophical, though the Auditor constantly passed over him for another speaker. On one occasion, when he rose to speak, the Auditor told him to sit down, saying he was an alien and could not speak. Gerald remained standing and speaking. Then, he said, he met Tomás Óg Mac Curtain, of the IRA, and told him about this treatment. On the next occasion when Gerald rose to speak and was told to sit down, Mac Curtain interjected and said: "No, Mr. Auditor, the next speaker is Mr. Goldberg." (I cannot vouch for this story though it was told to me by two independent sources, who also heard it from Gerald. The problem is that, according to UCC's records, which I have checked, Tomás Óg Mac Curtain, son of the murdered Lord Mayor Mac Curtain, was only 15 at that time, and did not enter the College until 1936 when Gerald had already graduated and was commencing his practice. The rescuer must have been someone other than Tomás Óg – otherwise the story is not credible.) However, later, at a general meeting of the Law Debating Society on December 9, 1932, Gerald was elected a member of the Committee.

Gerald, after being conferred with an Honorary Doctorate of Law, at University College Cork with the then President, Prof. Michael Mortell.

Gerald's last interaction with UCC was in 1993, when he was awarded an Honorary Doctorate of Law. That was a lovely day. We were all there. Sheila was beaming from ear to ear, as she did whenever success came. It did come late: Gerald was then 81. In the evening, there was a *Vin d'Honneur* in Fleming's restaurant. It was a very special occasion as Gerald looked splendid in his Rembrandt hat and robes.

Chapter 2

SHEILA: EARLY DAYS

Say little, do much.

Shammai, *Pirket Avot*

heila's father was Alec Smith, known as Ben, though no one knows why. Her mother was Gertrude Rachel Cristol, known as Rachel by friends and as Trudi within the family, from 92 Hibernian Buildings in Cork. Born on October 25, 1883, Rachel was the daughter of Michael and Esther, and was a first cousin of Rachel Sandler, Gerald's mother. Ben and Trudi lived at 50 Landscape Terrace, Crumlin Road, Belfast. This large, red brick Victorian house, which stood at the top of the terrace, was also just in front of the Crumlin Road Gaol. A warder patrolled the area night and day.

The Smiths were also from Lithuania, and may have been from Siauliai (*Shavl* in Yiddish), but moved to Palanga, a holiday town on the Baltic coast. Ben's father, Todres Schmid or Schmit, was born *circa* 1850 in Gargzdai, near Klaipedos. He was first a draper, then a financier, whereas the Goldbergs had kept a *shenk* (tavern) and chickens. Todres' wife was Chana Esther and they had five children: Alec, Abe, Harry, Minnie and Frieda. Chana Esther moved to Ireland in the early 1900s, which I cannot explain, and brought some of her children. Both Ben and Abe went to South Africa as teenagers. Again, the myth of draft dodging appears: it was said that both boys were in South Africa avoiding conscription. Ben, who was very young, was possibly in Muizenburg in the Southern Cape, where he may have contracted malaria while working in the mines. Others of his family were already in Ireland, so when he recovered, he came to Ireland to join an uncle in Dundalk. During his long and slow recovery, he met Rachel (Trudi) Cristol. They became engaged and married in Dublin on December 28, 1909. Abe came from South Africa for the wedding, and met Eva Cristol, Trudi's sister, whom he later married in Chicago. Two brothers married two sisters! When Ben and Trudi settled in Belfast, Chana Esther went to live with them.

Todres stayed in Palanga until Abe bought him to Ireland in April-May 1921. Abe's passport specified he was going to Latvia (*sic*) to see his parents. Abe went back to the United States, and Todres died in February 1922 (David Wilson, email to Debbie Levi, April 26, 2020; emails between George Smith, Debbie Levi and John Goldberg, 2005.)

The Cristol family all went to America and mostly resided in Chicago, although Eva and Abe went to Dallas. When Sheila was six years old, her mother took her three children on a sea voyage to see the family in Chicago. Sheila's ticket stated she was then "6 and married"! I remember Sheila telling me about that great voyage to her Uncle Tommy. They also went to Dallas. It must have been quite the trip.

Sheila, later in life. (Photo: Debbie Levy Archive)

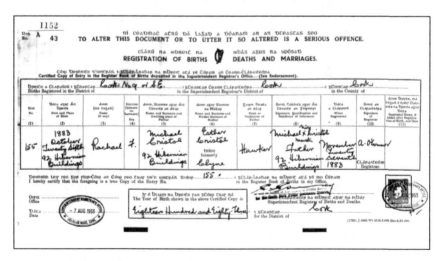

Birth certificate of Rachel Smith (née Cristol), Sheila's mother.

Sheila's family – the Smiths: 1. Abe Isaacson, 2. Lily Isaacson, 3. Archie Isaacson, 4. Freda Isaacson, 5. Solomon Green, 6. Minnie Green (aunt), 7. Mome Isaacson, 8. Harry Smith (uncle), 9. Rachel (Trudi) Smith (Sheila's mother), 10. Abe Smith (uncle), 11. Sapsa Isaacson, 12. Todres Smith (grandfather), 13. Sidney Smith (older brother), 14. Chana Smith (grandmother), 15. Alexander (Ben) Smith (Sheila's father), 16. Sidney Isaacson, 17. Stanley Smith (younger brother), 18. Sadie Isaacson, 19. Lena Isaacson, 20. Stella Green, 21. Sheila Smith. (Photo: Debbie Levy Archive)

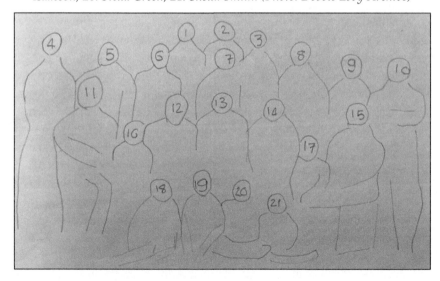

Of Ben and Trudi's five children, only three survived: Sidney, born April 12, 1912; Sheila, born August 20, 1916; and Stanley, born September 19, 1919. As a child, Sidney was often ill with pleurisy and bronchitis which kept him at home, missing much school. A nurse was hired to look after him during these bouts of illness, and he did many sketches of her coming and going through the door of his bedroom. He became a portrait and mural painter, especially on ships for the Union Castle Line. Stanley became a radiologist. He was also an awarded photographer, and he served with the 6th Airborne Royal Army Medical Corps, the Red Berets. The three children went to Methodist College in Belfast, known popularly as "Methody."

Sheila was very close to all her family, especially her mother. When she came to Cork, Sheila left what she called a close-knit community. Many of the Cork community were related to each other, and at first she found it difficult to be included.

My memories of those times are few. Sheila would take us on the train to Belfast. I loved crossing the bridge at Drogheda. It seemed so long, as if it went on forever. Of course, it didn't, yet that memory still remains. The house in Landscape Terrace was demolished during the Troubles for security reasons. As a boy, I can remember a small garden at the back, where a cinder track ran between the garden railings and the gaol wall. I also remember that, in Belfast, there was a man we visited called Abraham Hurwitz, who I think was a relation. He sat in his shirt, without the collar, just the stud, and he had a waxed moustache, the only time I recall a man with a waxed moustache.

Sometimes, in the evenings, Ben used to get us kids to count his three-penny pieces which he kept in Dimple Haig bottles. He was fond of a drop. Very occasionally, we went for a drive in his car which was kept in a garage somewhere else, and was driven by his man, Billy. Other days, we ran up and down the long landings on the first and second floors. They were nice visits.

Our grandmother, Bubbe Smithy, as we called her, was a warm, gentle and loving woman. She often spoke Yiddish to Sheila and would pat me on the head, saying "*Kinahora*," meaning "no evil eye." She was a good cook and baker. One thing she made was *Lockshen Kugel* or pudding with dried fruit, apple, spices and with noodles. Sheila told us how Bubbe rolled the dough very thin, and cut it very fine: it was good. I recollect other delights, such as wonderful ginger *Kugel* knuckles and macaroons for *Pesach*, when she also made mead. Preparations began weeks and months before.

One day, Sheila came home feeling very pleased and told her father that she had done exceptionally well in her exams and showed him the results.

Ben was a short-tempered man, and had little time for girls' education. His response was: "Vhat bleddy use is exams?" He frequently put people down with phrases like that or he would say: "Vhat de bleddy hell do you vant it for?" Sheila always regretted that she never went to university. She would have done well, but her father's attitude to women's education was common for the period.

Ben, despite all his years in Belfast, never quite mastered English. He was an austere authoritarian with a very thick Eastern European accent. He had a "delightful" habit of chewing tobacco, and wasn't too careful about where he spat it out. Perhaps it was an old custom from Russia. After Trudi died, he came to live with us for half of each year. Every day, at about 12.15 or 12.30 p.m., our dog Orange could be seen sitting outside O'Driscoll's pub in Douglas. When Ben came home, he always gave each of us a bar of chocolate. Then he planted bottles of beer and sherry in the garage. Those were trying times for Sheila.

Marriage and Ben-Truda

In 1928, Gerald visited Donaghadee, a small coastal town in Co. Down, Northern Ireland, where he met a girl named Sheila Smith. Between the time Sheila and Gerald first met and their engagement in 1934, they did not see each other. They wrote. Only one letter is extant which I found in the Jewish Museum. It is now in a delicate state, but some of it is worth quoting as it gives us a further image of how intellectual Gerald was. It was not an ordinary passionate love letter. He wrote on March 19, 1935. He was just starting his practice and had a lot of time on his hands waiting for clients.

> My dearest Sheila, here I am in the office trying to tell you on paper, not as durable as that required, how dearly and tenderly I love you. I could not wait to buy parchment on which to write, but, I must boast that my love will be more durable, more lasting and infinitely more strong than any parchment in the world.

He went on to say that he wasn't very good at saying the things he wanted to say. He remarked how much a part of his life she had become "even though you only came to me in pen and ink for five years." And he always thought of her as more than a 99th cousin three times removed. He declared that he would be faithful and loyal always and would never let her down, and then he said he knew there was something in him which would never allow him to fail. With her by his side, he could not fail. He saw the legal business as "a slow game, and must be … *illegible* … harder and harder without fear or failure until ultimately I am established." These were words not just of love and endearment to Sheila, but prophetic too. He fulfilled his obligations and became very successful much quicker than he expected, though he did not admit it.

Sheila and Gerald at the Giant's Causeway, c. 1934/35.
(Photo: Debbie Levy Archive)

Sheila married Gerald on August 8, 1937. They had three sons: John, 1938, named Lewis John after Laban; Theodore Michael, 1943, named after Todres Micha, and David Simon (myself), 1945, named after Gerald's grandfather.

Gerald and Sheila on honeymoon in Juan-les-Pins.
(Photo: Irish Jewish Museum, Dublin)

Sheila and Gerald honeymooned in Juan-les-Pins and Nice, enjoying the *Promenade des Anglais*. Family lore has it that, on their honeymoon, Sheila told Gerald that they must agree never to go to bed on a row. If there was a disagreement, then they would agree to differ and sort it out in the morning.

INTERLUDE

Chapter 3

THE VOYAGE OF THE IMMIGRANT

The voice of myth is powerful.

Lefteri, *Songbirds*

Can you find another homeland?
I don't believe you can.
I don't believe he did.

Louis Lentin, *Grandpa, Speak to Me in Russian*

G erald repeated, in innumerable interviews, the story of how his father left Lithuania, escaping conscription, fleeing persecution, and heading for America, when he was put ashore in Cobh, Co. Cork, by a rogue sea-captain who told him, "This is the next parish to New York." I grew up with these stories, but later discovered that historians have contradicted them. In fact, when Gerald's father left his *shtetl*, Akmian, and travelled to Ireland in search of a better life, he went straight to Limerick where his uncles, Marcus and Benjamin Greenfield, who must have been economic migrants, arriving in the 1870s (Ryan, 2014), took him in. I wanted to find the truth, but I also wanted to learn why Gerald believed these stories, and how they made him the sort of man he was.

The stories of the "voyage of the immigrant" have been told all around the world by Litvaks. Robert Alter (2013) distinguishes between those stories which are part of cultural memory and those which are part of historical memory:

> They are not historical memory... what is reported as the national past is grounded not in the factual historical experience of the nation, but in the image of the nation that the guardians of the national literary legacy seek to fix for their audiences and for future generations.

Historians call cultural memory "myth" and historical memory "fact." I prefer the term "cultural memory" to "myth." The stories I want to tell are part of cultural memory. Throughout his life, Gerald told many stories about his father's travails, both in Lithuania and Ireland, and those stories belong to cultural memory. He said that the three things which influenced him were his father, his Uncle Sol, and Cork. Of these, his father is of particular importance, and I want to try and create as accurate an image of him as possible.

In what Gerald called "an attempt to write an autobiography" (never completed or published) (GSA, UCC), he spoke at length about his father's life in *"der heim"*: Jewish persecution, the effects of the Pale of Settlement and the May Laws of 1882. Also, he often talked about conscription, which he said his father avoided. There were degrees of persecution: the Pale of Settlement and May Laws of 1882 were restrictive and oppressive; and there was conscription of Jews into the Russian Army. That is historical memory. There is some information which is accurate: then there is – and has to be – some elements of speculation, and educated guesswork. I will reiterate Gerald's stories and compare them with historical memory.

Life in Akmian

Gerald's father was named Louis. According to Esther Hesselberg, who knew him in Cork, he was called by his Hebrew name, Laban (pronounced *Layben*). His eldest daughter, Fanny Marcus (Marcus, GSA, UCC), said he was a thin, medium-sized man, good-looking, with a reddish beard. He had a lovely smile and fine baritone voice. I will call him Laban, though I never knew him. I will look at three major events: life in Lithuania; a *broiges* within the Limerick community (**Chapter 4**), and a Limerick Pogrom (**Chapter 5**).

Yehuda Leib (John Lewis) Goldberg, known as Laban.
(Photo: Goldberg Special Archive, UCC)

Elka Goldberg (née Karlin): Shimon's second wife, Laban's mother, and Gerald's grandmother. (Photo: Goldberg Special Archive, UCC)

Certificate of Naturalization to an Alien.

Whereas *Louis Goldberg*

an Alien, now residing at *67 Henry Street, Limerick Ireland*

has presented to me, the Right Honourable *Aretas Akers-Douglas* one of His Majesty's Principal Secretaries of State, a Memorial, praying for a Certificate of Naturalization, and alleging that he is a Subject of *Russia having been born at Achmehan, Kovna; and is the son of Simon and Elka Goldberg both subjects of Russia – Of the age of thirty two years a Draper – is married and has three children under age residing with his*

viz:–

Fanny Goldberg aged 9 years
Marrie   "   7
Sidney Henry   "   4

Laban's certificate of naturalization – page 1.

and that in the period of eight years preceding his application he has resided for five years within the United Kingdom, and intends, when naturalized, to reside therein :

And whereas I have inquired into the circumstances of the case, and have received such evidence as I have deemed necessary for proving the truth of the allegations contained in such Memorial, so far as the same relate to the Memorialist :

Now, in pursuance of the authority given to me by the said Acts, I grant to the aforesaid *Louis Goldberg* this Certificate, and declare that he is hereby naturalized as a British Subject, and that, upon taking the Oath of Allegiance, he shall in the United Kingdom be entitled to all political and other rights, powers, and privileges, and be subject to all obligations, to which a natural-born British Subject is entitled or subject in the United Kingdom ; with this qualification, that he shall not, when within the limits of the Foreign State of which he was a Subject, be deemed to be a British Subject, unless he has ceased to be a Subject of that State in pursuance of the laws thereof, or in pursuance of a Treaty to that effect.

In witness whereof I have hereto subscribed my Name this 20th day of *August* 1902.

HOME OFFICE,
LONDON.   *A. Akers Douglas*

Oath of Allegiance.

I, *Louis Goldberg*

do swear that I will be faithful and bear true allegiance to His Majesty King Edward, His Heirs and Successors, according to law.

(Signature of Alien) *Louis Goldberg*

Sworn and subscribed this 26th day of *August* 1902, before me

(Signature) *John Guinian E.*

Justice of the Peace for *City of Limerick*

30 August 1902   A Commissioner for Oaths.

Laban's certificate of naturalization – signature page.

Laban was born in Akmian, a small *shtetl* (village) in Lithuania, called *Akmene* in Lithuanian, and *Ockmyenya* in Russian, on the banks of the Dibikine river. Akmian is now a substantial industrial town in the northwest of Lithuania, on the border with Latvia, where there is now no trace of the Jews, except a cemetery.

There was no register of births, deaths, or marriages there until the 20th century, so the year of Laban's birth is uncertain, though, strangely, not so in the case of his siblings. Gerald surmised 1867, although it was certainly not later than 1870.

The registration of his death states he died from pneumonia and cardiac failure in the Bons Secours Hospital, Cork, and gives his age as 62.

Laban's father was Shimon, who twice married. He had a son and two daughters by his first wife. After she died, he married a 15-year-old girl, Elka Karlin, from Zagges in Kurland. She may have been known in English as Elie, as that is how she appears on the census of 1901. She came from a prosperous family and brought with her a substantial wedding trousseau (Marcus, GSA, UCC). Shimon and Elka had five children: twins, Rachel and Berra; Laban; Yerukim Shia; and Sol.

Shimon kept a *shenk* (inn or tavern) which was a commonplace business and one of the few that Jews could engage in. Elka was a confectioner. Because they were wooden structures, it was not unusual for *shenken* to burn down, sometimes from non-violent causes, but often by groups of customers, including soldiers, who engaged in fights with each other and caused fires (Citvarienė, 2022). When their *shenk* suffered this fate, Shimon and Elka were devastated, and he lived only a few more years, leaving her destitute.

Clearly a determined woman, Elka re-organized herself and children. She sent Rachel to be apprenticed to a dressmaker, Berra to a builder, and fitted out Laban as a peddler. I know nothing about Yerukim, but Sol was too young to work. At that time, Laban was between 7 and 10, and had to stop *cheder*. Elka baked, selling her bread, cakes and biscuits (Marcus, GSA, UCC).

The language of the house was Yiddish. Gerald said that Laban spoke six languages, but that is unlikely. He certainly would have spoken Russian, because that was then the language of Lithuania. Historians (Sirutavičius & Staliūnas, 2010) agree that only 2% of the population spoke Lithuanian. Akmian was owned by a Russian general, who in about 1800 gave it as a gift to his wife (Indre Joffyte, email, 2021). Structures in the 19th century were wooden, and not in the best condition. Overall, the place was small, grey and bleak. Houses may have been low, and the entrances partially below ground level. There was a Catholic church, meadows and vegetable plots, and unmade roads. The synagogue was likely in the center, possibly in the middle of "heaps of crooked houses," near the central market. It was a center of religious devotion, culture, trade, gossip, rows, and settling disputes (Chessman, 1967). The *shtetleh* (villages) were very religious, and when he came to Ireland, Laban took lessons every day in Hebrew and the Liturgy, and became competent in conducting services and home ceremonies (Marcus, GSA, UCC).

Life revolved around market days, fixed in each town, based on the Catholic liturgical calendar. On those days, everyone came from nearby towns. There were many horse-drawn wagons with much jostling and movement (Chessman, 1967). Jewish traders, usually carpenters, shoe-makers, tailors, craftsmen, and peddlers collected together, pushing, shoving, and feeling the produce such as chickens, eggs, hides, gloves, wagons. There was bargaining, doing the best deal they could. Quarrels and retractions: turning their backs, walking away, waiting, coming forward again, until hands were shaken and deals were done. Then to the *shenk* for a celebratory drink of beer, vodka, or brandy. Neighbors met with others, and discussed issues which had arisen, trying to get a resolution to problems and quarrels. There was a lot of matchmaking. Horses left piles of green manure all over the streets which were covered with straw. In the evening, traders sat in their little shops counting their takings and ascertaining whether they had made a profit or loss (Chessman, 1967).

A typical Lithuanian house of the time – photographer unknown.

Gerald wrote that Shimon and Elka's house, which he called a "shack," was on the outskirts of the *shtetl*. In the living area, there was a large Lithuanian range or stove with a long, wide shelf on top. The range was kept lighting during the winter. Shimon and Elka slept in a small room off the kitchen-living area. The boys slept on or near the range. There was another room occupied by the girls. The family had to wash in a barrel outside, and break the ice in winter, but maybe they were able to heat water on the range. Then they went to *cheder* and had breakfast afterwards: black bread and tea. But on Friday nights, *Kabbalah Shabbat*, they had *challah* baked by Elka. The *challah* was covered with a cloth called a *challah dekel*.

In Gerald's childhood, he said, it was the same in his house, and it was a custom he himself later observed "more in the breach than in the observance." I can remember Friday nights very well, and I cannot recall much breach.

Lithuania was known as the country of *yeshivas* (seminaries), to which many boys were sent. If they did well, they stayed and became rabbis. If not, they were sent to be apprenticed to a cobbler or tailor. That was a rough life. Sol Goldberg wrote an article for *The Jewish Chronicle* (August 10, 1928), in which he calls himself "Smerke." At the age of 9, these boys were apprenticed to a cobbler:

> He had to do all the rough work at the bench, and all of the dirty work in the house. He got very little food, but a lot of beating from everyone. He was bitter. When he was 18 years old, he looked 30. He started in business himself. He knew that when he was 20, he would be called for military service, so he decided to leave for England. He left his town with a heavy heart. "Whoever forgets?" he asked. "Even when we lived in London, we still dreamt of our little town in Russia, with its little river, its beautiful walks, its woods and marketplace, where the cattle would be gathered in the summer before the shepherds drove them to the woods, and then in the evening they would return... Ah, happy dream of childhood." But one thing Smerke noticed, with the exception of his father and mother, who shed bitter tears, no one saw him off. His feeling of bitterness increased.

These accounts give us a glimpse into life in the *shtetl*, what life was like, and how they found a new world when they left. In 1874, there were 667 Jewish souls in Akmian; by 1897, there were only 543, out of a total population of 1,501 (Chessman, 1967).

Emigration

Emigration began in the 1860s and continued until 1914-1917 (Klier, 2011), by which time the Jewish population was much reduced. This raises two issues: *Why* did they leave? And *how* did they leave?

Gerald always said that Laban left because of the antisemitism, persecution, conscription and pogroms. Then he often described the voyage and how they reached Cork. Let me look at these in turn.

There is no doubting that there was serious antisemitism, degrees of persecution, and conscription, but historians are firm in that there were no pogroms in Lithuania in the 1880s (Klier, 2011; Staliūnas, 2015; Cesarini, 1996).

Gerald referred to the Pale of Settlement and the May Laws of 1882 and conscription as though they were the causes of emigration. However, this does not seem to be correct. He always conflated conscription during the reign of Nicholas I with that of Alexander II. The difference was enormous: under Nicholas, Jews had to serve for 25 years, but this was reduced to 15 years in 1834 (Petrovosky-Shtern, 2014). It was a severe and brutal regime. Nicholas died in 1855 and was succeeded by Alexander II, called "The Great Reformer," though there is some doubt about that. His minister, Milyutin, introduced reforms: conscription reduced to six years, with the last two years suspended, but there was also a nine-year period as a reserve (Drury, 1994).

Another drum which Gerald beat was the May Laws of 1882. These were restrictive, but not the reason for emigration. Prof. Hasia Diner, New York University, said in *The Accidental Irish* (2003):

[The Jews emigrated]... from the deliverance of the absolutely bleak economic prospects made worse by the May Law of 1882, but *not created* by them (italics mine).

She said the timing of migration, based on gender, occupation, and class:

... all pointed to the movement as a deliberate and rational choice taken in the face of grim realities that staying put involved. The young were chosen first, and those in the peddling trade.

This points to Laban's decision at the age of about 14 to leave Lithuania and go to Ireland. Although Gerald said Laban was on his way to America, it is clear he was going to Limerick because he was a peddler, and because he had uncles, the Greenfields, who had settled there. Fanny Marcus said that there was correspondence between them. Perhaps Elka was involved. And the economic historian Cormac Ó Gráda (2006) mentioned Laban when he wrote:

> ... given however, that the 11-year-old Louis Goldberg who had settled in Limerick was at first sheltered by relatives and would marry into a Litvak family that had been in Cork since 1875, surely a straight forward economic interpretation of his emigration is more probable.

It was an economic migration. Another fact which confirms this is offered by Prof. Diner (personal email, 2021) who told me that, once the railway was laid from Germany to Ukraine, including Poland and Latvia, cheap imports were brought in, and this caused competition for low priced goods with which the peddlers could not compete. Also, despite the antisemitism and tensions, Jews went down to Ukraine to work in factories where they could make a better living.

When Laban was leaving, he promised that he would bring his whole family over to Limerick. His mother, Elka, was the first to come, followed by his sister, brothers and their families. They were all in Cork on September 18, 1891, for his wedding to Rachel Sandler (Marcus, GSA, UCC).

No one should think that leaving *der heim* was easy. Boys, perhaps as young as 14 years old, some travelling alone, others accompanied, left the home place knowing they would never see their land again. It was the same for Irish emigrants on their own journeys to a new life across the seas. People had to be mentally tough and courageous to survive. The journeys were long, and food had to be carried with them.

The telling and re-telling of these stories of the voyages gave the immigrant a bridge between *der heim* and the new land. They were leaving the repression of life in Russia, and looking forward to the bright new future without a repeat of oppression. Those who came to Ireland found the people tolerant, and they were able to go amongst the populace of Limerick without a repeat of the violence that occurred in the homeland – although there were some isolated incidents. Nonetheless, this is what enabled them to put down roots.

How did they leave, and why did they come? The first stories I ever heard were from Gerald. He told the story of immigration in many interviews on radio, television, and the print media. The essence of his story was that Laban went to Riga in Latvia and took a boat, which he believed was intended for America, but when it reached Queenstown (Cobh), Co. Cork, the captain told the passengers that they were in the next parish to

New York, and put them all ashore. It may be that Laban travelled with another boy called Louis Tevye Clein. Gerald claimed that Laban was dodging the draft, and that, after failing to get the captain to explain when the ship would continue to America, he went ashore where a man named Itsa (Isaac) Marcus was waiting at the quayside, to look after Jewish migrants on board.

This story, or something similar, is told by many Litvak families. However, according to current historical thinking, it cannot be correct. It is more likely that, leaving *der heim*, Laban probably bought a combination ticket for the train and boat from one of many local agents who were in competition with each other. Various historians have said that passports could be obtained in Libau (Evans, 2021).

The story that Gerald told does not fit the time frame of Laban's emigration in about 1882. Itsa came from Akmian too, but did not leave until about 1890/1891. He lived in Cork city where he had a shop which sold delph and toys. He also opened a chandlers in Cobh which was managed by his son Solly. In 1906, the White Star Shipping Line was running liners between Southampton and New York, stopping at Cobh. Itsa was retained as an interpreter to help any Yiddish-speaking passengers who disembarked. (Mike Solomons, e-mail, December 2021, and personal communication)

It is certain also that the story of the rogue captain is part of cultural memory. It is unlikely that Laban would have had the means to travel on expensive liners from Southampton. He could have come on the Packet from Fishguard in Wales to Cork, but even that seems unlikely as his destination was Limerick. Another problem is that Riga was not a port from which the ships sailed to Ireland. They sailed from Libau (as it was known then; to-day, it is Liapage), and there were no direct shipping routes from any part of Latvia, Eastern Europe, or Russia into any port in Ireland. In addition, Queenstown was a deep-water port for transatlantic liners; liners did not berth at the quayside. (When I was a child, we sometimes used to take a spin down to Cobh to look at the ships, and occasionally to meet a passenger from New York when we took the tender out to board the ship.) I am grateful to the historian Nicholas Evans, Hull University, for his email of January 28, 2021.

> Not a single vessel Ever, Ever, Ever arrived in Ireland (not just Cork) from Russia. It is most likely that Laban arrived through the east coast of England, probably Hull, London, West Hartlepool, or Scotland's Leith. The latter two are doubted, so probably Hull. Again, it is likely they stayed in Leeds or Manchester for a short

time and then made the onward journey to Ireland via Liverpool
or Holyhead. They could have taken a migrant vessel for the USA,
but it is more probable they journeyed on a direct shipping route
because of the disease risk.

Some immigrants came to different parts of England, Scotland and Ireland,
and after some time made the onward journey to America, South Africa and
Palestine. When Gerald and Sheila visited Chicago in the 1970s, they looked
for Goldberg relations but did not find any.

Gerald's version of the story said that Itsa Marcus took Laban up to Cork
to Hibernian Buildings, now known as Jewtown. There, Laban was housed
by Abraham and Mira Sandler who came from Akmian in 1875. Gerald said
that Laban got a loan of some money, walked to Dublin where he bought a
peddler's license, and some goods which he sold while walking back to
Cork. He rested there, and then walked to Limerick.

Gerald's story is very colorful, and he believed it, but two things help
me to think that Laban arrived in Dublin first. If Laban's destination was
Limerick, then why would he go to Cork at all? The idea that he was
supposed to be going to America does not seem likely as he had no relations
there that I know of. Immigrants only went where they had contacts. It is
called chain-migration and Fanny Marcus said there was correspondence
between Laban and his relations, the Greenfields. Is it not more likely that
he came from either Liverpool or Holyhead to Dublin and possibly was met
by a member of a Jewish charity which looked after arriving immigrants, as
they did in England?

But the story told by Sandy Hotz (a South African Weinronk cousin) and
accepted by Gerald and by Fanny Marcus is that, when Laban was in
Dublin, he met a man named Zellig Zackson, who loaned him 10 shillings.
Did he buy a peddler's license, as Gerald said? If he did, then why did he
not have one on March 23, 1888, when he was summoned, with a few other
Jewish peddlers, for trading without a certificate? (Ryan, personal
communication, August 2021). At the time, he was living with his relations,
the Greenfields, at 1 Westland Street (an earlier name for Colooney Street),
in Limerick. They took him in when he arrived, as arranged.

The part of Gerald's story which is almost certainly right is that Laban
walked to Limerick. At that time, walking was a common phenomenon in
Ireland. People walked everywhere, and cottagers were often
accommodating to strangers. They often made "shake-down" beds of loose
straw in a barn or thrown on the floor in a corner of the living room, and
sometimes they provided a rug. Often, strangers worked for their food.

Gerald said Laban brought food with him, and wouldn't accept any from the lady of the house because it was not *kosher*. But sometimes needs must and, in any event, Laban could have eaten potatoes, eggs, and soda bread. Gerald said he would only have taken milk if he could milk the cow himself, but he brought a billy can with him for hot water.

Walking would not have been a hardship. As a peddler, he would have walked from one village to the next in Lithuania selling his wares. He would have had decent boots, and possibly a second pair which he might have worn around his neck. If the boots broke, they could be repaired by almost any man on the way, as they all had the materials and tools to do that. There were only roads between major towns, and these were unmade. Mostly people walked through tracks, and one followed the crowd. There were travelling companions too who walked the route together. Language would not have been a real problem, though there was little signage.

Another reason why Laban would have walked is that the train fare from Dublin to Limerick in 1882 was 17/9d for 2nd Class and 10/9d for 3rd class (Rev. Dr. Norman Gamble, email, May 2022). That was a king's ransom. Even Bianconi's coaches, still running at the time, cost two shillings.

Some immigrants did make the onward journey from Ireland to America. Gerald recounted that, years later, Laban was leaving Cork for Queenstown by rail to take the boat to America, with his family when his son, Sidney Henry, got his hand caught in the railway carriage door. He saw this as a portent. But Gerald also told another version of this story in the RTÉ documentary, *An Irishman, a Corkman and a Jew* (1983), in which he said that when Laban was in Leeds and decided to go to America, one of his daughters got her fingertips caught in the carriage door. It is possible that this story exists in the cultural memory of other Litvaks, but I have not yet found it.

These are some of the stories which shaped our antecedents and which shape each of us to-day. I believe they shaped and made Gerald, which is why I am telling them. Perhaps it is easier to remember coming out from Lithuania as fleeing from conscription, pogroms, antisemitism, and persecution, rather than tell of the economic hardship, and poor conditions: the snow, the dark, and cold, the misery of ill-health, and the bleakness of winter.

Prof. Diner said:

> In all of these accounts, the immigrants, dazed, ignorant, and impecunious, not only had no idea where they were going, but by necessity had to be *leaving something horrendous rather than going towards something more positive* (italics mine).

> Those who came to Ireland – and there is no reason to assume
> that any somehow landed there by accident or chicanery – did so
> because they saw in John Bull's other island the prospect for
> economic success. They learned that in Ireland a living could be
> had whereas in Lithuania it could not. Here they could go into
> business, in particular peddling.

Yet, the cultural memories are extremely strong. As a judge once said, sometimes it is very difficult to dig out errors in law. They somehow become embedded, not only into consciousness, but also the traditional fabric of story-telling. It is likely that these stories will long outlive the historical memory, despite the work of many historians.

Life in Limerick

When Laban arrived in Limerick, he was fitted out as a peddler, and put to work immediately. He joined the men of the fledgling community in going door to door and village to village selling on the "vickla" system which was an early form of hire purchase. It was called "vickla" because they didn't know English and couldn't say "weekly." They wrote their sales in a book, and at the end of the week they tallied each account – as a result, they were called the "tallymen." Fanny Marcus (GSA, UCC) recalls:

> They had a back-pack on each shoulder and went out in all
> weathers. There was no slack: they had families to feed and put
> bread on the table. They often went through the streets with
> their backs bent followed by children shouting at them: "A pitchy
> man, a tallyman, a Jew, Jew, Jew."

Laban learned to read and write English. He also learned to read Hebrew and became proficient in the liturgy so he could take a service in later years.

Having begun as a boy peddling goods around the southwest of the country, he learned business very well and within a few years he went into wholesale drapery, which he found more lucrative. He also opened a grocery shop in his house at 50 Coloney Street but that does not seem to have been particularly successful, so he closed it. Much later in life, when he came back from Leeds to live in Cork, he had a business card which was headed "Wholesale rag and metal merchant." He also sold feathers and various hairs for stuffing, and Gerald said he had a contract with the Cross & Blackwell Company to provide them with jam jars for their preserves. In those days, jam jars were a valuable commodity.

L. GOLDBERG,

Offices : IO, Warren's Place, CORK.

Stores : 25, Cattle Market Avenue Shandon St.

and 3, French's Quay,

Wholesale Rag and Metal Merchant.

CURRENT PRICE LIST.

Iron—Mixed

Copper   ,,

Brass   ,,

Lead   ,,

Zinc   ,,

Pewter ,,

Woollen Rags

Mixed Rags

Tailors' Clippings

Feathers

Horse Hair

Cow Hair

Curled Hair

N.B.—All Goods to be delivered Free.   Cash by return.

Laban's business card, when he later had become established in Cork.
(Photo: Goldman Special Archive, UCC)

Laban married Rachel Sandler in 1891. As a wholesale draper, he frequently went to Cork to buy stock. He visited people Elka had known in Akmian, amongst whom were the Sandler family. Abraham and Miriam (Mira) were living in 13 Elizabeth Terrace, Hibernian Buildings, Cork.

Laban and Rachel on their wedding day in Cork, 1891.

Page 2.

iage solemnized at _the Synagogue_ in the _Parish_ of _St Nicholas_ in the _City of Cork._

.	Name and Surname.	Age.	Condition.	Rank or Profession.	Residence at the Time of Marriage.	Father's Name and Surname.	Rank or Profes Father.
1	Louis Goldberg	Full	Bachelor	Dealer	23 Mount pleasant avenue Limerick	Simon Goldberg	decease
2	Rachel Sandler	Minor	Spinster	—	14 Elizabeth Terrace Buck St Nicholas Cork	Abraham Sandler	Drape

Synagogue _____ according to _rites of the Jews_ by _Certificate_   by me,

Louis Goldberg
Rachel Sandler   } in the Presence of us, {   Lewis Ellin   Minister + head of Synagog
                                                                Jacob Cristol

Laban and Rachel's certificate of marriage.

Laban and his daughter, Molly (date unknown).
(Photo: Goldman Special Archive, UCC)

Rachel was one of five children; the others were Isaac, Thomas, Harry and Fanny. Rachel is not entered in the 1901 census, though she was the eldest. She was one year old when she was brought to Cork in 1875. I only knew her when I was a small child. She lived in a house which Gerald rented for her on the South Douglas Road. We went to see Rachel on Sundays when Gerald gave her money. The room was dark because the curtains were always drawn. Archie, Yanks and Ernie – Gerald's brothers – lived there too, but they did not work. The boys took naps in chairs during the day before going out at night. Sheila was most displeased, and never came on those visits. My recollection of Rachel is of an elderly, frail woman, who must have had a very hard life.

How Rachel met Laban is told by Fanny Marcus. One day, when Laban was visiting the Sandlers, he found a beautiful young girl, wearing a calico apron, on her knees scrubbing the floor. When Mira entered the room from the back yard, she introduced them. Fanny described Rachel as having a complexion of "milk roses, light brown hair with natural waves. She was of medium height, slim and dainty." Rachel always regretted her lack of education, only attending school to 3rd class. This may account for her lack of English, as she might not have mixed with English-speaking girls at school. When Laban saw Rachel, he was struck by her beauty, and asked two friends, Zalman and Nelkin Clein, to arrange the *shidduch* (match).

The house at 13 Elizabeth Terrace had a short hall, parlor, and kitchen, from which there was a stairway to the bedrooms. A small yard at the back was packed with wooden boxes around the walls, planted with various flowers and shrubs, with more plants in old buckets and pans. Mira kept hens in a coop which had a door. The hens were kept in at night to prevent the cats attacking them (Marcus, GSA, UCC). Jewish women came around selling hens. Farmers came with eggs, chickens and butter. Mira would put down a clutch of eggs for the hens to sit on and Fanny remembered seeing them and delighting in watching the chicks break out of the shells.

When Fanny and Molly were brought to Cork to see their grandparents, they went by train. Fanny wrote in her memoir describing the excitement of the journey:

> Looking at miles of green fields with animals running around small farmhouses, some with thatched roofs. Men in their heavy farming boots and clothes, some patiently walking up and down and leading a horse and plough. Women standing at the door of the whitewashed cottage, and all flashing by the train's windows, all too quickly.

When they reached Cork, they took a ferry boat from near the station to the other side of the River Lee, and then walked the short distance to the Sandlers' house. One of the family, Harry, played a small stringed instrument and sang (Marcus, GSA, UCC).

After their marriage, Laban and Rachel went to live at 23 Mount Pleasant Avenue in Limerick. They started a family, but their first child, Gertrude (1892), only lived a short time. Two other children – Sidney Henry (1898) and Simon (1901) – died between infancy and five years, and Necha (Nella) when she was 24. Of those who survived, there were three daughters: Fanny (1894), Molly (1896) and Hycie (Hyacinth Rose) (1907); and five sons: Arthur (Archie) (1904), Isadore (Swanee) (1905), Jocelyn (Josh/Yanks) (1910), Yael (Gerald) (1912) and Aaron (Ernie) (1914). Fanny, Molly and Arthur were born in Limerick; Isadore and Hycie in Leeds; and Yanks, Gerald, and Ernie were in Cork. All the men were known by their nicknames, which were given to them by their sisters.

When researching, I found a reference in Rosenblatt's *Irish Jewish Genealogy* (2014-2018) to another daughter, Laura. She is said to have been born in 1919 and to have died in 1920. However, neither Theo nor I ever heard Gerald mention a lost younger sister.

Laban and Rachel lived in five different houses in Limerick. From the first house in 23 Mount Pleasant Avenue, in 1894 they moved to 48 Coloney Street, and in 1897 to 50 Coloney Street. Fanny Marcus described Coloney Street as dirty and smelly. The road was made of mud and stone. There was no sanitation, the houses were crowded and there were frequent fights in the streets between drunks. Poverty was rife. There was domestic violence, women were dragged into the street by their hair and children had neither shoes nor socks. Many men were out of work. These were the humble beginnings for Laban and Rachel.

Then, in 1900, they moved around the corner to a bigger and better house in 67 Henry Street. This house was double-fronted and had washbasins in each room. 67 Henry Street was their best house. Their cousins, the Barrons, lived next door, and when they moved, David Weinronk and his family, also cousins, moved in. The parlor was upstairs, the kitchen and dining room downstairs. Elka did the cooking and baked the bread, while Rachel looked after the children (Marcus, GSA, UCC).

Their last house in Limerick was in 47 Henry Street only a few doors away, but according to Des Ryan there is some doubt about this Census entry.

Laban kept two horses and traps which were used all week. Men only came home at the week-ends. The horses were Polly and Julia, and were stabled behind the Theatre Royal where Laban enjoyed plays (Marcus, GSA, UCC).

Fanny described Laban as a generous man. He helped his family even when they weren't good in business. He had an account in McBirney's and his brothers-in-law, among others, were able to buy on his account. He occasionally found himself in financial difficulties, particularly when his brother Sol went into a jewelry business with Philip Blond and Laban had to bail him out at considerable cost. But he was not perturbed (Marcus, GSA, UCC). Gerald had the same charitable trait as Laban and helped many people within, and outside, the family.

It was a strictly orthodox household. On Friday nights, the sabbath table was laid with a white damask cloth, and the girls wore white dresses. Candlesticks had been brought from Russia, and were polished for the night. These were lit before Laban intoned the *Kiddush* (blessing over wine and bread). There was no possibility of importing *kosher* wine, so Elka made it from raisins. When it was made, she said in Yiddish: *"es muy zech upliegen"* (the wine must lie up). Then it was poured into a glass decanter. The meal was traditional: *Gefilte* fish, soup with *lochshan* and "crocodilian," small meal balls or soft herring and *tsimmis* with roast chicken or meat with pickled cucumbers. Saffron was used in the cooking. The room was lit with paraffin lamps and candles. A *shabbes goy* came in to light them for four pennies and four lumps of sugar. When there was no maid living in the house, Mrs. Burns came to clean (Marcus, GSA, UCC).

They lived in number 48 in 1894 and, in 1887, they moved to number 50. When I looked at these houses at the top of Colooney Street, I noticed the numbering went 48, 49, 51. There is no number 50 today. Number 48 is a blue color and number 51 is grey; both one-storey over ground. However, Fanny Marcus described number 50 in her time as a two-storey dwelling. On the first floor was the parlor, with a flowery carpet and mahogany furniture. There was a glass case inside the door, in which were kept volumes of prayer books. A table with a plush red tasseled cloth draped over it was in front of the case, which was filled with photographs in velvet frames, and countless ornaments, some of which were attached to velvet brackets in various colors. Rachel loved red glass and had a collection. There were many ornaments and a lot of household wares, many of which were purchased in Auchmaty (*sic*) in William Street and Goodbody (*sic*) in George's Street. Women came around bartering old clothes for these ornaments and household wares (Marcus, GSA, UCC).

About every three months, the carpet was rolled and carried to Byrne's Field where it was hung on a line and beaten aggressively. Byrne's Field is now Byrne Avenue, with new houses. It is near Caledonia Place where Jacob Barron and his family lived. In between carpet beatings, Rachel saved tea leaves, dried, and sprinkled them on the carpet and floor and brushed them (Marcus, GSA, UCC).

Laban and Rachel's bedroom was on the first floor next to the parlor. Elka slept on the next floor and may have shared the room with Fanny. The other room was occupied by the maid. In the morning when Elka and Rachel came down to the kitchen, they wore blue check cotton aprons, and Elka always wore a *tichel* (a head band) in the house (Marcus, GSA, UCC).

All the Festivals and High Holidays would have been fully observed. *Pesach* (Passover) required considerable preparations which Rachel and Elka made when they lived in Limerick around the end of the 1900s. Rachel had the kitchen whitewashed, and the brick part of the range painted. The shelves were scrubbed, but the inside of the chiffonier and the kitchen table Elka reserved to herself as she couldn't trust anyone else to get all the *hametz* (unleavened agents) out of it. The table was turned up, and the underside was also scrubbed down to the feet. It was left to dry overnight, and next day it was covered with several sheets of newspaper, on top of that there was a clean canvas bag with draw strings which had been put away from last year and only used for this purpose. On top of that, a thick tablecloth, which in turn was covered by an American cloth, similar to an oil cloth. It was then ready to be laid and used. All the tableware and cooking utensils were cleaned. Elka got a large pot of cold water. She took all the cutlery and tied each piece to a string. There were spaces between each piece. Then the water was boiled, and the pieces of cutlery were dipped in and out by the string until she was satisfied they were free from *hametz* (Marcus, GSA, UCC).

During their time in Limerick there was a lot of illness. In 1898, Molly had bronchitis and then Laban contracted typhoid fever. One day a priest, Fr. Cregan, knocked on the door of 50 Coloney Street. Rachel answered. The priest said he was collecting for a Catholic charity and asked her if she would like to contribute. Rachel gave him a shilling. Next door was Coll's pub, run by Mary Coll. The priest went into the pub and told Mary that a beautiful woman next door had given him a shilling, and she was crying. Mary told him they were Jews, and her husband was seriously ill. Fr. Cregan was impressed that a Jewish family would give so much to a Catholic charity, and he was sorry to hear that her husband was so ill. Then

Fr. Cregan wondered if he could say Mass for Laban. Mary thought they wouldn't mind. The next Sunday, their maid servant, Mary Morrissey, was at the Mass. She came back very excited, shouting: "Oh Mam, the boss is going to get better. Fr. Cregan told the people about him and said Mass for him in the chapel and everyone prayed for him. He is going to get better, I tell you." He did. Such is the power of prayer that none should ever be eschewed (Marcus, GSA, UCC).

Later Fr. Cregan came to visit when Laban was convalescing. His physician, Dr. Myles, made a professional call at the same time. Tea was brought up and served with *kes cuchen* (cheesecake) made by Elka. The three men met together again to play cards, and this became a regular gathering until Fr. Cregan was moved. Laban gave him a travelling rug as a gift (Marcus, GSA, UCC).

Elka's gravestone; she died in Leeds in 1922, aged 78.

On Saturday and Sunday evenings, there was singing in 67 Henry Street. A lot of people came: one of them was a Sandler who played the melodeon or concertina. They danced half sets of eight. Harry, son of Berra, sang a ballad about Robert Emmet. Fanny remembered the words: "Bold Robert Emmet the darling of Erin / Bold Robert Emmet who died with a smile." The singing drew a crowd outside on the street. As they were attracting too many people, Rachel decided they should stop (Marcus, GSA, UCC).

Chapter 4

A LIMERICK
BROIGES

Look, how good and how pleasant is the dwelling of brothers
together.

Psalm 133 (Trans. Robert Alter)

D es Ryan, Limerick historian, has investigated this period, and I am grateful to him for his generous assistance.

Broiges is a Yiddish word, and means a bitter dispute or feud within a community. In 1900, such a dispute occurred in the Hebrew congregation of Limerick. What caused it, what it was about, why it was so bitter is hard to comprehend. In retrospect it seems trivial enough, yet it caused great bitterness and damage and was a source of grief, anger, and disillusionment to Gerald. His father, Laban was at the center of it.

Rev. Elias Bere Levin (1863-1936) was ordained a rabbi at the famous *yeshiva* of Tels, Lithuania, at the age of 19. He first took up a post in Vilna. Then, in 1882, he accepted the position as Minister to the small Limerick community where he was always known as a Reverend. When he arrived, he found the tiny community "riven with doctrinal difference and divided into two groups" (Feeley, 1980). Since Laban can barely have arrived before Levin, and was then only in his early teens, he can hardly have been involved in the origins of the quarrels. Some of these disputes were determined in the courts before Judge Adams, who was well known to the community, and had attended some of their functions.

As early as 1881-1882, and continuing until 1900, there were at least 23 cases consisting of various assaults, embezzlements, and monies owing. There were others due to rows in the synagogue over business dealings. What the differences were between the factions is not clear, but if they were doctrinal, then Rev. Levin ought to have been able to resolve them. Apparently he did not; or, if he tried, he was unsuccessful. The two factions continued to war with each other up to 1904, when the antisemitic attacks by Fr. John Creagh, Redemptorist leader of the Arch Confraternity in St. Alphonsus Church (**Chapter 5**) forced them together. The *broiges* exploded in 1901-1902 like an atomic blast which left a cloud hanging over the Limerick *shtetl*, until the restoration of the cemetery in the mid-1980s. This story is the worst of many arising from the history of this community. In telling it, I wonder where the actual truth lies.

Financial Lending and a New Synagogue and Cemetery

By 1896, Laban was President of the community, and on June 28, he called a meeting to elicit advice and support for a new synagogue because "the present one was too small, and deficient in other purposes" (trove.nla.gov.au, courtesy Ryan). "A committee was formed and was progressing most favorably" (*ibid.*). Laban's view was that a cemetery should be opened before a synagogue. His authority was Genesis 23:3: Abraham buys land to bury his wife. Others disagreed with this interpretation.

In September 1898, Rabbi Adler, Chief Rabbi of Great Britain and the Commonwealth, made his third visit to Limerick where he repeated what he had said on his second visit in 1892, namely, that no members of the community should engage in financial lending. There were no more than five families engaged in that business. Laban and some others expressed their displeasure at this practice, but I do not think that it was the central core of the *broiges*. Very serious rows and unhappy differences broke out in 1900, resulting in violence, which ended before the courts. A law report in *The Irish Times* (September 1, 1900), gives as clear an account as any other source:

A Curious Dispute in Limerick

At Limerick Petty Sessions yesterday, a number of cases were heard arising out of a dispute among the members of the Jewish community in Limerick. In September last, there was an election for president and Louis Goldberg was elected to the office of President by a majority over Mr. Aronovich. Dissention among the members followed, respecting burial and pew fees.

Mr. Goldberg resigned and was succeeded by Mr. Aronovich, who held office only for a week. At the outcome of arbitration proceedings, Mr. Goldberg was reinstated, culminating on Saturday 25th August, 1900, when the service of the Jewish Sabbath was interrupted and the synagogue was more or less wrecked by the party opposed to Mr. Goldberg. Some 20 of the Jews arrived with sticks and missiles, entered the synagogue, broke the chandeliers, smashed the furniture and ended with a general tumult during which assaults were committed.

In court, Goldberg's case was that any complaint should have been made after the service but Levin, the officiating priest [*sic*], stated that the time for such was after prayers and before the Scroll of the Law was taken from the ark.

As a result of these disturbances, proceedings were issued in the police court and upheld on appeal to the magistrates, which according to Hymen Graffe and Barney Jaffe (*Limerick Leader*, March 23, 1902), resulted in damages being paid out to Laban and his party. Laban entered into an agreement never to have any claim against the Limerick Hebrew Congregation (Ryan, 2002). The amount is unknown, and there is no record of this settlement.

Further trouble arose between Laban and Wolf Toohey (Ryan, 2014). Laban had sought subscriptions for a burial fund which he had started, but Toohey, Graffe and others refused to subscribe. Laban asked them to give up their seats so that he could rent them to other members who had no objection to making a payment (Ryan, 2014).

The *broiges* worsened. There seems to have been more than one attempt at arbitration. One, by Leopold Greenberg, failed in January 1902 (*The Jewish Chronicle*, January 10, 1902). He proposed that the United Synagogues Council in London would buy the cemetery for the whole community. This was considered carefully in Limerick at a general meeting, where a motion was proposed by D. Weinronk and S. Ginsberg that this proposition should be opposed, because it was already agreed that the subscribers of the Limerick Hebrew Congregation should be the exclusive owners of the ground (*The Jewish Chronicle*, January 10, 1902.)

Two synagogues emerged soon after the disturbances in 63 Coloney Street that August. When the *broiges* seems to have been most intractable, Laban converted the upstairs front room of his house at 67 Henry Street into a synagogue where about 10 families worshipped (Marcus, GSA, UCC). Later he moved it around the corner to 72 Coloney Street. Ryan cites a letter from Marcus Blond, dated January 9, 1901 (*Limerick Leader*), in which Blond said that Laban "was inviting people to come to the 'so called synagogue' at 72 Coloney Street. For our Christian neighbors and friends not to be misled, I hasten to inform the public... that there is no other synagogue authorized by Chief Rabbi Adler." Laban replied on January 10, 1901, that he did this because he did not want to be associated with those few who engaged in financial lending. As I delve further into these muddy waters, this does not seem to be the core reason, but it must have been a contributing factor. Gerald always said that Laban was following *Halacha* (Jewish law), which he said required that a burial ground should be opened before a synagogue.

I have investigated this as thoroughly as I can by consulting three rabbis, and none of them could confirm that such was a required law. Rather, it seems that it is a rule or custom and practice based on commonsense, because prayers and services can be said anywhere, and in Limerick, for a long time, they were held in Rev. Levin's house amongst others. Another reason to open a burial ground was because all funerals were brought to Cork, a requirement that took its physical and financial toll. What emerges is that there was a split in the community, perhaps since it began. The dispute over financial lending and the opening of a burial ground were, I think, just the catalysts which brought a festering feud to a head. But of these, there is no doubt that the opening of the burial ground was the more significant.

Rev. Levin does not appear to have called the sides together to try and resolve these differences, which seem to have been doctrinal. Rather, he took sides or stayed faithfully with the Toohey-Graffe faction from 63 Coloney Street by whom he was employed.

One unexpected and extraordinary consequence of the *broiges* was that Rev. Levin could not, or would not, kill meat for the Goldberg faction, since he did not support them. Laban, therefore, undertook a course with a rabbi in Cork and acquired the qualification for killing fowl, but Fanny Marcus said that he was neither a comfortable nor a competent butcher. He could just about handle chickens, and he paid for those that he killed while learning, and for those that could not be eaten if they were not then *kosher* (GSA, UCC). Laban went to England and brought over Rev. Velitzkin, who only stayed a few years (Ryan, 2014). Fanny Marcus said that one day she was asked by Elka to ask Rev. Levin to kill a chicken for her because she felt very sick, and a chicken, especially as soup, is a legendary Jewish cure. Levin said he was sorry she was ill, but he could not do it: he had been warned by his community, who employed him, not to do anything to assist the Goldbergs.

Trying to disentangle the various threads in this story is difficult. They become both hard to follow and to understand. Apparently, Laban proceeded with his plan to buy a plot of land at Kilmurry, outside Limerick, and raised £41 (Ryan, 2014). At the same time, and unknown to him, Toohey, Graffe and others were collecting from their non-Jewish neighbors to help finance the cemetery (Ryan, 2014). Laban wanted the names of all the community in the deed, but he discovered that Toohey, Graffe and others had signed a deed on February 17, 1902, which only recorded the names of the 63 Coloney Street congregation. The Rules provided that anyone who is Jewish could be buried there (Ryan, 2014).

The deed was signed, and Laban was excluded not only from it but from having anything to do with the burial ground. Rev. Levin not only issued a *pinkus* (a deed of excommunication), but also wrote a "Prologue" as a record of the proceedings of the Holy Burial Society of the Limerick Hebrew Congregation. It was written in classical Hebrew (Benson, 2005).

> In order that the coming generation, with the help of God, our
> future descendants and all those that succeed us, may know

what happened to us from the time we settled here in the city of
Limerick... when one soul from the congregation of Jacob left us,
we were obliged to transport the person to the nearby city of
Cork, in order to perform a Jewish Burial. This was done at high
financial cost and physical expense... It has not been possible for
us to act in accordance with these holy customs... sometimes
because of the pressing demands of the steam train and at other
times because of the hardship of the road, and laws of the land.

Rev. Levin continued expressing the need to buy a tract of land for burial,
to avoid "derision from the gentiles... who say, 'It is not enough that the
Hebrews be wandering through their lifetimes, but also after their death.'"

In this Prologue, Levin claims that the endeavor was obstructed, until
Leopold Jacob Greenberg, the publisher and editor-in-chief of *The Jewish
Chronicle*, promised to raise the balance required, if the community raised
£50. He said that Greenberg fulfilled his commitment, but none of that
money was received, though it was not his fault. He said: "Those
responsible were the *Beni Korach* who had not yet died... quarrel mongers...
who harm every proper and useful matter. David Weinronk, Leib
Goldberg, Saul Ginzberg, Azriel Shabbatia Aronowitz, who intrigued
against us at every stage, because they were not appointed by our
community as its leaders...." He is likening them to the followers of Korach
who had challenged Moses' authority and were swallowed by an
earthquake (Numbers 16:1–18:32). Rev. Levin could not forgive "those
mentioned earlier in the Prologue who are doomed to eternal shame,
because they did us great harm and defiled the name of the congregation of
Israel before the gentiles... they can never hold office nor accept any
appointment in the Holy Burial Society." And so, they were excluded from
the deed, and the memorial tablet in the prayer house at the cemetery, until
this day. This always upset Gerald. He wanted his father's name on it, but
it was not possible.

The *broiges* even engaged Judge Richard Adams K.C., judge of the
County Court of Limerick. who was a reader of *The Jewish Chronicle*. He
observed correspondence about the Limerick Jews of whom he was a
"sincere well-wisher" (*The Jewish Chronicle*, March 14, 1902). He called them
"a most industrious and well conducted body, at once respectable and
respected." He said they had received great kindness and fair play to the
honor of the Catholics and Celtic community amongst whom they live. He
said they had got themselves into a very bitter feud:

... two rival synagogues confront each other, and the feeling
between the parties is so strong that more than once it has given
rise to assaults, which have been investigated in my court. I never
could make out what all the trouble was about; some obscure
point of ritual, I imagine.

He then sought the intervention of someone of tact and standing from the
London Jews "to try and compose a feud which injures the honor of an
honorable community; and is a source of dissension to men who require
unity for their happiness, being, however well treated, but 'strangers in a
strange land.'" Sol Goldberg replied to the Judge in *The Jewish Chronicle*
(March 21, 1902), agreeing that he did not know, and could not get to the
bottom of the matter, and nobody else could – "for the Limerick Jews do
not know themselves." That letter gave rise to a leader column in the same
issue in which it praised the Judge. But it noted, sadly, that such occurrences
were common amongst communities throughout the United Kingdom.
There was, it said a "lack of peaceable disposition and self-control" shown
by burial societies. It endorsed the Judge's suggestion of sending an
arbitrator to Limerick, which had been done before on many occasions. It
noted the Chief Rabbi on his pastoral visits had done this many times, but
the feuds were too numerous for him to be able to deal with all of them. The
Judge's letter and the leader article did have effect: on March 21, 1902, *The
Jewish Chronicle* reported that the suggestion was considered by the Board
of Guardians, and they were prepared to offer their good offices.

On September 12, 1902, Laban took up his pen again to write to *The
Jewish Chronicle* to advise that they had accepted the offer of arbitration. He
accused Rev. Levin and his party of "blankly refusing arbitration." The
deed had been signed several months previously, and now the row seems
to have been about the money. £41 had been collected and was in a bank. It
had never been paid over to the Graffe faction of 63 Colooney Street,
perhaps because the deed was done behind the backs of Laban's group, and
they were excluded. Laban said he was willing to release the sum
"provided we obtain the same voice in the management as originally
agreed." Alternatively, he was prepared to give back half the money or just
arbitrate. Blond replied on September 19, 1902, acknowledging the offer of
arbitration from the Board, but "as to the burial ground" his claim was to
recover the portion of the £41 which had been collected from his
community. Graffe and his party had now issued proceedings before the
Recorder's Court returnable for hearing on October 7 to recover the money.
On September 26, 1902, Laban wrote to *The Jewish Chronicle*, reporting that

the matter had been settled. There is no further mention of this case, and in all probability it was struck out on October 7.

While the men from Akmian were short-tempered, resolute, determined, unstoppable, quick to take offence and bear grudges, they were also their own worst enemies. The story I have just described is the worst of all. Yet, there are some puzzling aspects. They probably brought many grudges and resentments with them from Lithuania where they were a close-knit community, and existing feuds may not have been resolved by changing countries. Such is likely to occur in many small communities, irrespective of their ethnicity.

Gerald was born long after these events. He and his sister Fanny had a warm, loving view of Laban. Fanny knew him for 16 years longer than Gerald, who only knew him for 20 years, and it is not improbable that he had developed an idealized vision of Laban. Gerald was a very conservative man. He formed opinions and ideas and stuck to them. When he knew of these stories, it caused him much dismay. Could these terrible things really have happened to his father? Was there no justice in the world? How many trials and tribulations did his father have to endure? He did not consider defeat in his own life. It was not a word he knew, but he had to come to terms with the fact that his father had been defeated. To me, it is clear that these episodes in his father's life had a huge influence in shaping Gerald.

It seems unlikely that Gerald had all the minutiae of his father's various dealings, and many appearances in court as a plaintiff, defendant or witness. Gerald would have been greatly upset had he known that Laban traded without a peddler's certificate in 1888; was first assaulted in Vize's Field in 1892; was fined for riding the trains without a ticket in 1895; and fined again for failing to pay rates in 1901 (Ryan, personal communication). Laban was not a stranger to court, and neither were the other members of the community. A point to remember about them is that many were related: Weinronks, Goldbergs, Barrons, Greenfields, and Martinsons were cousins. For some reason, Gerald felt the responsibility of this. For him, it was a terrible outcome, despite great efforts to do what he believed was right. When he talked about these events, it was always with great bitterness.

Restoration of the Cemetery, 1980s

The outcome of this feud affected Gerald in one other way. He corresponded with Denis Leonard, Chairman of the Limerick Civic Trust, who undertook the restoration and maintenance of the Burial Ground in the mid-1980s. Gerald and Denis Leonard had a very good relationship. There is a small cache of letters written by Gerald, which exhibit a more emotional side.

Leonard wrote to Gerald (December 13, 1983) that the Trust would conduct the restoration of the cemetery. Gerald had visited Kilmurry with RTÉ in March 1983 when they were filming the documentary *An Irishman, a Corkman and a Jew,* and was shocked by its condition, being completely overgrown with brambles and weeds. He visited later in July with his cousin Jack Weinronk, from Port Elizabeth, South Africa. Jack's grandfather was David Weinronk, who had been a member of the community. On that visit, Gerald said they were both "broken hearted. Recriminations about the past were not acceptable." Leonard's reply to Gerald (January 14, 1984) said it was far worse than he expected. Gerald wrote a very long letter on January 21, 1984: "… the condition of the cemetery was only part of my reaction. I had that sense of grief as well as the realization that the picture might have been otherwise." Gerald described a book which he said was a record by Rev. Levin. It contained the names of those on the memorial plaque in the prayer house, but not of those interred. He said he tried to find records of the deaths of his own immediate family, and he had found the death certificate of his brother, Sidney Henry, who died in 1903. I have not managed to locate this document. On February 13, 1984, Leonard replied, advising there would be a joint approach with Limerick County Council to clear the debris and begin restoration as soon as the weather improved. He wrote: "Mr. Goldberg, I really enjoy our letters…" A sketch of the restored cemetery was approved by Gerald as "admirable."

When I visited the cemetery in August 2021, I was impressed by its tranquility and spaciousness. There are very few stones, and some graves are unmarked. There had been two plaques; one relating to the cemetery, and one to the synagogue. Gerald wanted, and was so advised by Jack Weinronk, to take the memorial plaque from the cemetery, but he didn't. As he said to Leonard, "I am now 72 and can't live forever. What will happen to it after my death?" That plaque is now placed on the wall inside the prayer house. Then on a subsequent visit to Limerick, he found the plaque, I know not how, that had been over the synagogue. It was in pieces under a heap of scrap in a man's yard. Gerald had to pay a considerable sum for it, which he didn't mind doing, although he said, "It was my duty to redeem it, not ransom it." He sought Leonard's advice on what should happen to the stone plaque. It is now in the Irish Jewish Museum, Dublin, but not in good condition.

The Jewish cemetery, Kilmurry, Limerick – now restored.

The last letter I have is dated November 28, 1990, and it reveals a little more about the *broiges*. The restoration and re-consecration of the cemetery could never have happened without Gerald and Denis Leonard. Gerald sent Leonard a copy of the deed and the Rules of the Burial Society. He said they were the most unusual rules he had come across. The cemetery was acquired on February 17, 1902, and the synagogue on December 16, 1904.

> Rule 12. "That no member mentioned in the Deed shall ever have the right or power, under any circumstances whatsoever, to transfer his title as member in the Deed to any person, but that it shall be hereditary, his place being taken by his eldest son, or whoever may be his heir at law."

Gerald remarked that "…it was quite clear that the rule was deliberate. Also clear is that it was wholly undemocratic and intended to ensure that the Trusteeship should be kept within what may be called an 'elitist' group of people and in particular, against two. One of those was my father and the other was his cousin, both of whom were expelled from the congregation. The reason lay in what, on one side, was a bitter reaction to the view expressed by the other that a Synagogue was a priority and that the acquisition of a Cemetery should take second place thereto."

When he visited the prayer house after reconstruction and saw the tablet which had been erected, and that his father's name did not appear on it, Gerald expressed to Leonard this feeling: "It would have been what my father wished, and in itself, would have marked a reconciliation between our side and the Trustees. It was not to be, however, and must be forgotten." He was at least pleased that on the Order of the Commissioners of Charitable Donations and Bequests, which he obtained, his name appeared on the back of the original. So, in a small way, Gerald took some comfort from that. But he was really disappointed that, even in death, the two sides could not be brought together, and they never will be now.

Postscript

For all of Gerald's long life, he grieved over this row and wanted somehow to bring about a reconciliation. He died resigned to the irreconcilable. But sometimes things happen or occur in the most inexplicable ways. The word may be accident or serendipity, but whatever it is, this story does have an end which I tell with the permission of Theo and Val.

After I began researching and writing this book in about 2020, I was in conversation with my nephew, Rabbi Alex, Theo's son. Alex has a very strong interest in the family and its genealogy. We talked at length about Limerick on a number of occasions. He told me that Val was a descendant from the Blond family who featured prominently in Limerick. It was some months later that I put the obvious conclusion together. So, this is its significance and how it now ends.

Theo, the grandson of Laban, married Valerie Silverman in 1971. Val is a granddaughter of Zila Blond, who was from Manchester and a sister of Marcus Blond from Limerick. By this marriage, it occurred to me that the reconciliation which Gerald craved, and had tried so hard to bring about, had been achieved. Gerald never knew that justice had, at last, been done, and the two sides of that small and fractious community had been brought together by the solemnization of a marriage, closing the circle.

Chapter 5

A LIMERICK POGROM, 1904

The Rascal Monk

Judge Richard Adams. *The Jewish Chronicle* (May 12, 1922)

The ochres give one a long sense of antisemitism.

Sasha Dugdale, *Pigment*, in *Deformations*

I am grateful to the Limerick historian, Des Ryan, for his assistance with the material in this chapter.

I have often heard it said that Ireland was unique in never having had an antisemitic episode; and while there has not been a major event, antisemitism has sporadically occurred, specifically in Limerick in January 1904. However, I do not think this episode was the start of such hatred.

Ryan found incidents in a report of the *Cork Examiner* (October 12, 1886): "The Polish Jews and the Kanturk Trades' Union." This article reported that the Union passed a motion protesting at the system of trading carried on by a number of Polish Jews in the Kanturk area, which was claimed to be "adverse" to the "legitimate traders," and they vowed to have nothing to do with "those imported hawkers." They urged all others not to deal with them. Copies of the resolution were sent to neighboring branches of the trades unions and National League. This is classic antisemitism, driven by a resistance to commercial competition. The Jewish traders operated an early form of hire purchase.

A similar report in the *Aberdeen Journal* (March 17, 1888), quotes an even more venomous meeting of the Cork Trades' Council, proposing to "hunt the Jews out of Cork" on the grounds that "they were ruining honest trade." The Jewish community was characterized as "crucifying gypsies" and "vampires" who should not "be tolerated in a Christian community" but should be "exterminated." At that time, there were about 300 Jews in Cork, all living in one locality in the south of the city. Another strange report from *The Jewish Chronicle* (July 15, 1887), states that "at the Assizes before Judge O'Brien, application was made to exempt Jews from jury service in Limerick due to *hostility* against them" (*italics mine*).

However, what happened in Limerick in 1904 was far more significant than these earlier episodes. In Limerick, there were rabble-rousing sermons from the pulpit by a respected local cleric, mob attacks on Jews and their property, and a refusal to pay bills to them or sell them food. The affair garnered world-wide coverage.

While the episode is often said to be a totally isolated and atypical event, the fact is that what happened on January 11, 1904, was the culmination of sporadic tensions which had existed in Limerick from as early as 1879, when there was an assault on a member of the Jewish community. A more serious attack occurred on Easter Sunday, 1884 (Ryan, 1984), when the house of Leib Siev was attacked by 100 people; glass and doors were broken, and stones thrown, injuring some of the family. Ryan further relates that two weeks later, Jacob Barron was attacked in the same road. He was saved by a woman who took him into her house. In November 1886, three dockers attacked Moses Leone outside his house on Colooney Street. The windows were smashed and the ruffians shouted: "These dirty Jews should not be allowed to live at all." Later that same day, Rev. Levin was attacked by other dock laborers (Ryan, 1984). Another more serious assault occurred on August 27, 1892. It was a Sunday: Benjamin Jaffe and his family were walking down Military Road (now O'Connell Avenue), when they were assaulted and knocked to the ground by three men. When Jaffe's brother-in-law tried to assist Mrs. Jaffe, he was also assaulted. They were saved by a passer-by (Ryan, 1984).

Laban was assaulted at Vize's Field, off Bowman Street, by John and William Tracey who threw stones at him. In his evidence, Laban said that the community lived in Westland Street, and were subjected to "continued persecution by numbers of young urchins like the accused who not alone attacked their houses but also followed them individually in the streets, and flung stones at them." (*Munster News*, February 20, 1892). Both John and William Tracey were sentenced to one week in gaol.

Between 1897 and 1900, there were at least 24 such assaults on Jews, leading to prosecutions and convictions. The police were unable to monitor all the streets, or give protection to all the traders as they went into "back streets" without their knowledge (Keogh & McCarthy, 2005, p.49). Thus, it cannot be said that the incidents of 1904 were not without precedent, though the scale and ferocity of the attack by Fr. Creagh was of a different order.

Fr. Creagh's attack

Ryan (1984) describes how Fr. John Creagh, a young Redemptorist priest, was appointed the spiritual director of the Arch Confraternity of the Holy Family, located in St. Alphonsus' Church, opposite Colooney Street. The sodality numbered some 6,500 men and boys, and was so big that it assembled from Monday to Friday nights. (There was a separate Confraternity for women in a different church with a different spiritual director.) In December 1903, Fr. Creagh told the Confraternity that he would discuss a special subject in the New Year, and hoped for a big attendance. It was a big subject, which would take him some time to explain fully. The statement caused much speculation, but the sodality had to wait until January 11 before he was ready. He was always controversial, but Ryan says: "It was his campaign against the Jews which was to write the names of Fr. Creagh and Limerick into the history books for all time" (Ryan, 1984).

Fr. John Creagh. (Photo: Limerick Museum)

The pulpit in St. Alphonsus Church, Limerick, from which Fr. John Creagh preached his sermons.

Fr. Creagh's First Sermon

In this sermon, Fr. Creagh said that the common good of his community must be guarded and never sacrificed. When a common danger is "pointed out," then they (the community) must do everything to preserve themselves. He continued: "It would be madness for a man to nourish in his breast a viper that might slay its benefactor with its poisonous bite." He said it would be "madness for a people to allow an evil to grow in their midst that would cause them ruin... they were allowing themselves to become slaves to Jew usurers... They knew who they were. The Jews were once the chosen people of God. God's mercy towards them was boundless. They were the people of whom was born the Messiah, Jesus Christ, Our Lord and Master. But they rejected Jesus: they crucified Him. They called down the curse of His precious blood upon their heads... I do not hesitate to say there are no greater enemies of the Catholic Church than the Jews...." He urged his audience to stand outside the houses of Jews at night to see those in shawls, going to pay the "usurious Jew." This sermon (January 11, 1904) was reproduced in full by the Limerick newspapers of the time, and is quoted in historical texts (Keogh, 1998).

Fr. Creagh sought to persuade his men and boys to engage in racism and to wreak socio-economic havoc on the Jewish community. In both of these endeavors, he was extremely successful. After his sermon that is what some of the sodality did, but although they saw no nefarious activity, several of the Jewish community were insulted, assaulted and abused (Keogh & McCarthy, 2005). Steps were taken to protect them.

Davitt's Letter

Rev. Levin and Sol Goldberg sent a letter to Michael Davitt, founder of the Land League, and to John Redmond M.P. Letters and telegrams also went to the Chief Rabbi of the United Kingdom, the Dublin Community, and others.

Redmond responded with a brief letter to the newspapers hoping common sense would prevail.

Davitt responded with an open letter in *The Freeman's Journal* (January 16, 1904), taking Fr. Creagh to task for the serious distortion of facts, and saying there was no truth to the "horrible allegations about ritual murder here insinuated against the persecuted race. I protest as an Irishman," he wrote, "and as a Catholic against this spirit of barbarous malignity being introduced into Ireland under the form of material regard for the welfare of our workers." He said Fr. Creagh deliberately incited the people to hunt the Jews from their midst.

Davitt asked Bishop O'Dwyer to intervene, but he refused. And when Rev. Levin and Sol Goldberg sought a meeting, O'Dwyer would not meet them. Instead, his secretary met them, and asked them to refrain from making any public statements. They complied, but doing so did not assist.

The police protected the community who were now in a siege situation. Without protection, the injury would have been quite serious (Keogh & McCarthy, 2005).

Fr. Creagh's Second Sermon

Fr. Creagh's second sermon, a week later, was a very long rebuke to Davitt, in which a number of the antisemitic tropes, and materials from the first sermon, were repeated. It too was reported in the newspapers of the time. The combined length of both sermons is in excess of 4,000 words. Fr. Creagh was very eloquent, and had a florid turn of phrase. He was a considerable orator.

Fr. Creagh said: "... I knew very well I would be the object of much attack from the enemies of God, and from those who had been duped by the Jews, by those who were in their hands and wanted to screen themselves; but I did not expect such a letter from Mr. Davitt."

He pondered that the Catholics and Ireland had suffered every kind of repression, but asked if that was a reason why they should submit to voluntary persecution by the Jews.

> Let us defend ourselves before their heels are too firmly planted on our necks... Nowadays they do not dare slay Christian children, but will not hesitate to expose them to a longer and even more cruel martyrdom by taking the cloths off their backs and the bit out of their mouths... Twenty years ago and fewer, Jews were only known by name and evil repute in Limerick. They were sucking the blood of other nations, but these nations rose up and threw them out. But they came to our land and fastened themselves on us like leeches, and to draw our blood when they had been forced away from other countries. They have indeed fastened themselves upon us and now the question is whether or not we will allow them fasten themselves still more upon us, until we and our children are the helpless victims of their rapacity.

The Aftermath

There were some assaults soon after the first sermon, but on the morning of Monday, January 18, 1904, even before the second sermon, when the Jewish men tried to make their weekly collections, they were met with hostility. In this section I rely on work by Keogh & McCarthy (2005). The *Limerick Leader* reported that there were mobs of 300 people in Irishtown (January 22, 1904, evidence of Constable Bell; also *Limerick Echo*, January 23, 1904, evidence of Constable Portobello). There were many women, girls and boys who threw mud, milk and stones. District Inspector O'Hara reported that the Jews were hunted and, in some cases, it was difficult to keep an eye on them all as many times they went into back streets without the knowledge or protection of the police (Keogh & McCarthy, 2005).

Isolated incidents occurred in different parts of the city. A man who was called to a house in Nelson Street was hemmed in at one end by a hostile crowd. He tried to flee, but there was another crowd at the opposite end. Stones were thrown at him (Shillman, unpublished mss, GSA, UCC). Samuel Sochat (named as Shokett in the press reports) had a whole bucket of sour milk poured over him (Shillman). Louis Cramer was badly assaulted by a threatening mob (Shillman). Some shops were attacked. There had been assaults during the day. There were some further incidents in February when four horse collars were stolen from Max Blond, President of the Community. On St. Patrick's Day, March 17, Samuel Racussen was assaulted in Henry Street (Ryan, 1984) and on March 25 Patrick Sheehan was fined £1 for this assault. Trade had ceased in the city but continued in the county, according to the police. Shops refused to sell goods to the Jewish community, and children were shunned at school (Keogh & McCarthy, 2005). Fanny Marcus also experienced antisemitism at school, and when she complained she came off worse (GSA, UCC).

Gannon (2020) writes: "What can be said with certainty is that between 40 and 50 sporadic anti-Jewish incidents were reported between February and July 1904, a very small number of which caused some degree of 'bodily harm.'" Rev. Levin was attacked on between three and five occasions. The community had some lucky escapes due to the police intervention. There were about 10 prosecutions and convictions quite early on, six by the State and four privately. Yet, despite Fr. Creagh's plea that "the Jews need have no fear of violence, intimidation or assault," it persisted for another six months. Nor did Fr. Creagh desist from his antisemitic utterances. When removed to Belfast two weeks after the sermons, ostensibly on a mission, he continued to speak about the Jews. And when Julian Grande met him in April 1904, Fr. Creagh said he would continue his campaign (Keogh & McCarthy, 2005).

After the rioting on January 18, Rev. Levin panicked, not unreasonably, and called on District Inspector O'Hara for assistance. On the same day, Levin reported that the traders were ruined; they had not collected 10% of their usual collection, and they had sold nothing in a fortnight. On the evening of January 18, Levin sent cables to the Chief Rabbi in London and E. "Wormser" Harris in Dublin: "Antisemitic riots took place throughout the day and general boycott in force. Community in peril. Every member assaulted" (Keogh & McCarthy, 2005). *The Jewish Chronicle* had a reporter there who said that he was fearful of what was likely to happen. There were slogans: "Down with the Jews," "They kill our innocent children," Death to the Jews," and "We must hunt them out" – the same slogans were as in Lithuania. The reporter wrote: "When I witnessed the organized attacks today, all the horrors of Kisninev came back to me, and then, and only then, I was able to realize what Kisninev meant." (Kisninev was a pogrom in Moldova in 1903.) Of course, it was not the same, but the Jews were living in a state of terror, not knowing how it would all end (Keogh & McCarthy, 2005).

Fr. Creagh had told the people not to pay their debts. Six petty huckster shops lost all their trade to Christians. Bills from wholesalers continued to arrive. Milk supply stopped briefly. O'Hara reported the Jews got nothing but abuse. He opined that, after a while, the "excitement will subside." The *Limerick Leader* advised people to avoid violence, and reported "… in the last few days, Jews have been subjected to ill treatment and assault in the street." It was thought that sending in reinforcements would have had an adverse effect. Deputy Inspector General Considine said: "They should act as if nothing had happened." He expected the matter to "blow over" (Keogh & McCarthy, 2005).

The police also took a low-key approach to Fr. Creagh's second sermon. They ignored the antisemitism, and concentrated on the single last sentence that he did not want any violence – although an unidentified senior officer said, "this may be the beginning of a very serious business" (Keogh & McCarthy, 2005).

The Duke of Norfolk and the British Board of Jewish Deputies both asked Cardinal Logue of Armagh to intervene but he declined on grounds of jurisdiction (Keogh & McCarthy, 2005). Towards the end of January, the Chairman of the British Board of Jewish Deputies, Charles Emanuel, petitioned the Lord Lieutenant of Ireland to have Fr. Creagh prosecuted. But the police advised the Secretary to the Lord Lieutenant that "it might do more harm than good, and there was not enough evidence." On April 5, 1904, the Board sent another letter referring to the plight of 20 of the 35 families. They said they were ruined and compelled to beg for bare sustenance. No one could step outside their door without fear of bodily injury (Keogh & McCarthy, 2005).

In April, Julian Grande, Chairman of the Irish Mission to the Jews, wrote letters to *The Times, Daily Express* and *The Irish Times* in which he rejected the contention of the Lord Lieutenant who said that matters were better now. Grande said the boycott was in full force, and the police had only provided "passive" assistance. This annoyed the police who responded that these comments were "highly colored and not in accordance with the facts." Nonetheless, Sgt. Moore accepted the Jews were hardly doing any business. He said: "If this state of affairs continues – and it is likely to continue – they must either leave the city or fall into a condition of want if they do not get assistance from outside" (Keogh & McCarthy, 2005). District Inspector O'Hara said that the claims that the police only gave passive assistance were completely unfounded. But then came the extraordinary – though not surprising – statement that the "methods of doing business practiced by the Jews was entirely responsible for the agitation." In other words, the old trope: the Jews bring trouble on themselves. This was repeated in a number of documents and press comment. O'Hara also issued a report in which he said: "the Jews were not so badly off as they themselves made out." Many times, both he and other officers repeated that they had given every protection to the community.

While the police will rarely show themselves in a bad light or admit to any errors, these last two statements cause me concern. They were agreeing with Fr. Creagh, and they were downplaying the extent and severity of the boycott and violence. George Wyndham M.P., Chief Secretary for Ireland, was told by McDonnell, his under-secretary, the history of the events, and he too added that the Jews were responsible for the episodes because of their method of business. Wyndham advised the House of Commons on April 14, in reply to a question from Mr. Sloan M.P. for Belfast, that people had ceased to deal with them (the Jews) but any money due is gradually being paid. "The police received special instructions to use every exertion to protect the Jews from acts of molestation or violence; eight such cases have been brought and two ... are pending. It is not correct to say that individuals are starving; they are able to obtain supplies and necessities in the locality" (Keogh & McCarthy, 2005).

The infamous Raleigh case on April 4, 1904, shows how local loyalty favored a youth of 14 years old, and two friends (not prosecuted), who stoned Rev. Levin on Carey's Road. Raleigh received a month's sentence in Mountjoy Prison, Dublin, with hard labor. There, he was known as the "the Jew Slayer." When he was released a crowd with a brass band met the train, and wanted to parade around Colooney Street, but were stopped by the police. The crowd carried Raleigh shoulder high to his house on Carey's Road, and presented him with a silver watch and chain (*Limerick Chronicle*, April 21, 1904).

On May 21, another case was before the court presided over by Judge Adams who had been at a Jewish wedding previously. In this case, Henry Blond sued John Rahilly, publican, for £1. 3s. 2d for goods sold and delivered (*Limerick Chronicle*, May 31, 1904). Adams said he did not think he should hear the case now in the interest of the city. "He only looked to the interest of the city, to the interest of its peace, and would not therefore hear one of those Jewish-Christian cases" (*Limerick Chronicle*, May 31, 1904). Adams asked if the city was quiet, and Sgt. Lonergan told him: "It is quiet at the present time." The Judge said he "hoped there would be no more trouble over this unfortunate business." He wouldn't try a Jew case at the sessions. He would not have trouble stirred up which was "happily dying away." He hoped that things would gradually return to normal. The case was adjourned (*Limerick Chronicle*, May 31, 1904).

No incidents were reported in June. However, on Sunday, July 17, Laban Goldberg was walking with David Weinronk, when they were attacked by a man with a shillelagh. The attack was committed by Patrick Berkley who ran at them and said: "I'll kill those bloody Jews" (Marcus, GSA, UCC). Weinronk was struck on the skull and fell. He was struck again on his leg, which fractured. Laban was struck on the back of the head, which knocked him down. He suffered a scalp wound and went to Barrington's Hospital. They were both badly shaken. When Berkley was prosecuted, Weinronk was unable to give evidence (Keogh & McCarthy, 2005; Marcus, GSA, UCC).

Marcus described how some men had gone to houses on the morning of Monday, January 18, 1904, for their collections. "They were beaten up and glad to get home with their lives." She also describes how Sprinza Weinronk, wife of David, was in Bowman's Street, searching for food, when she was attacked by a man who jumped on her and banged her head against the wall. She somehow got away, and spent several days or weeks in bed (Marcus, GSA, UCC).

Grande referred to cases where the police asked Jews not to prosecute. As a result, families began to leave. The police reported that only eight families (49 people) left but that, of those, three were going to go anyway. By the end of July 1904, seven months later, a large number of members had left or were leaving. Some say it was about 80 souls, but it is hard to provide accurate figures. It wasn't quite the end, but it was devastation and desolation nonetheless. Numbers declined, and in the 1926 census there were only 33 Jews living in Limerick city and county. By 1946, the number was reduced to 10. The seeds of destruction had been sown that January day in 1904.

Fr. Creagh remained in Limerick until 1906, when he was sent to the Philippines. It was said that this transfer was not demotion, but it follows a consistent pattern of the Church that, when someone caused trouble, they were moved. He left to a fanfare of applause and acclamation. In this story, the Jews lost again. From the short resume of the foregoing, the people, the press, the officials, the Mayor and Corporation, even the police, sided with Fr. Creagh, whose parting shot was not one of apology but continued conviction of his stance: "The Jews are a curse to Limerick, and if I am the means of driving them out, I shall have accomplished one good thing in my life" (*Limerick Leader*, April 20, 1904).

Leaving

That same year, Laban took his family to Leeds where his brother Sol was then living. Sol had married Mellie Velonsky, whose father Abraham was a tailor in Whitechapel, London. They were married on March 16, 1904, in Leeds, and Sol did not return to Limerick. His other brother, Berra, also left and went to Glasgow. I have no knowledge of the other siblings.

Laban lived in Leeds for a few years. Two more children were born there: Isidore (Swanee) in 1905 and Hycie in 1907. The family returned to Ireland, to live in Cork.

What is a Pogrom?

At the time, and for more than 100 years thereafter, these events were described as a "pogrom," (Gannon, 2020; Keogh 1998). Today, the word "boycott" is applied by historians, including Keogh, Wynn and Gannon.

While the events encompassed a vigorous boycott, there was also considerable violence on January 18. That is why I call this chapter "A Limerick Pogrom." It was unique in the history of pogroms, and a little different from Eastern European pogroms. In my view, and it may only be a matter of semantics, it is not correct to separate these two aspects of boycott and pogrom. One cannot ignore that there was a large crowd chasing Jews on January 18, 1904, in different parts of the city from Irishtown to Coloney Street, about a 25-minute walk apart. At that time, Limerick had many laneways where several incidents occurred in which Jews were not protected by the police (Keogh & McCarthy, 2005). Some of these were never investigated or prosecuted. Nor can one ignore that assaults did occur, some of which resulted in injury to the person, and to property (Keogh & McCarthy, 2005). All these incidents might not have amounted to much in and of themselves, but they must be looked at all together as one continuous episode, all of which are connected to the sermons of Fr. Creagh; it was a continuous chain with unbroken links, all part of a single objective: to drive the Jews out of Limerick.

In the months that followed his sermons (on January 11 and 18, 1904), Fr. Creagh privately continued his crusade against the Jews. He succeeded, to a substantial extent, in destroying the community. When looked at in the round, in context of the overall scheme of the assaults and attacks, then the Russian definition of pogrom is applicable. "Pogrom" is a Russian word, with two definitions:

> Пазорение, опустошение, уничтожение.
> *Devastation, desolation, destruction.*

> Пеакционно-шовинистическое высчтучплене против какойл. национальной группы населення, сопровждаюшэщееся пэразграбпением имущества и убийстбамн.
> *Reactionary, extremely nationalistic actions against any national group accompanied by evisceration of property and murders.*

> [Personal communication, Nataly Eremina, 2021]

Thus, a boycott only differs from a pogrom in the *modus operandi*. A boycott is a pogrom without violence. The ultimate aim of both is the destruction of property and the routing of a person or group of people from a particular place, which is what Fr. Creagh intended and achieved.

A pogrom can occur without any loss of life. A riot or mob violence is sufficient. A pogrom does not have to include casualties. Yannay Spitzer (personal communication, July 2, 2021) confirms and adopts the definition in the *Jewish Encyclopedia* that it is an anti-Jewish violent riot that is first directed against property, and when it escalates, may end up with the wounded and dead. Many pogroms had no casualties (Spitzer, personal communication, July 2, 2021). Both he and Darius Staliūnas, a Lithuanian historian, raise the question of what constitutes a pogrom: duration, intensity or degrees of violence? Spitzer distinguishes between a brawl, a street fight, some small group riot, and a pogrom. He said that "to me it seems like the riot at the beginning of events at Limerick could pass as one, but reasonable people could disagree on whether it was above or below the threshold." Threshold is a very legal word: the balance of probabilities? Beyond a reasonable doubt or something less weighty, such as a statable case? He said that "there were many similarities [in Limerick] to the dynamics of a Russian style pogrom, such as the incitement speech that started it and the themes of grievances against the Jews. What seems to me different is the protracted boycott that ensued." That is why I call it "A Limerick Pogrom."

A boycott and a pogrom are both an attack on property. The right to earn a living is a fundamental property right. It is as old a human right as the right to marry or have a family. The first Lord Chief Justice of England, Sir Edward Coke (1552-1634), wrote that *Magna Carta* and the common law protected the right of "any man to use any trade thereby to maintain himself and his family" (Sandefur, 2010). And it is also the most precious liberty man possesses (*ibid*). As 1904 was before the Irish Constitution of 1937, the right to earn a living was protected under English law. If it had been post-1937, then it is a property right enshrined in Arts. 40.3.1, 40.3.2, and 45.2. and also, later, Art. 15 of the *Charter of Fundamental Rights of the European Union*.

There are two citations which reinforce this view. Costello J. in *Caffola v O'Mahony 1985 IR 486* wrote:

> Generally speaking, the right to earn a livelihood can properly be regarded as an unspecified personal right first protected by Art. 40.3.1. But this right may also exist as one of a bundle of rights arising from the ownership of private property capable of being commercially used and so received the protection of Art 40.3.2.

See also *Murphy v Stewart 1973 IR 117, in re Art 26 and the Equality Employment Bill 1996, 1997 2 IR 321, Cox v Ireland 2 IR 563*, and *NH v Minister for Justice 2016 IECA 86* in which Hogan J. delivered a very strong dissenting judgement. He said:

Employment is not just a means of making a living. Employment gives dignity to what would be a soulless existence and for those of us fortunate enough to have an occupation, trade or employment this may be said to be one of the key defining features of our lives. The protection of the dignity of the individual (and not just citizens) is of course one of the objectives of the Preamble to the Constitution seeks to secure.

A boycott uses no violence. Section 7 of the *Prevention of Crime (Ireland) Act, 1882, 45 & 46 Vic. 25*, made it an offence to intimidate others to instigate a boycott. The important word in the section is "intimidation." This is defined specifically in the Act as:

In this Act the expression 'intimidation' includes any word spoken or any act done in order to and calculated to put any person in fear of any injury or damage to himself, or to any member of his family, or to any person in his employment, or in fear of any injury to or loss of property, business or means of living.

This was a very repressive Act which said the ordinary laws were not adequate to deal with the agrarian disturbances. Because it was so controversial it had a sunset clause; it died after three years – in 1885. So, it was gone before Fr. Creagh's attacks.

I am arguing this discussion as the lawyer I am, not as an historian. I take the view that a pogrom is an attack on, and the destruction of, property. It makes no difference whether it is realty or personalty. They both arise as a result of physical interference with the person's right. In Limerick, a few shops were badly damaged. Gerald said that the family could not buy food, and the two girls, Fanny and Molly, were sent out to source supplies. He said that the house at 67 Henry Street was attacked by the mob on January 18, and the family had to take shelter upstairs. Several traders lost their businesses.

Whatever word historians like to use to describe the events of Limerick, and they can use both, or even στάσιο (*stasis*, civil conflict), there is no doubt that there was considerable antisemitism, and antipathy towards the Jewish community and the violence would have been infinitely worse were it not for the vigilance of the police. Although scrutiny of the police records shows they were also antipathetic towards the community, they did not want civil disorder and so sought to prevent and avoid it.

The Russian definition places much more emphasis on the devastation, desolation and destruction of property rather than massacre of people, although the latter is usually how pogrom is now understood. Devastation and desolation are precisely what occurred in Limerick, and that was the result of the violence and boycott which lasted for a minimum of seven months, some say up to two years (Ryan, 2002). It must have been a most terrifying experience. The community was devastated, desolate and partially destroyed, and damage to property took place. These words amount to desperation, which means without hope. Limerick Jews were without hope during those months. They required help from the Board of Deputies of Jews in London, and the community in Dublin, which did come, but very slowly, beginning in April 1904. Assistance also came from the Protestant community, through the intervention of Julian Grande, Chairman of the Irish Mission for Jews (Keogh & McCarthy, 2005).

The Redemptorists' Apology

2003 was the year of repentance for the Redemptorist Order. They sought "repentance for hurting the Jewish community early this century" (*Limerick Leader*, November 29, 2003. The report meant the previous century).

> At a ceremony, alive with music and dance in the Redemptorist Church in Mount St. Alphonsus last Sunday, Fr. McNamara, principal of the Order in Limerick, while outlining the community's history, commented how they had badly hurt the Jews of Limerick. "Sometimes, we Redemptorists put a foot wrong and badly hurt our Jewish brothers and sisters for which we seek repentance."

Postscript

These events have been long discussed by historians who debate both their classification and severity. My purpose in telling the story is to offer an interpretation, and to understand how important these events were to Gerald, even though they took place eight years before he was born. He had no first-hand knowledge of how they had unfolded and yet it was an overwhelming element in his life. He frequently talked about it in conversation, he lectured on it, and referred to it in some of his interviews.

In 1965, he went to Limerick to address a large audience at a meeting organized by Tuairim (**Chapter 7**). When the matter erupted again in 1970, after the then Mayor of Limerick resurrected and minimized the incident, Gerald was at the forefront of the riposte (**Chapter 8**).

The incident stalked him all his life; it sat in his mind like a burning bush, occasionally sending out waves of anger and revulsion. He was angry that it happened, angry at the instigator, Fr. Creagh; angry at the insult and the assaults on the community; angry that his family was involved; angry because they thought they had left persecution and antisemitism in Lithuania, only to find it again in Limerick; angry that his father was injured; and angry that the Church did nothing to stop it. He was particularly angry at the failure and refusal of Bishop O'Dwyer of Limerick and Cardinal Logue of Armagh to intervene with the Redemptorists; even the head of the Order refused.

Historians have now revised this story. No longer is it referred to as a pogrom. It is described only as a boycott, and really, they say, in the final analysis, no destruction of the community occurred; it was a minor event. I do not agree with them.

Chapter 6

THE CASE OF THE JEHOVAH'S WITNESSES

Justice, justice shall you pursue.

Deuteronomy, 16:20.

There is an important reason for telling this story: of all the cases that Gerald did in his 63 years of practice, covering almost every type of case both criminal and civil, this was the one which upset him more than any other. For him, it revived echoes of the Limerick Pogrom (**Chapter 5**), and so it affected him deeply. I recall him saying that on his way back from court that day he had to stop and get sick. When he got home, he was totally dejected and depressed. It was a case which he never forgot, nor really recovered from. He retold many times how horrified he was at the way the District Justice, Gordon Hurley, whom he knew well, dealt with it.

This case demonstrates Gerald's thinking and courage and illustrates his hunger for justice and fair play, even for those with whom he fundamentally disagreed. In the case, Gerald took on a "watching brief" on behalf of two Jehovah's Witnesses who were involved in a trial in Limerick. A watching brief is where a lawyer attends court on behalf of someone other than the accused or the plaintiff. It usually occurs where there is a victim of a criminal offence who contemplates a civil action, so what happened in the trial might be important in the civil proceeding. The lawyer does not, however, have a part to play in the current trial. It is surprising that he took the case at all, as he did not have any particular regard for the Sect. When their magazine would arrive in the post, he would put it out immediately.

Background

The background to the case was this: two members of the Jehovah's Witness community, Mr. Miller and Mr. Bond, were in the town of Clonlara, Co. Clare, on May 13, 1956, knocking on doors and trying to distribute their literature. Miller later told the court that he was going from house to house "preaching the Gospel." Although this was a very conservative area, there were no objections and they were well received. Mr. Miller was riding a motorcycle, with Mr. Bond on the pillion. About a mile from *The Angler's Rest*, a car pulled across the road in front of them blocking them. A crowd of men appeared; one tried to pull Mr. Bond from the motorcycle. Miller and Bond both tried to push the men away to escape. They struggled to the pub to phone the Gardaí, but the pub had no phone. The first person they saw when they came out of the pub was Fr. Ryan, a local priest, who told them they were selling heretical books and to take them away. Mr. Miller told Fr. Ryan he would call a Garda, but Fr. Ryan said they did not need Gardaí. Mr. Miller was knocked backwards, and someone grabbed his arm and held him. A man holding a hurley told him to "take his glasses off." Mr. Miller asked Fr. Ryan if he approved, and Fr. Ryan told him he could leave. The roadblock was removed, and Miller and Bond returned to Limerick. The books were taken from them and publicly burned.

The Court Case

In the subsequent court case, Fr. Patrick Ryan and nine lay members of the parish were charged with malicious damage of all the papers valued at £3, and with assaulting the Jehovah's Witnesses. All 10 were represented by Mr. Ignatius Houlihan, Solicitor, of Ennis, Co. Clare. He and Gerald were contemporaries and extremely good friends. Houlihan was a superb solicitor and had a very large firm. The court was packed, according to the report in the *Irish Press* (July 28, 1956). The case lasted two hours, and in the well of the court was the Bishop of Killaloe, Dr. Rogers.

Mr. Houlihan's cross-examination of Mr. Miller was notable for his concentration, not on the alleged assault, but on Miller's religious beliefs. Miller told him he had been "ordained by God to preach the Gospel." God had informed him of this through spirit. He accepted that he and Mr. Bond distributed a booklet called *Let God be True.*

Mr. Houlihan:	In this booklet you say there is no Blessed Trinity?
Mr. Miller:	I think the Doctrine of the Blessed Trinity is of pagan origin.
Mr. Houlihan:	In fact, you believe that Satan is the author of the Blessed Trinity?
Mr. Miller:	I believe Satan is the author of the laws of the land, which had been formed under the authorship of the Blessed Trinity.
Mr. Houlihan:	If that were so, then the Constitution and laws of the country were under the authority of Satan himself?
Mr. Miller:	I believe the Blessed Trinity was of pagan origin. It is my duty to honor God.
Mr. Houlihan:	Do you also claim that Our Blessed Lady is not the Mother of God?
Mr. Miller:	I believe Mary is the Mother of the Son of God as Scripture says. I believe that Jesus is the Son of God. He is a God, but not *the* God.

Certainly, these were outrageous concepts to the ears of conservative rural Ireland in the 1950s. Mr. Miller was asked questions about Pastor Russell, the founder of the Jehovah's Witnesses and said he was a clever man. Mr.

Houlihan disagreed, saying he had denounced all churches, religions and clergy. Mr. Miller responded that they were denounced because they were not in accord with Scripture. He accepted that Russell had produced some scandalous cartoons about the Catholic religion, but he commended them if they were going to help people to see the truth.

The cross-examination continued:

Mr. Houlihan: Do you know that Pastor Russell was divorced for infidelity?

Mr. Miller: He was a man of dignity, and legally he had nothing against him.

It was put to Mr. Miller that Pastor Russell sold "miracle wheat" to farmers and was prosecuted in the US Federal Courts. Russell had sued a US newspaper but lost his case. Mr. Miller said he himself was a minister of religion, unpaid, and provided with accommodation plus a very small stipend. It was put to him that the laws of England had decided that "you and your equals are not ministers of religion?" He replied: "I claim to be a Christian and a lover of Jesus."

Mr. Bond said he was pushed around but could not identify who did it. He heard someone say they would burn the literature. He thought Mr. Miller heard someone say something like "Look here, my good chappie" to Fr. Ryan.

The owner of the pub said she saw five men but did not see Mr. Miller being assaulted. She heard him address Fr. Ryan as "My dear fellow" and took objection to the way Mr. Miller addressed Fr. Ryan in calling him "My dear fellow" rather than "Father."

Garda Sgt. Lewis said he interviewed Fr. Ryan who told him that the Jehovah's Witnesses had been around Clonlara a year earlier. He had warned them to leave the parish, which they did, and told his men that if they returned he was to be informed. When he heard they had returned, he gathered some men and interviewed Mr. Miller and Mr. Bond at *The Angler's Rest*. They took literature from them and burned it. He did not assault either of the men.

Garda Sgt. Lewis said he had interviewed one man, Sheedy, who admitted assault.

Mr. Houlihan made a storming submission, really "pushing the boat out," as Gerald had done in many cases, though in a very different direction. He referred to the law of blasphemy. "What they had heard was most unusual and unprecedented." A Jehovah's Witness had told the court that Satan was the author of the doctrine of the Blessed Trinity; he had committed blasphemy in open court. He had claimed that the Constitution was of pagan origin and dishonored the Christian religion. In England, a judge had described the Jehovah's Witnesses as "a band of humbugs who had commercialized religion." "This case is so serious," Houlihan submitted, "that the Bishop of Killaloe has instructed me to state that any penalty you impose will be accepted readily. The people in court today are defending themselves against the most arrant blasphemy started by a person of ill repute." It was his considered opinion that the Attorney General had no idea of what filth and blasphemy the Jehovah's Witnesses were selling for their livelihood. The natural law gave people the right to protect themselves against such evil in their midst. When the Attorney General learned what was being done by the Jehovah's Witnesses, he would have to take action to protect the people from them.

District Justice Hurley, in his decision, said it was the duty of the court to maintain law and order and to be impartial and non-sectarian. Persons had a right of personal liberty but no man had absolute liberty, which was "a much abused word." There should be religious tolerance but did that tolerance extend to accepting the Gospel disseminated by "persons like Miller and company?" Persons like Miller had set out to attack and outrage that religion which was held dear by the people of the country. Treating the case on its broadest basis, were the people of Clonlara to lie down and put their hands to their ears when Miller and his friends came in their midst? Miller and his friends had escaped very lightly.

The Judge held that the charge of assault against Sheedy had been proven but he dismissed the charge under the *Probation Act* in view of the provocation, and he dismissed the charges against all other defendants. He declared that it was his duty to ensure that this sort of thing did not happen again and so he proposed binding both Mr. Miller and Mr. Bond to the peace in their own bond of £100 and two sureties of £100. In default, they were to go to prison for three months.

Gerald's intervention
Gerald then asked the Judge if he proposed binding the two men to the peace despite the fact that they appeared as witnesses and not defendants. If he was going to do that, he asked the Judge to fix recognizances in the event of an appeal. The Judge refused and said: "You have no right of audience in this court, Mr. Goldberg."

Mr. Miller said he was representing both himself and Mr. Bond. Gerald said it was unprecedented for a Judge to refuse to fix recognizances and be obviously biased against them. "I submit that, whatever the consequences."

Later, Gerald returned to court and apologized for suggesting the judge was biased in refusing to fix recognizances. The Judge said he was glad the allegation was being withdrawn. He then fixed recognizances in the event of an appeal.

Gerald was instructed to seek Senior Counsel's opinion on a constitutional issue arising from the order: whether it should be challenged by way of an application for *certiorari* to the High Court. When the matter was listed before the Circuit Court, it was adjourned by consent.

What distressed Gerald so much was the fact that a case that should have enquired into alleged assault had brought in a verdict *against* the alleged victims, and that their religious beliefs had been used against them. Perhaps what shocked him more than anything was the burning of the books, with all the associations that act has in Jewish history. This was Limerick once more; Lithuania once more; religious intolerance once more, another familiar injustice. Gerald took these matters to heart, and they churned his stomach.

Chapter 7

THE TUAIRIM MEETING, 1965

Justice is my fellow countryman.

Gerald Y. Goldberg, *Sunday Independent* (December 5, 1965)

I will never be free of the effect of this act.

Boris Pasternak, letter to his father,
quoted by Maria Stepanova in *In Memory of Memory*.

*T*uairim is an Irish word which means "opinion." It was the name of a society established in Dublin, possibly by Dr. David Thornley, a lecturer in politics in Trinity College, and later a Labour Party T.D. in Dáil Éireann. There was a branch in Cork and Limerick. The latter was chaired by John Dillon, then a young school-teacher at Glenstal Abbey. Gerald was a member of the Cork branch.

When I began researching for this book, I clearly recalled a meeting in Limerick about the Pogrom and Fr. Creagh (**Chapter 5**) which Gerald addressed, held in the Ballroom of Jury's Hotel, Limerick, in 1965. I was there with Sheila, Sean Collins, Melba Footte and several others. Cars full of interested people came from Cork and other parts of the country. I remembered that the meeting was ably chaired by John Dillon. I wondered whether he could be found – indeed, whether he was still alive, as it was 56 years ago. Most of the people who knew my parents were not. If so, how could I find him? Would he still be in Limerick?

I made a phone call to a friend of mine, Anne Noonan, who was very well connected in Limerick. She said she didn't know, but could make enquiries. A few days later, she called me and gave me a phone number. I phoned the number and got a reply from a man with a mature firm voice. He said he was John Dillon, and I told him who I was, and why I was calling. He was very glad to tell me what he could on the phone. I couldn't take notes, and so we arranged that we would meet in Dublin, where John was now living, when Covid permitted. As we were not far apart in age, we were both fully vaccinated. Carla and I went to meet John and Jean Dillon in their home on the Summit of Howth, Co. Dublin. It was a great meeting.

The RTÉ Program

In November 1965, Radio Telefís Éireann broadcast a program in its Discovery series on the Jews in Ireland. In the course of this program, it was stated that there had been a "pogrom" in Limerick in 1904, caused by the sermons of Fr. Creagh (see **Chapter 5**).

The TV critic of the *Sunday Independent*, Peter Cleary, in his piece on November 14, 1965, headlined "Let Limerick make amends to the Jews," expressed great praise for the program and thought it one of the best of the week. He wrote:

> Having sat down with a feeling of smug complacency that the
> program would be about the Jews in Ireland and somewhere in

> the script there would certainly be a self-congratulatory
> sentence that the Irish people have never shown intolerance
> towards the Jews, I was shocked to learn that Limerick city – of
> all places – had driven out a small community of Jews away back
> in 1904 at the urgings of a priest. It is a measure of the silent
> manner in which the Jewish community bear their afflictions
> that this information must have come with the same sense of
> shock to many thousands as it came to me. Maybe Limerick
> should make amends by inviting this year or next year the Chief
> Rabbi to become a freeman of that historic city. I believe that the
> people of the rest of Ireland would appreciate it.

He concluded his short piece by saying that "with knowledge, there comes the true basis of friendship."

This was followed a week later by two letters to the Editor of the *Sunday Independent* which rejected the story that anything had happened to the Jews of Limerick and that Fr. Creagh had done anything other than good work against the usurious money lenders. In addition, William "Wacker" O'Brien, a Councilor in Limerick Country Council, said that no "pogrom" ever happened in Limerick and that the program was completely wrong.

Gerald wrote a lengthy letter to the *Sunday Independent*, published on December 5, 1965, at the end of which he offered to go to Limerick, if people wanted it, and speak of what happened there. He mentioned that he was a member of Tuairim and thought that perhaps Tuairim might organize a meeting. John said he made immediate contact with Gerald and invited him to speak. A notice appeared in the *Limerick Echo* on December 11, 1965, that the next meeting of Tuairim would be on the Jews of Limerick. The headline to the press release read: "Mr. Goldberg will speak on the Jews in Limerick" and it continued:

> Mr. Goldberg, a distinguished member of Tuairim from Cork, will
> relate the experiences of his family among others, in the terrible
> months of early 1904. Neither Tuairim nor Mr. Goldberg would
> have revived this subject, but for the publicity which it has
> received in the last few weeks as a result of the Discovery TV
> program. Tuairim hopes, however, at this meeting to lay finally
> an old ghost haunting the name of Limerick, rather than to stir
> up any further ill feeling. As is Tuairim's custom, a fact-sheet will
> be distributed before the meeting. It is hoped, also, to play a
> recording of Father Creagh's original speech.

The Meeting

The meeting was scheduled for December 14, 1965. It caused the Arch Confraternity of the Holy Family to take umbrage as they did not want the issue raised again. John Dillon received a delegation from the Confraternity and some members of the Redemptorist Order who run it who wanted John to cancel the meeting, but he refused. He told the delegation that Tuairim didn't start this, it was raised in the newspapers and denied by Councilor O'Brien. The members of this delegation left without the result they wanted, so they then went to see the headmaster of Glenstal Abbey where John taught. But the principal was not entertaining the delegation either, and they left. John then talked to the Mayor of Limerick, Councilor Frank Leddin, who agreed to back the meeting which he personally attended and at which he spoke. This was important. It was rumored that the Confraternity would break up the meeting, so before it commenced there was a very tense atmosphere.

John had gone to the offices of the *Limerick Leader*. He knew the editor, and got his permission to research the issues of 1904. These were housed in what he described as a shed at the back of the premises. Then he decided that it would be a good idea to have a recording of the sermon of Fr. Creagh. He brought in a tape recorder and read it with *brio*. He also changed it into the first person. He said Fr. Creagh's sermon was "hot stuff." His reading was memorable.

When the meeting started, John didn't know how many people were sent by the Confraternity. When a group came in and sat in the front row, John thought this was "trouble" and feared they would break up the meeting. Then before introducing Gerald, John asked the audience if they would like to hear the sermon. There was an overwhelmingly positive response. At this point, the people in the front row walked out. Then John handed over the floor to Gerald.

The ballroom was full to capacity with people standing all around the sides. There was a lobby outside the room, and this was also packed. The doors were open so they could see and possibly hear. There were several hundred people in attendance. It was difficult to know how this was going to develop. But Gerald produced the speech of his life, and used all his courtroom skills as if addressing a jury. There was hushed silence. He was very good at using the pause. It created anticipation. The meeting remained quiet according to the *Evening Herald* of December 15, 1965, until Gerald stated that he could not forgive a Limerick priest of that period because of a libel which he alleged he had made against the Jewish people. At that point, a man in the room shouted, "That is a shocking statement. No Catholic should listen to that," and left the meeting. Apart from that man and those who left before the sermon was played, no one else moved. Gerald had the whole audience in the palm of his hand.

He described how his father Laban was beaten in 1904, together with other members of his family and the community, when they were chased and stoned by local people. He described how the riots and assaults followed the sermon by Fr. Creagh, who made charges of usury. Gerald said he did not come with any sense of bitterness or resentment; he only wanted to put the facts before the people. In the course of his speech, he quoted from news reports of court proceedings at the time. He said that the community offered to open their books for inspection, but this was not taken up. The Bishop had made an appeal that there should be no violence, and Fr. Creagh himself had not advocated any. Gerald said he regretted that the whole matter had been revived.

I recall as best I can that, possibly at the beginning of that speech, Gerald referred to his identity. He is likely to have told the audience where his loyalties lay. He might have put it like this: "Next, let me say, that firstly I am an Irishman, secondly a Corkman, and as both I am a Jew." He would have said this to quell the question that sometimes has arisen as to the loyalty of the Jewish community to Ireland.

After he finished, it was open to the floor. Councilor Leddin, Mayor of Limerick, proposed a vote of thanks. He put out his hand and said: "On behalf of the people of Limerick, I offer you my hand in friendship and ask you to forget the past." Gerald shook it warmly, and replied: "As far as I am concerned the past is forgotten and you will not hear me refer to this again. I have found tolerance in Limerick."

Gerald received a great ovation at the end of a long, difficult and emotional night. There were members from the local Confraternity there who challenged him but did so "courteously and with tolerance." A number of those men shook his hand at the end of the meeting. Gerald had appealed both at the meeting and in the newspapers for an end to the Limerick affair.

Regrettably it was not to be. Within five years, it arose again in a most unexpected way.

Chapter 8

STEVE COUGHLAN

Rudeness is the weak man's imitation of strength.
Edmund Burke

The greater the power, the more dangerous the abuse.
Edmund Burke

S teve Coughlan was Mayor of Limerick in 1970. He was an Alderman of Limerick Corporation, a member of the Labour Party and an elected member of Dáil Éireann. On April 18, 1970, he opened the 10th annual convention of the Credit Union League of Ireland (now the Irish League of Credit Unions) at the Parkway Motel, Limerick. Present were 1,000 delegates, representing 350 credit unions throughout the country. After Dan Morrison, president of the League, welcomed the delegates, the Mayor read his official script. Then he departed from it and said: "And now I want to talk to you as Steve Coughlan."

This was the beginning of an outburst of antisemitism unparalleled since the time of Fr. Creagh. Mayor Coughlan maintained that he remembered 60 years earlier (though he was not born then) how the Jews had afflicted Limerick. He said that Fr. Creagh was courageous in his declaration of war on the Jews of Coloney Street, saying they were "bloodsuckers and extortionists." The Arch Confraternity had recently been misrepresented, and it was they "who, as a result of this action, set up a movement which developed into the credit union in Limerick."

At this point of his speech, he was interrupted by a delegate from Dublin who jumped up and said: "We want to be disassociated from this and we can get a two-thirds majority to support us." Mayor Coughlan continued his speech through slow hand-clapping and shouts of "Stop talking" and "Shut up" and further shouts of "Sit down." But he refused to be interrupted.

He then told a story about a woman who was having a baby:

> ... and in they came, getting their 5/- a week, 10/- and 7/6, scourging her and the unfortunate people of Limerick who were overcharged. They took the bed from under this unfortunate woman, and it is tragic for me, as Mayor of Limerick, to have to say this but it is true.

According to the *Cork Examiner* report of April 20, 1970, Coughlan appeared to break down and cry at that point. The hall became a "seething mass of heckling and booing and slow handclapping which started at the rear *(sic)* of the assembly."

This speech had serious consequences. The first action was taken immediately by the Credit Union League, which passed an emergency motion unanimously. This "condemned in the strongest possible terms his (the Mayor's) abuse of our national platform to attempt to justify his personal views and activities." Further it added: "This convention deplores the untrue, biased, unjustifiable and damaging press report, arising out of the speech from the Mayor of Limerick to this convention" (*Cork Examiner*, April 20, 1970).

Gerald was contacted by Chief Rabbi Isaac Cohen, who asked him to issue a statement. He did so in trenchant terms (*Cork Examiner*, April 20, 1970). Gerald said that he intended to propose a motion to the next meeting of Cork Corporation, "expressing its concern with the unbridled and uncalled for attack made by the Mayor of Limerick on the former Limerick Jewish community which was destroyed by a pogrom and boycott in 1904." He went on to deplore the "intemperate remarks, inaccuracies, and false picture as to the happiness, friendships and tolerance enjoyed and exchanged by all sections of our people" and called for the rejection of Alderman Coughlan's remarks "with the contempt they deserve." Gerald accused Mayor Coughlan of lying.

Mayor Coughlan responded that he felt he "was taken up wrongly by the Credit Union meeting." He was linking the creation of the credit union movement with the events of 1904. Then he continued: "The furthest thing in my mind is to attack any section of people, be they Catholics, Protestants, Jews, or any other section. But in this case it was the Jews who were extracting from the poorer classes the money which they could ill afford to repay" (*Irish Independent*, April 21, 1970). "It was the Jews who scourged these poorer classes in the lanes and alleyways of Limerick and it is for this reason they should not escape criticism." He went on to claim that they could have been any other section of the people, but: "No matter who they were," he stated, "even people of our own denomination, I would have attacked them for this terrible abuse which brought such sorrow and misery."

Mayor Coughlan also referred to the Tuairim meeting five years previously. He is reported in the *Irish Independent* (April 21, 1970) as saying: "About five years ago, Mr. Goldberg had come to Limerick to speak at a Tuairim meeting in the city regarding the Jewish problem in the 1900s in Limerick and raised 'all the old sores' at a public gathering. If Mr. Goldberg wished to let this problem and this controversial issue lie dead, he surely would have not been so fast to speak on that occasion."

Mayor Coughlan went on to say that "what had primarily to be broken at the time in question in Limerick was the system of money lending which was threatening to wreck to (*sic*) community. Unless it was stopped, it would have taken a fierce grip. But it was taken in hand by Fr. Creagh and the problem had been solved because of his efforts." Suffice it to say that, in 1904, no one would have dared to rebuke a priest for what he said. They were beyond any challenge, and the Confraternity numbered in excess of 6,000 men and boys.

Mayor Coughlan said that the Credit Union League had misinterpreted what he said. "We cannot close our eyes to a situation which was a fact at a particular time in our city. Thankfully, things have changed. The war against extortionists was won."

The leader of the Labour Party, Brendan Corish T.D., and the chairman of the Party, Dan Browne, issued statements immediately disassociating themselves and the Party from Mayor Coughlan's remarks which they denounced. Mr. Corish said:

> I wish to disassociate myself and the Labour Party totally from Saturday's statement by Alderman Stephen Coughlan as reported in Sunday's press regarding the Jewish community in Limerick. If Mr. Coughlan was reported incorrectly, and I understand the press was not present at the function in question, then he has a duty, in fairness to himself and his colleagues, to set the record straight as his reported views certainly do not represent those of the Labour Party.

The Chairman of the Party issued a statement in similar terms (*Irish Press*, April 21, 1970). In fact, the press was present at the Conference.

Gerald then sharpened his pens again and took on Coughlan in a full scale, withering, broadside attack. He challenged him to fight "anywhere, anytime" (*Irish Press*, April 21, 1970). He referred to the Tuairim meeting in 1965 at which he had spoken, because "of a resurgence of anti-Jewish lies." He confronted the "scandal mongers, and [wanted] to offer facts not 'stories.'" Gerald repeated the injuries to his father, and how his sisters Fanny and Molly were the only ones who could source food. He repeated how his father's house was attacked and the front door broken down, while the family took refuge upstairs. He wrote:

> Now, I will not stand by and allow Mayor Coughlan to get away with lies. Father Creagh is dead, but Father Coughlan is alive. Where was this gentleman with his fictitious impossible story, which not even Fr. Creagh mentioned, when I spoke in Limerick? Behind whose priestly cassock was he hiding then? The world must know the truth and the truth will now be told – here and elsewhere. History must be written.

There was ferocious anger and steel in what he wrote. He continued:

I will not stand by while fascism rears its ugly head in Ireland,
whether it be the Paisley or Coughlan type, and if necessary to
do so, I will fight Coughlanism if he is man enough to fight,
anywhere, anytime. The people of Limerick have a chance now to
make amends to do so.

An important member of the Limerick Corporation, also a former Mayor,
and a member of Dáil Éireann for the Labour Party, Jim Kemmy, issued a
strong statement condemning Coughlan's outburst. "It was irresponsible,"
he said, "to use the words 'bloodsuckers and extortionists.'" He said that
the vast majority of the Limerick Jewish community had no connection with
money lending whatsoever (*Irish Independent*, April 21, 1970).

Several newspapers – the *Irish Press, Irish Independent, Limerick Leader,*
and *The Irish Times* – issued critical editorials. The *Independent* (April 24,
1970) put it:

The Mayor of Limerick has put his civic foot in it again, and by
offering to fight he seems bent on putting the other foot in it too.

It went on to say: "He could end his forays into the news with a period of
decent silence – even if he cannot bring himself to apologize."

The *Irish Press* (April 21, 1970) referred to the 1904 pogrom as "a stain on
the City of Limerick... [which] its people should be allowed to forget." It
claimed that the Mayor had given "this discreditable skeleton another
unwelcome airing." It said that Gerald's response was dignified and
convincing. The *Limerick Leader* (April 25, 1970) wrote in a very similar vein
to the *Irish Press,* but it was more critical of Gerald's response. It thought: "it
might have been a bit too harsh, though fully within his rights." They
thought he might have been "a little unfair to the people of Limerick."

The entire matter put the Labour Party in a difficult position. Steve
Coughlan had been controversial over two previous issues: first, the visit of
the South African rugby team to Ireland, and second, the Maoists. But his
attack on the Jews of Limerick was far more serious. Other members of the
party issued statements criticizing him. Some members were upset because
the Party's statement did not condemn him. Coughlan's second statement,
in which he attempted to explain his remarks to the credit union conference,
moved some members to call for his expulsion. A motion of expulsion was
put down but not moved.

Most of the Church's Archbishops and Bishops did not issue any
statement, except for the Catholic Bishop of Limerick, Ardfert and
Aghadoe, Dr. Murphy (*Limerick Leader*, April 22, 1970). He said he hadn't

studied the history of the incident because it was so long ago and not relevant to the present. He felt it dangerous to drag up "stories of abuse, errors, and pogroms." He continued to say that "Christianity owes a great debt of guilt to the Jewish people." He wanted Limerick to think of itself as a wide community with a variety of race, religions and nationalities. He wanted to "tell my many Jewish friends that they have a valued and much-loved place in our Irish community which is also their community as of right." He did not think that Steve Coughlan was fully conscious of the implications of what he said. Dr. Murphy accepted Coughlan was not antisemitic.

Then the Protestant Bishop of Limerick, Reverend Dr. Wyse Jackson, issued a statement, saying he "did not believe the Mayor was fully conscious of the implications of what he was saying in his official opening speech to the Credit Union League." The Bishop repeated the use of the words "extortionists" and "bloodsuckers" when referring to the usury at the time. He also repeated the explanation that "the Mayor was referring to the system in operation at the time, and not specifically to the Jews." Then the Bishop said he "gladly believed the Mayor when he said he was not antisemitic." His statement then echoes in some respects the Catholic Bishop's statement. It concluded that he would like to tell his many Jewish friends that they had a valued and much-loved place in the Irish community, which was also their community as of right (*Irish Independent*, April 22, 1970).

A statement then issued from Mr. William Peacock, the president of Tuairim, who said the Mayor was "misleading" when he referred to the meeting of Tuairim five years previously. Mr. Peacock said the suggestion that "Mr. Goldberg had gone to Limerick un-invited at that time and used a platform for his own advantage" was wrong. He went on to explain that Tuairim had decided to hold a public meeting following a television program concerning the Jewish community in Ireland and an article in the *Sunday Independent* suggesting that Limerick owed the Jews an apology. That gave rise to correspondence in the newspapers which was unfavorable and "at that point, Mr. Goldberg requested the discussion be closed." Mr. Peacock said he regretted that Mayor Coughlan had used this meeting to attack Mr. Goldberg: he was an invited speaker and was welcomed by the Limerick citizens, including the then Mayor, Mr. Frank Leddin (*Irish Independent*, April 22, 1970).

After a week of very intense pressure which came in many columns of the newspapers, including letter writers and editorials, there were resolutions from Labour Party branches, such as Donnycarney, Dublin, as well as from individual members of the Administrative Council threatening to resign if Coughlan was not expelled. This would have had serious consequences for both Coughlan and the Party.

Coughlan issued a further statement (*Irish Independent*, April 25, 1970), in which he said:

> It was never my intention to insult any minority group, and, if I did this, it was unintentional and I sincerely regret it. I am not antisemitic and I never was. Indeed, my relations with the Jews of Limerick go back more than 40 years and they have always been very good relations.

He said he tried to honor the Credit Union League for the great work they had done. They had eliminated the embarrassment of borrowing money. He put it on record that the credit unions ought to be appreciated in "their efforts to tide people over in their financial difficulties." He was making comparisons between past and present. He wanted to show to people that out of evil had come a great deal of good. He referred to his reason for his remarks. He said it came as a result of an attack in a certain magazine and it was only to "defend our people that I tried to make comparisons with the past and present living conditions in Limerick." He continued: "It would seem to me that all the extremists or the fanatics can say what they like, but when someone talks back to them he is accused of being out of turn. It has become a one-way traffic of abuse."

Gerald issued a statement (*Sunday Press*, April 26, 1970) in which he rejected the apology. He said: "This is a limited apology. I do not regard it as sufficient. It has reservations." He also expressed regret that the Bishop of Limerick did not call on Coughlan to apologize. He said he could only accept a clear and unqualified statement from Coughlan that it intended to cover his remarks concerning the Jewish community in Limerick in 1904. "There is no point in apologizing to the Jewish community of 1970 if the apology is limited to any upset or affront given to them". Gerald's lengthy statement rehearses most of what he had said in previous statements.

He said he was prepared to meet Alderman Coughlan in Limerick or anywhere else for a "full and frank discussion. I will meet him, if he is prepared to do so, on television. I will answer any questions and will hold back nothing. But I must know whether or not his apology is limited or full."

The statement continued that Gerald: "… did not want to prolong this 'unhappy situation'" but he expressed his determination "in fairness to the memory of the Jews of 1904 to see that the record was set down in writing so that future generations may have some source from which to draw if this sort of conduct from a person, whether in high office or otherwise, should ever again occur in the City of Limerick."

In rejecting Coughlan's apology, Gerald said he was speaking with the full authority of the Chief Rabbi. This was unfortunate, as the Chief Rabbi accepted the apology (*The Irish Times*, April 27, 1970). When asked about Gerald's rejection of the apology, the Chief Rabbi said: "This is his personal view of the matter. I am speaking on behalf of the Jewish community of Ireland and Mr. Goldberg agrees with me. This was his first reaction, but I think in discussion and consultation with me and in examining the remarks which have been made we feel we are happy to welcome the statements of the two bishops and Alderman Coughlan." After all that, there was a possibility that Gerald and Coughlan would meet on the TV program *7 Days* the following Tuesday. But this did not happen.

There also had been correspondence in the letter pages to which Gerald contributed. One of the letter writers was Michael McInerney, then foreign correspondent to *The Irish Times*, who said he was born in Wolfe Tone Street (Coolooney Street as it then was), a few years after that infamous pogrom. He thought Gerald was unfair to attack "all the people of Limerick" (*The Irish Times*, April 22, 1970). He extolled all the well-known people who came from Limerick. Then he said: "… as a boy I was sent to all the Jewish shops in the street for family groceries and never heard an unkind word against the Jews." This "… proves that ordinary decent people of Limerick do not hate Jews – or anybody – unless they are incited to do so, and their fears and illiteracy exploited by supposedly educated and civilized men. A few years after that incitement, the ordinary people of Limerick were friends with the Jewish community when the incitement had died down. Sometimes illiterate men are called the rabble, but the real rabble are educated 'cultured' men who incite fear, and its concomitant, hate, among simple people: such 'educated' men surely are the real rabble."

McInerney said that men and women used to work from 6.00 am to 6.00 pm and often to 8.00 pm. Children were also forced to work. Limerick had notorious slums (which were all located around Coolooney Street). He said these were the social evils which should have been attacked by Fr. Creagh and his Confraternity. There were still social evils there today. He concluded: "I am sure that all of the ordinary decent people of Limerick today, with their knowledge that the original Holy Family, after which the Confraternity is called, was a Jewish family, will abhor this most recent attempt at a new incitement against a harmless and kindly people."

Gerald ended his contribution to this affair with a very long letter to *The Irish Times* (April 27, 1970). He wrote: "In a few days' time I shall make specific charges against Fr. Creagh and others in relation to the events..." He then launched into a ferocious attack on those involved in the original affair, accusing them of deeds far beyond anything that had actually happened, including lies and near genocide. The complete letter makes uncomfortable reading for me, as his anger is so extreme, and would be understandable if Coughlan had not been so outrightly condemned from the outset.

Michael McInerney wrote a sensitive reply which is best quoted in full. He wrote in *The Irish Times*, April 29, 1970, as follows:

> The trouble with Mr. Goldberg is that, having shot down in flames Mr. Coughlan, the Redemptorists and the Bishop of Limerick, having routed his enemies and won the war, he still persists in fighting the battles all over again, starting a new siege of Limerick. The danger in this is that he may soon lose the peace. Again, he himself will not give an inch. Even after acknowledging the generosity and courage of many Limerick people, he cancels out these otherwise admirable gestures in the same letter (April 27) with his continuous charges of the collective guilt of Limerick. Not only is this unfair but it is bad tactics, particularly when he has won. He has no idea of the extent of his victory in securing an apology from the Redemptorist Fathers, even though the apology is somewhat late. Mr. Goldberg should identify his enemy and concentrate his fire, not scatter it over a whole city...

Postscript

The matter seems to end there, and there has not been any controversy in the last nearly 50 years. Trying to put all of this into perspective is not easy. It offers a number of interpretations.

One, which I referred to in the earlier chapters, is that the entire episode consumed Gerald's conscious and unconscious mind. It came to the front of his mind after the Jehovah Witnesses' case, and again after the *Discovery* TV program (RTÉ, 1965) which led to the Tuairim meeting. In all probability, Gerald must have thought he had laid the issue to rest at that meeting. When it arose again after Coughlan's remarks to the Credit Union League conference, it re-ignited in Gerald's head. It is clear from his statements and letters that he was not unlike King Lear: howling, howling, howling. Some of his statements were accurate, but there were a few which were not. Interestingly, the word "pogrom" was used in many statements and letters by different people. But Gerald used the word "genocide." There was no genocide in Limerick. No one was killed.

Chapter 9

MY VISIT TO COLOONEY STREET

Limerick, you're a lady.

Denis Allen

When I started researching, it quickly became obvious that I needed to visit the Jewish Quarter of Limerick. It was August 2021 when Carla and I took the train. We were met at the station by Des Ryan, who has been enormously helpful. He has been researching this subject for over 40 years and knows more about the Jewish Community in Limerick than anyone else.

Des drove us to Coolooney Street, and I was surprised to find it was so close to the station, just around the corner. We stopped at the top of the street. The first building he pointed out was number 63, a fine double-fronted house. In 1884, this was the Royal Constabulary Barracks (RIC). After they vacated, it became the first "official" synagogue. There is nothing on the walls to indicate its past, but in the Irish Jewish Museum, Dublin, is the stone on which are inscribed the words in English "United Hebrew Congregation" and in Hebrew "*Beit Knesset Hakowdesh*" (the Holy Meeting House). This is the stone which Gerald redeemed from a builder's yard in the 1980s. In about 1884 when it was the police barracks, Ryan told me that it was only around the corner from Edward Street, where there was a mob riot in front of Leib Siev's house. It was a tumultuous riot, but the RIC heard nothing until someone made a complaint to them.

As I was taking photographs, a lady came up to me with a broad smile on her face. I introduced myself and explained my connection with the street. She told me her name was Sylvia Hogan and introduced her husband, Tom. She told me that she had lived in number 63 for over 50 years now. She was very gracious and invited us inside. The hall divided the house: on the right and left, there were two identical rooms, both quite dark and small. These have not changed. There was a fixed table in each, with bench seating around the wall. I sat down and thought about the men who sat here over 100 years ago. I could see them, squeezed in, arguing loudly in Yiddish. Perhaps a hand banged the table! I wondered did any smoke? These were likely used as meeting rooms. Maybe it was in this room in 1896 that Laban presided, when he called a meeting asking for guidance on the size of the synagogue. There was a stairwell on the right which was original. It led to the sanctuary, now bedrooms. Beyond the stairwell downstairs was a kitchen which was added by the present residents.

Thanking Sylvia, we went into the street again, and I looked across at two houses which were strangely numbered 48, 49 and 51 – no sign of number 50. Laban lived in number 50 in 1897 when he had typhoid fever. This was the house that Fr. Cregan called on, and from which Rachel gave him the shilling. Fr. Cregan came frequently to play cards with Laban and

Dr. Myles and to eat Elka's *cuchen*. I found it difficult to comprehend how
one priest could be a friend of Laban's, while another, Fr. John Creagh,
could launch such a vitriolic attack.

We walked only nine doors down the street and stopped at number 72.
This was the Goldberg synagogue. It is a large, imposing house, set on its own
plot with an entrance gate big enough for a coach and horse. There is space
all around it. Today, it looks unoccupied, though it is not. I did not feel
comfortable knocking on the door. Yet, I could see the separate factions
walking up and down the street going into and coming out of their respective
synagogues. When Laban left Limerick in the summer of 1904, number 72
was taken over by the Tooheys, Blonds and others as the synagogue.

The street has now changed completely from what it was in the 1890s.
Then it was a slum area; the peddlers could not afford anything else. It has
been tarmacadamed and many houses have been renovated. It is now busy,
with a lot of traffic. As I walked down the street, I noticed one house had a
memorial plaque to an IRA man, and there is another at number 47 Henry
Street to honor and remember Sean South who was with Arthur Griffith, an
antisemite. But there is nothing to indicate this was the Jewish Quarter, not
a sign or plaque. That tells its own story.

I noticed numbers 18 and 18A where Rev. Levin lived, and where there
was much activity in 1904. I don't know why he moved from one house to
the other, but before number 63 was leased, this is where services were
conducted. It was down those steps that Fanny went to ask the minister to
kill a chicken for Elka when she was ill. I could see one incident in my mind,
which was when Laban and David Weinronk were walking down the street
and were assaulted and injured by Patrick Berkley in July 1904. There was
a constable close and he intervened but not quickly enough.

Visiting this area gives a strange feeling which I cannot really explain. I
know something about who these people were, where they came from,
something of their personality traits, about the remarkable voyages they
made to get to this place, and the difficulties they encountered, especially
in 1904. From the tables of family names and places of residence, I could see
that the Jews moved around from one house to another on a regular basis.
Ryan said that Limerick people did that too.

We went down to the bottom of the street where there is a cul-de-sac of
small single-storey red brick houses. This is Emmet Place. Moses
Greenfield, Laban's uncle, Laban's brother Jeremiah and several other
members of the community lived there. When Laban arrived, he was taken
in by his uncle Benjamin who lived at 1 Westland Street (as it then was).

63 Wolfe Tone Street (formerly Colooney Street), Limerick – now Sylvia & Tom Hogan's home.

72 Wolfe Tone Street (formerly Colooney Street), Limerick – Laban's first synagogue.

67 Henry Street, Limerick – Laban's last home in Limerick.

We left the street, and turned the corner into Henry Street and walked a little further towards the city center. Des Ryan pointed out number 47 but said he thought that Laban did not live there, and that the entry on the census might have been a mistake, but he could only surmise. Number 67 was a large double-fronted house, certainly a change from Colooney Street. It must have been grand in its time. It was here that Laban first opened the synagogue upstairs; it was here that there were sing-songs on Saturday nights when Harry played. I got a feeling for the singing as I stood outside on the street. I was glad to have seen all the places where both Laban and many others lived.

Another place Des Ryan took us was Vize's Field, which is in the same area. This has a row of cottages down one side which look original. Perhaps there was a field on the opposite side, where today there are blocks of apartments. But it was in Vize's Field that Laban encountered his first assault in 1892.

Then we turned and walked to Mount St. Alphonsus Church and Monastery on the other side of the road. We crossed and entered the church.

I was impressed by its grandeur and scale – big enough to accommodate 1,000 people. And there on the right towards the altar is the stone pulpit from which Fr. Creagh delivered his two antisemitic sermons in January 1904. I stood in the pulpit and declared this was where the sermons were uttered. As this is so close to Colooney Street, it is not surprising the community were terrified to go out when there was a large mob stalking them. I felt a shiver and was not comfortable.

After we had completed our visit to this area, Des Ryan took us to see the house where Fr. Creagh was born. There is nothing particular about it.

Then we went out to the cemetery at Kilmurry. Today it is all built up, but in 1902 this was countryside. When Gerald visited here it was overgrown, but now it is well maintained. It is a quiet peaceful plot with some nice mature trees, but there are very few stones: not more than 10, and some are unmarked. Do I have a great uncle buried here? Gerald said Shia Sapsa (Sidney Henry) is buried here, but I am not sure.

Looking at this quiet pleasant place, I wonder what all the fuss was about in 1902. How could people behave in that way – and so publicly? Nor can I feel the sense of anger which Gerald expressed, nor his desire to have his or his father's name added to the memorial tablet in the little prayer house, now used for storage.

There is a right of way through the cemetery, making it easier to go from one housing estate to another. Women with shopping bags walked through unaware of the place they were in, or so it seemed to me. I wonder what they think of it, if anything?

Postscript

I now know the names of all the community which Des Ryan has researched. He told me where they lived, where they moved from and to, all the different houses they lived in. They were all peddlers for several years after they arrived, and where they remained until the community was sundered in 1904.

They were all from Akmian, all quarrelsome, difficult people with hot tempers. Today I can remember them. Sadly, there is no acknowledgment that they existed at all. There is no star of David in the sky over Colooney Street.

PART
TWO

Chapter 10

GERALD: THE LAWYER

The passion for justice, like the obsessive scratching of a rash, tears any system from the inside, forcing us to seek and demand retribution, especially on behalf of the dead – for who will defend them, if not us?

Maria Stepanova, *In Memory of Memory*

When Gerald finished his two years in college, he went to the Incorporated Law Society (ILS) in Dublin, and lived with his sister Molly and her husband, Bernard (Barney) Shillman. After his first exam, he wrote home in very nervous terms. The letter is incomplete and undated, but likely written in 1931/1932.

> Dear Mother and Dad,
>
> Well, here I am once again after the exam, and I suppose you are all anxious to know how I got on. Well, in order that there may be no excuses when the results come out, I had better tell you that I don't think I have any possible chance of passing.
>
> The first paper in the morning was the hardest I have ever seen. Every question had about three possible answers to it and unfortunately I chose the wrong ones. In one question, there were 15 distinct and separate
>
> – *(the next page is missing)* –
>
> I don't think I have any more to write. Please do not be downhearted. Results are not worth worrying about. I certainly am not worrying.
>
> I expect results in about three weeks, but as I said I cannot hold out any hope at all.
>
> With best regards to all.
>
> I remain
>
> Your affec. (*sic*) Son
>
> Gerald.

When his father Laban died in 1932, Gerald was in Dublin and unable to get back for the funeral in time. The community did not wait for him.

Gerald continued his law studies and, in 1934, qualified as a solicitor, obtaining his practicing certificate. Then he returned to Cork and set up on his own at 96 Patrick Street.

Gerald excelled at studying, it was his passion and his comfort. Books were his friends. Consequently, it was no trouble for him to read law reports, textbooks, even statutes. What assisted him most of all was his prodigious memory. A good lawyer must be able to remember the evidence, the questions you ask on your feet, and the replies. Also, you must be able to immediately find the passages in the cases or texts. Equally, you must be able to unravel the complicated machinations of statutory language. He could do all that.

In addition, he was capable of making good fees and collecting them. John Fitzgerald, UCC's Librarian, became a friend of Gerald late in his life. He repeats a story Gerald told him about collecting fees:

> Gerald defended an IRA client who was in some difficulty. The man was acquitted. He said to the client: "You have to pay my fee." "How much is it?" asked the client. "250 guineas," Gerald replied. The client's face sank like a stone. "But, sure I don't have anything like that sort of money, Mr. Goldberg." Gerald replied: "But I did what you asked me to do. I defended you and got you off. Now I am asking you to pay me." A day later, a man ran up to him in the street with 250 guineas held tightly in his hand. He shook hands with Gerald, exchanging the money. "Take this quickly." And he vanished.

Just suppose the man had been arrested for robbing a post office and asked Gerald to defend him? Gerald also told John Fitzgerald that sometimes fees were left in a cask on a milk tray outside the house.

Early Days at Law

Gerald's practice grew from very humble beginnings. He said he only earned about £300 in his first year, 1936. He told me that he sat on the top step of the stairs to his office at 96 Patrick Street, waiting for clients to come, and while he waited, he read law reports or textbooks. He dictated his letters and briefs onto wax cylinders which, because of their fragility, were stored in fleece-lined tubes. During the war, there was petrol rationing, so he could not drive although he did have a car. Instead, he used a bicycle to go to the office. He brought these discs home on the back of the bike. He was not very practical about securing them, and once lost a whole brief when they fell off.

Despite his own comments about his slow start as a solicitor, I noticed that there were many reports in the newspapers from 1940 onwards, reporting some quite serious cases, both criminal and civil, in which he was involved. This shows that he began to make his name in that early period. In the next chapter, I will refer to some major cases.

When he was in the office, Kathleen, his first secretary, brought him tea at about 4.00 pm every afternoon. In the mornings he was usually in court, and afterwards the solicitors repaired to Rearden's Hole in the Wall pub for coffee and banter. I remember Rearden's very well. It was a grocery provisions shop located across the street from the Courthouse on

Washington Street. It was where Sheila, my brother Theo and I went shopping on Saturday afternoon. It was a big shop but dark, and in the front, as you went in, there were big glass-topped tins of biscuits. We could see right into them. I remember Mr. Cremin there, who wore a grey, light-weight jacket. "Oh, good afternoon, Mrs. Goldberg. A seat for Mrs. Goldberg, please. And would Mrs. Goldberg like a glass of sherry, and would Master Goldberg like a biscuit?" Those were the days!

When there was no High Court, the Cork solicitors went to Rearden's for coffee or something stronger, though Gerald did not drink: he could get drunk on the smell of a brandy! Rearden's pub was very small and dim. I remember years later, when I was a practicing barrister, often going over there in the company of several eminent Senior Counsel who came for the High Court sessions twice a year. It was full after the call over of the day's list of cases at 10.00 am. Many of the silks drank hard liquor before going back to start trials at 11.00 am. The place was always filled with smoke.

One of the most eminent Senior Counsel was Ernest Wood, who was fearless and acerbic. Gerald briefed him in several cases. Ernest didn't care who he was speaking or writing to; everyone was treated with equal disdain. Recently, I met a colleague who told me he was in the pub one morning when Ernest said to Gerald in his rasping voice: "Gerald, you think everyone hates you because you are a Jew. You're wrong. They hate you because you are a shit!" This was meant, and accepted, as a joust.

Gerald's practice grew slowly. He took on whatever work came his way. Several of his early cases were debt collections, but he also got other work including industrial accidents, then called Workman's Compensation Claims. The leading expert on that subject was Barney Shillman, his brother-in-law. Barney had written the textbook, and Gerald instructed him in some cases. Barney was first a civil servant and then a barrister.

A typical case related to his life-long interest in the arts. Sometime in the early 1940s, Gerald and Sheila became friendly with Miss Joan Denise Moriarty who had started a ballet school in Patrick Street. Later, she founded the professional Irish Ballet Company. Gerald and Sheila were directors and supporters. In 1944 when Miss Moriarty (as she was universally known) had a school of dance in Patrick Street, the lady who resided overhead was so exasperated by the constant music, the clacking, and tapping that she sued Miss Moriarty for nuisance and an injunction to stop the classes. Miss Moriarty retained Gerald as her solicitor. The action was brought in the Circuit Court. Ruth Fleischmann wrote to me in an email: "The judge patiently listened to the case and then dismissed it. He accepted Goldberg's argument that the studio was located in a business area of the city and that tenants could not be denied the right to work in such premises, even if a certain amount of noise was unavoidable." It was an ingenious argument. Costs were awarded against the plaintiff tenant, and Gerald returned £5.5.0 to Miss Moriarty.

Even then, he was without doubt a brilliant solicitor. Senior Counsel who worked with him said he was the best in the country. Another brief example illustrates this.

He was defending a soldier at Court Martial charged with drinking while on duty. The hearing opened before the Judge Advocate and proceeded all morning. After lunch, the Superior Officers gave evidence, and Gerald cross-examined:

Gerald: What did you do over luncheon?

Officer: We went to the Mess.

Gerald: And what did you do there?

Officer: Had lunch.

Gerald: Did you have anything to drink before lunch?

Officer: Oh yes, of course, a Gin and Tonic.

Gerald: And were you not on duty then?

That was the end of it.

Discipline was key to keeping on top of his legal practice. I recall him telling his standing Senior Counsel, Tommy Doyle, that he had a recurring dream about a mountain growing bigger all the time, so he had to take a machete to it and keep cutting it down. Gerald didn't work in the evenings. Usually, he and Sheila listened to music and read, but he would rise anywhere between 5.30 am and 6.00 am, when he would go downstairs and start dictating. I remember his voice bellowing into the Dictaphone as though he was already in court and in full flight of argument, thrashing the opponent. The letters he wrote on behalf of his clients were withering. Through the meticulous preparation of his cases, Gerald established himself as an erudite, consummate solicitor. From the beginning, he maintained a large and complete law library. When clients came, he read the law as well as taking very careful instructions. He was unusual in that when he briefed counsel, he briefed them fully on the law as well as fact. When needed, he placed advertisements in the newspapers looking for witnesses to accidents.

At that time, until about the beginning of the 1960s, Sheila cooked the main meal in the middle of the day and Gerald always came home for lunch. He was quite crestfallen when she told him she had decided she would change dinner to the evening, and he should have a sandwich in town. He only stayed away overnight when he went to Dublin for High Court cases; otherwise, they always travelled together.

The Struggle with Growth

By the 1960s, his practice had grown exponentially. His first assistant was Harry Shanahan, who was with him from very early on. Later, Tommy Bernardi joined him. There was a time when Gerald had many apprentice solicitors who chose him because they wanted to be well trained. At one time, there were more than 10, but sadly they did not stay to join the firm, other than Peter Fleming, son of a barrister whom Gerald briefed. Anne O'Mahony was the last solicitor to join. Gerald sold her the practice, but she did not remain in law, retiring very early on. She sold her interest to another solicitor who got into difficulty with the Law Society. The practice had to close, and now the name Gerald Y. Goldberg, Solicitor, is no more in Cork. The only Goldberg now in Cork is a pub in Jewtown, but *sin scéal eile.*

There were many missteps, such as not expanding when he had the opportunity, failing to bring his young trainee solicitors into the practice or offering them partnerships, and then leaving it too late to sell his practice. By the time he did sell the practice, he was 80 years old and much of it had gone. Although Gerald thought he still had the same capacity for work that he had had when he was younger, it was not so, and he could not keep up with the demands, nor the many changes that were fast-occurring, especially in European Law. What grieves me, and is so tragic about this, is that he could have built an empire. He had the opportunity, but he was unable to divide the spoils of his success.

One of the most significant contributions to this was, undoubtedly, his inability both to work with others and to delegate. It is a trait I believe he inherited from his father. He could not trust others to do things as well as he did; no one was good enough. For a long time, he was able to handle a mammoth workload: practice in the District Court nearly every day, the Circuit Court, the High Court, and the Courts of Appeal, including the Supreme Court. But others had difficulty working with him. One example was my brother, John, who qualified as a solicitor and joined the practice in 1962. They did not work well together. Consequently, John went to New

York, and after his marriage, he and his wife Nancy returned to Cork, John re-joining the practice in 1963. John had ideas to modernize and expand, and to make changes to the way things were done. Gerald would not countenance any changes. John and Nancy decided to go back to America in 1964. They never returned. Peter Fleming, after he joined the practice, was ultimately made a partner, but reluctantly. That relationship, too, did not survive. Peter left and set up on his own. The inability to keep his excellent solicitors in the expansion of the firm was, I believe, a personality trait which occurs in brilliant people who are high-functioning on the autistic spectrum. I don't think Gerald could help it as it runs in the genes, and no one knew of such a thing in those days.

Gerald & Sheila with the staff of Gerald's practice at the office Christmas party, 1969. Back: Pat Horgan, Mary Porteus, Michael Rearden, Sheila, Tommy Bernardi, Mrs. Bernardi, Gerald, and Peter Fleming. Front: Breda Holland, Eileen Dinan, Kathleen Barry, and Kay Mulqueen. (Photo: Goldberg Special Archive, UCC)

Gerald struggled with himself and many others. When he disliked someone, he frequently cut them out of his life, like an amputated limb. If he felt he had been slighted or had had a serious row with someone, he might never have contact with them again; this is what happened with some of the solicitors who trained with him.

However, he could also inspire great loyalty, as shown by the secretaries who stayed throughout his career. Kathleen Barry was his principal secretary, then came Eileen Dinan, and then Edith Murphy. They all joined the firm when they were young. None of them married. Edith was only 15 when she started. Her father had died young, and she had to leave school to support her mother. Edith eventually left the firm and became a solicitor herself.

Gerald's reputation attracted interest: for example, one day, a young red-headed boy came into the office and got a meeting with him. The boy's name was Pat Horgan. He said: "Mr. Goldberg, teach me the law." He didn't become an apprentice. He went to the Bar, but he spent a lot of time with Gerald.

"Go to Goldberg"

Gerald had a reputation for taking the hard cases. Many people said that "anyone can buy your house, but when you are in trouble, go to Goldberg." Even today, in doing research for this book, I have asked people for information, only to be told, "You know he was my solicitor, too." Eventually, clients came from all over the country to retain him because he was a great lawyer. Barry Galvin, principal of Barry C. Galvin & Co, solicitors, where Gerald was apprenticed in 1930, told me this story about a client of his known as "HA" because he had a stutter, and who, to prevent stuttering, would say "HA!"

> HA worked for a motorcycle company, and later was employed by a big manufacturing company. One day, HA was riding his motorcycle near Glanmire, just outside Cork. There was a small hump-backed bridge at Riverstown, and he alleged that a lady driver was coming over the bridge at speed. There was a collision. HA was knocked off his bike, and he brought a claim for damages. Gerald defended the lady driver. Some of the cross-examination went like this:
>
> **Gerald:**   Where did you go after work?
>
> **HA:**   The Elm Tree.
>
> **Gerald:**   What did you have there?
>
> **HA:**   Two pints.
>
> **Gerald:**   Where did you go then?

HA:	Another pub.
Gerald:	What did you have there?
HA: T	Two pints.
Gerald:	What did you do then?
HA:	I went to – HA! – O'Leary's in Glanmire.
Gerald:	What did you do there?
HA:	I met a few of me – HA! – friends.
Gerald:	What did you have?
HA:	I had three – HA! – pints.

Gerald sat down. It was the end of the case. HA's wife was with him. She was upset, and when they were outside the courtroom in consultation with Barry Galvin, Gerald passed by and said: "Bad luck".

HA's wife:	Is there no justice?
HA:	I told ya, we should – HA! – going to Goldieberg.

Many of Gerald's clients became his friends. I knew two of them from Scilly in Kinsale. In the 1960s, Kinsale was rocking and rolling. It was the place to be. The Spaniard pub in the town was completely new and refreshing; it was packed every night. Then there were two restaurants, The Spinnaker and Man Friday. The first was owned by Hedli MacNeice and the other by Jack Penfold; both were clients.

When Hedli was prosecuted for selling liquor after hours, she retained Gerald. He went down to Kinsale District Court with a barrow-load of books. His opponent was Michael Dempsey, State Solicitor for East Cork. Gerald and Michael did not get on at all. Gerald began addressing the Justice, informing him about his client's background. "She is the former wife of the great Irish poet Louis MacNeice. She is a singer and actress in her own right. She has appeared in New York Metropolitan Opera, appeared in La Scala Milan, and appeared in Covent Garden…." Dempsey was known to nod off a bit, but when Gerald got to "appeared in Covent Garden…," Dempsey woke up, pushed his teeth back into his mouth, and piped up in his droll Cork accent: "And now she's appearing in Kinsale District Court."

Postscript

Very revealing was an interview on July 24, 1977, on Radio Telefís Éireann (RTÉ), Ireland's State broadcaster. Gerald and Sheila were then the Lord Mayor and Lady Mayoress and gave an interview for the program *For Better, For Worse*. The interviewer, Tom Savage, asked Sheila about disappointments. She replied that one of the disappointments was: "… although two of our sons did law, neither of them are in the practice." She had hoped that one of us would stay with Gerald and "… help him, because I think he needed it." She said my leaving the Bar to paint was traumatic. Gerald was asked if he was conscious of the dynasty dying. He replied that to leave a lasting firm was what he had wanted and hoped for, as he wished "to found a Goldberg dynasty, especially in the legal profession." Then he said that he was the last of his family in Cork city and "… when I had three sons, I was so certain that my name would be carried on in Cork." He recognized that it was gone, and it was very disappointing. He had thought the name Goldberg would be associated with Cork forever; however, he was unable to see a way achieve that goal. It was a bridge too far, but not his fault.

Gerald and Sheila with David, on the occasion of his calling to the Bar of Ireland, 1967.

Chapter 11

GERALD: KEY CASES

The heart hates injustice.

Maria Stepanova, *In Memory of Memory*

Words are the tools of a Lawyer's trade.

Tan Twan Eng in *The Garden of Evening Mists*

There were many aspects to Gerald. He was a man of many interests, but he was first and foremost a great advocate. Advocacy is what he gave his life to, and it is how he is remembered. He was a lawyer who was not shy to take on a challenge; rather, he relished it. Many of his cases were straight forward and he often argued his own criminal trials with a jury. He was well schooled in both sides of the courts' jurisdiction.

David Gwynn Morgan, Professor of Law at UCC, said of Gerald: "His learning, far sightedness and resourcefulness were poured out in unstinting libations for his clients" (Keogh & Whelan, 2008). Morgan says that Gerald cut a swathe through administrative law, taking on local government for tenants long before it was practical. However, it is not administrative law I want to address.

I have chosen to present here three of Gerald's many cases, each very different, that demonstrate Gerald's courage and determination to follow justice and not to take the easy solution. The accounts have been gleaned from court records and newspaper reports.

The Case of the Ten Shilling Note

In 1947, a man named Trindle was charged before the Cork Circuit Court with breaking and entering the dwelling house and pub of a lady, and stealing £30. In the course of the trial, evidence was given that the accused was in the licensed premises on a Saturday night and bought a drink which he paid for with a very crumpled 10/- note. As he smoothed it out, he tore a corner. The note was put in the till, rolled up. The publican kept the takings in a wardrobe in an upstairs room with a skylight. The next morning, being Sunday, some of the family went to Mass but one aunt and some children stayed at home. The family came back by taxi and went to the wardrobe upstairs for cash to pay the fare. £30 was missing and they reported it to the Gardaí. It was noticed that the skylight was open and there were footprints on the floor. Also, the back door, which had been locked, was now open, which suggested entry through the skylight and exit through the back door.

Originally, Gerald was retained to act on behalf of the accused, but an odd set of circumstances obliged him to withdraw from the case. It was alleged that money from the robbery had been paid by the accused to Gerald for his fees, so Gerald was called as a State witness. He was asked questions bearing on receipt of the money which he refused to answer, claiming the privilege of lawyer-client confidentiality. The privilege belongs to the client, not the lawyer.

During the trial, evidence was given confirming this story. A Garda Superintendent said he had taken two statements from the accused. In the second, Mr. Trindle said he had given Mr. Goldberg £8: £7 in single notes, and two 10/- notes, one of which he thought might have been torn in the corner. A Garda Sergeant visited Mr. Goldberg's office and asked him if he had received anything from the accused. He was shown £7 single notes and two 10/- notes. One corner of one of the 10/- notes was torn. Gerald said the accused had consulted him at his office and the conversation was one between solicitor and client, and not in the furtherance of any criminal act on the part of the accused. When he was asked if Mr. Trindle had given him anything, Gerald claimed privilege. Counsel for the prosecution asked him on at least four occasions if he had received anything, perhaps a 10/- note, but Gerald refused to answer. Counsel then asked the Judge to intervene and direct an answer. The Judge said that he was satisfied from the evidence already given that Mr. Goldberg had received the money, and it was essential for the administration of justice that it be produced. "... I rule that privilege is gone, and I must ask you to produce it." Gerald respectfully declined. Counsel for the prosecution said this placed himself and the Judge in a very uncomfortable position and asked the Judge to treat Gerald in contempt and deal with him accordingly, since refusal to answer questions was a contempt of court.

The Judge in his ruling said: "I am very sorry, Mr. Goldberg, I must find you guilty of contempt of court. The suggestion of the State is that this money is a portion of stolen property and it ought to be produced ... I will have to fine you £50. It is a very important matter." The jury was then discharged. Gerald raised the issue of an appeal from the ruling, and the Judge said he would do anything to assist that and hoped the fine would never be collected (*Irish Examiner*, April 23, 1947). The Judge added: "You are taking a very courageous stand in the best interests of the profession, and in what you regard as the privilege of the profession."

When the court sat again the next morning, the Judge referred to the previous day's proceedings. He said he had been thinking the matter over, and that he wished it to be known that Mr. Goldberg's contempt was not contempt of court in the ordinary course of events. "It was a refusal to answer a question as to which, I am sure, Mr. Goldberg had legal advice on which he was acting, and on what he considered to be the best interests of the profession. When, therefore, this matter is finally determined, and if my ruling is upheld on appeal, I make an Order the £50 fine be reduced to 1/-, if Mr. Goldberg acts on the Order of the Appeal Court, and gives evidence accordingly."

The Retrial

When the case came back to court for rehearing in October 1947, the same witnesses gave the same evidence. Gerald told the court that Mr. Trindle was a client of his and had retained him previously for certain other business. Mr. Hooper was prosecuting; Mr. Wellwood acted for the accused.

Mr. Hooper SC:	While with you, Mr. Goldberg, did he give you anything?
Mr. Goldberg:	Before I answer that, my Lord, I would like to say that unless the accused either personally or through his counsel waives the privilege which I believe he has, I must claim on the grounds that the conversation which I had with him was one as between solicitor and client, and was not in the furtherance of crime or the commission of a crime.
Mr. Hooper SC	I did not ask you, Mr. Goldberg, about any conversation. I asked you did the accused give you anything?
Mr. Goldberg:	I have the same answer to make as that brings in a matter of professional conduct.
Mr. Wellwood:	I am happy to say, my Lord, on behalf of my client that he waives any privilege which might exist in relation to Mr. Goldberg.

That ended the stand-off and the case proceeded. Gerald said he was given a sum of £8: seven single £1 notes, and two 10/- notes. Asked if he had the notes, he produced them, saying that after the last trial he had given them to the solicitor for the accused for safe keeping, and received them back before this trial commenced. He said that a few minutes after his consultation with the accused, he had been visited by Detective Sergeant O'Riordan to whom he showed the notes. They had been in the same condition as they were, except that a small ink mark had appeared on one note. The 10/- note was torn in exactly the same fashion as when Mr. Trindle gave them to him but the piece which was torn from the note was missing.

On further questioning by Mr. Wellwood, it was determined that Gerald had had a further consultation with the accused after the visit of Detective Sergeant O'Riordan, and had asked Mr. Trindle about the source of the money. Gerald told the accused that unless he could be satisfied as to the source of the money, he would not be able to accept instructions from him. When asked if the accused accounted for the money, Mr. Hooper objected on the basis that it was a matter for the jury. The judge agreed.

Mr. Trindle denied breaking and entering the licensed premises and stealing £30. He said that he had been in the pub on the Saturday night and had bought some drinks. He changed a £1 note but could not remember whether he received a note or all silver in the change. On Sunday, he got up rather late. His wife had gone to 9 o'clock Mass. At about 9.30 am, he went to the pump for a bucket of water, wearing his best blue suit and a gun metal blue overcoat. He filled a white enamel bucket, then went home. He did not see anyone he knew, and he had not gone to Mass because there was no room on the bus.

He told the jury that, in the preceding week, he had sold some books for £3.13.0 and had also cut an inscription on a family memorial in a graveyard for which he was paid £4.18.0. This money was kept in a writing cabinet in the kitchen, and it was there when the Gardaí came. He said he had some business with Mr. Goldberg for which he paid him £8 and that was the money he had received from the sale of books and the stone-cutting. Cross-examined by Mr. Hooper, Mr. Trindle said that when he was paying Mr. Goldberg, he tore one of the notes, but could not remember which one. He added that he often tore notes.

Mr. Hooper SC: Do you remember Mr. Goldberg objecting to the production of these notes in court?

Mr. Trindle: Yes.

Mr. Hooper SC: Did you want that done?

Mr. Trindle: No, not at any time. From the first, I wanted them produced.

Mr. Hooper SC: It was your desire that these notes should be handed over to the police or produced in court?

Mr. Trindle: Produced in court.

Mr. Hooper SC: Did you take any steps to see that they would be produced before the court?

Mr. Trindle: No. I left that to Mr. Goldberg himself.

That was the end of Mr. Trindle's evidence. Two witnesses then gave evidence confirming Mr. Trindle's story of the books and the gravestone. The judge charged the jury and they retired to consider their verdict. They took only 20 minutes to acquit Mr. Trindle. The judge directed that the £8 be returned to Mr. Goldberg who undertook to produce it at another trial.

This case demonstrates how Gerald cared about the minutiae of the law, even to the point of unnecessary pedantry. Why did he not discuss it with Mr. Wellwood, whom he knew well, and discover what was Mr. Trindle's view? Why would a young solicitor with a young family and not a huge practice have submitted himself to a fine of £50, a considerable sum in 1947?

The Coroner's Court: An Inquest

This concerns the inquest into the death in 1967 of a man while in Garda custody. At that time, there was much emphasis in medical teaching on the importance of properly assessing the possible injuries that a drunken person might sustain, and that might be disguised by his inebriated condition (Dr. Carla Goldberg, personal communication). If there were any doubt, the person must be brought to an emergency department before a police cell. In this case, the deceased had asked for a doctor, while in a cell, but was ignored. Gerald was dissatisfied by the evidence of the Gardaí and of the pathologist who had done the *post mortem*. As a result of the unusual circumstances surrounding a death in custody, an investigation commenced and then an inquest was held. Gerald was retained by the next of kin.

Background
On May 30, 1967, Liam O'Mahony, a retired seaman, described as "very healthy, apart from a problem he had had with his foot for many years," was taken into custody in the Bridewell Garda Station, Cork. He had been arrested in Winthrop Street at about 6.00 pm, with two others, because they were drunk. The deceased was described in the *Evening Echo* (May 30, 1967) as "a big strong man" who had been drinking in the Long Valley Bar, a well-known pub on that street, with two other men, when a dispute occurred. The three men were put into a squad car, two of them peacefully, but O'Mahony resisted and force was required. All three were taken to the Bridewell, and O'Mahony was placed in a cell. The other two may have been released or transferred to hospital, but it is unclear, because it was not recorded what happened to them.

At about 11.00 pm, a Garda coming on duty had a conversation with the prisoner who told him "his side was hurt." When asked what was wrong, Mr. O'Mahony said he was kicked by a Garda. He asked for a doctor at about 12.30 am but the Garda to whom he spoke believed that a doctor was not necessary as he was sobering up and improving. He denied at the Inquest that he kicked the man.

Sometime later, when a duty Garda looked in on the prisoner, he saw him sitting up with his feet straight out in front of him, his back against the wall, and his hands on the ground. When the Garda looked at him, he knew immediately there was something wrong. The prisoner was pale and he could not discern any breathing. He was cold to the touch. The Garda concluded he was dead, and he told the other Gardaí in the public office. They placed O'Mahony on the bunk, and called a priest and a doctor.

The Coroner was called to the station at 4.00 am to view the body. The Deputy State Pathologist conducted a *post mortem* the next day which revealed considerable injuries to the head and chest. Some evidence at the inquest suggested that O'Mahony had suffered two falls from a bar-stool. Other evidence suggested that, between 11.30 pm and 1.30 am, he suffered very serious injuries to his body in the Bridewell. The report in the *Evening Echo* said that when the deceased's brother-in-law, also called O'Mahony but not a blood relation, went to the Bridewell to enquire what had happened, he was told he had fallen from the bunk "a few times." When Mr. O'Mahony pointed out a bruise on his brother-in-law's face, he was told that it was "his coloring."

Headlines in the *Evening Echo* put it rather starkly: "Mystery Death in Cork Garda Station – Inquiries Continued Through the Night." The police were tight-lipped when asked questions by reporters.

In the Inquest, it was stated that Mr. O'Mahony, the deceased man's brother-in-law, had come to the station to complain that the prisoner had been beaten. The Garda witness, Garda Power, reported that "this man" was drunk and that he told him on at least three occasions to go home and come back the next day. Garda Power swore that he did not see anyone else touch the prisoner other than himself. He had tried to rouse him by pushing his foot under the soft part of his thigh to shake him awake. Another Garda told him it was dangerous to allow him to sleep as he might smother or get sick. He saw nothing wrong with him, other than he was drunk. Garda Power said that he did not suspect the prisoner was suffering from anything other than the indulgence of drink. State Solicitor, Mr. Harvey, began.

Mr. Harvey: Was there any other signs on him of any other injuries?

Garda Power: There were no other signs shown to me that there was anything else wrong with him.

Gerald then began his cross-examination by asking for the Station Diary and asked whether the entries relating to each incident were written up at the time or later.

Mr. Goldberg: Am I right in saying also that there is no entry in the diary of his complaint that he had been kicked in the ribs?

Garda Power: I made a mention of that in my statement.

Mr. Goldberg: Am I right in saying that there is no reference to a complaint made by the prisoner that the kick had been received by the prisoner from a Guard?

Garda Power: The prisoner might not have made a complaint that he was kicked by a Guard. He said that he was kicked, and I asked him who kicked him and the prisoner replied, "Guard" and nothing else.

Mr. Goldberg: I have to suggest to you that you are telling lies.

Garda Power: I am not telling lies.

Mr. Goldberg: Did you suppress in a statement made to your superior officers on May 30 information that the prisoner made a complaint of being kicked in the ribs by a Guard?

Garda Power: I was asked on the night that the prisoner died what comments had the prisoner made and exactly what I told them was that the prisoner had told me that he had been kicked and when I asked him who had kicked him, and he replied "Guard."

Garda Power then said he had no reason to hide or conceal anything. He noticed no marks on the deceased man's face, except that he was pale. When he came into the cell first, he noticed that there was a bit of blood on his face.

Mr. Goldberg: The State Pathologist will be giving evidence and he will tell the Coroner and jury of the various marks on the deceased man's face. He will distinguish between two marks, the marks made by impact and what he calls "abrasions and dragging." The pathologist will say there were marks "indicating abrasions caused by dragging on both sides of the deceased man's face" and that dirt had penetrated. If these marks were found when the pathologist carried out his *post mortem* examination, can you tell us how they were caused?

Garda Power: I can safely say that the man was never touched.

Mr. Goldberg: Was he dragged?

Garda Power: He was dragged at no time. I never saw the man being dragged.

Mr. Goldberg: And there were no marks when you went into the cell, other than the pallor on his face?

Garda Power: Other than the pallor on his face. He had a bit of a nose bleed and there was a bit of blood on his face.

Garda Power also noticed a black eye which had shown up after he died.

Mr. Goldberg: Are you shocked to hear about the abrasive marks filled with dirt?

Garda Power: I never saw it.

Mr. Goldberg: In your first statement to your superior officers, you said: "When I was with the prisoner at about 1.30 am he said he had a pain in his ribs-side and complained that he got a kick in it. He agreed that it was a guard kicked him." That is what you told the Coroner and jury last week that it was "a guard" and not "guard," isn't that what you said?

Garda Power: If you read my statement, I put down the exact words of what the deceased man said to me.

Mr. Goldberg: May I take it you did not put down the exact words in the statement I read out?

Garda Power: No.

Mr. Goldberg: Were you suppressing something?

Garda Power: I was suppressing nothing. When the prisoner said to me that he got a kick and I asked him who kicked him, he said, "Guard." At that time, I thought he got a knock or something and he was blaming the guards. It was just a passing thought to me at the time.

Mr. Goldberg:	Will you concede that when I said last week that when the prisoner complained that he was kicked by a guard I was not making it up?
Garda Power:	It was in my statement.
Mr. Goldberg:	And now it is changed to "Guard."
Garda Power:	The exact words the prisoner said to me was "Guard." At the time he made it, I was busy. When he was under Garda O'Keeffe's care, I thought he could not have got a kick from a guard and it was one of those complaints that prisoners often make.

Garda Power told the Coroner that he knew of cases where the prisoner alleged that a guard did something to him but, in actual fact, there was never anything wrong with him.

Mr. Goldberg:	Was it your duty to enter that complaint into your diary?
Garda Power:	That complaint was not necessary.
Mr. Goldberg:	How then are your superiors to know what events took place in the Bridewell Garda Station and to which their attention should be attracted if the diary omits a complaint of this nature? In writing into the diary, you write in what you think is necessary? And also omit something which would arouse the suspicion of your superior officers? That never entered your mind? Are you satisfied now from what you have heard that this man was at death's door?
Garda Power:	I cannot answer that question.
Mr. Goldberg:	Have you any doubt at all?
Garda Power:	I am fully convinced that the man was....
Mr. Goldberg:	I am asking you if you now have any doubt at all that he was then at death's door?
Garda Power:	He may have been from what I have heard after the *post mortem*.
Mr. Goldberg:	I am advised by expert evidence that will be given that, in fact, I made an under-estimate last week, that there were 13 fractures involving nine ribs, and four of them were double fractures. You have told Mr. Coroner and the jury that the deceased said: "I have been kicked in the ribs," isn't that right?

Garda Power: Yes.

Mr. Goldberg: There is no doubt that he did not imagine the injury to his ribs wherever he got them, and he was quite genuine in saying there was something wrong with his ribs. From what you said, he appeared to be improving?

Garda Power: Yes, he did.

Mr. Goldberg: Were you convinced that, despite his complaint, he did not need a doctor?

Garda Power: That's right.

Then Garda Power said that when he was shaking him up, he heard a noise like a groan.

Mr. Goldberg: If you were shaking a man with 13 fractures of nine ribs, he would groan?

Garda Power: He would, I suppose.

Mr. Goldberg: I am suggesting to you that his breathing must have alerted you to his injuries.

Garda Power: Never at any time.

Mr. Goldberg: Do you say he was breathing normally?

Garda Power: He was.

Going on to describe how on one visit to the cell, Garda Power said he placed a blanket under the deceased man's head to prevent him hurting himself.

Garda Power: I put the blanket down alongside his head and I distinctly remember putting my hands down under the back of his neck, rising up his head a little bit, and putting it on the blanket and shoving the blanket in against the wall with my foot.

Mr. Goldberg: Patrick O'Mahony (brother-in-law) saw that...?

Garda Power: He did but he said I kicked the blanket under his head.

Mr. Goldberg: He was very fair. He said he saw you putting the blanket in with your foot?

Garda Power: I just shoved the blanket in not more than about an inch and a half or two inches.

Mr. Goldberg: This is what you said in your statement, that you used your foot: "I just lifted O'Mahony's head a little bit with my hand and pushed a loosely rolled blanket under his head with my foot." That is what you said in your second statement.

Garda Power: If that is what was put down, that's not what was meant to be put down. What I was fully convinced I put down there was "I lifted up this man's head." You see, you got the impression I'd kicked the thing under his head.

Mr. Goldberg: He did not say you kicked, he said "... pushed the blanket under his head with your foot."

Garda Power: I lifted up O'Mahony's head, put it on the blanket and pushed the lot into the wall an inch and a half.

Mr. Goldberg: All these tips that you describe and the manner in which you even put a blanket under his head – would you treat your mongrel dog in that way?

Garda Power: I was most careful in treating this man.

Mr. Goldberg: Would you kick your mongrel dog in the legs?

Garda Power: I kicked nobody in the legs.

Mr. Goldberg: Haven't you admitted, to use your own words, "tip," saying "Get up."

Garda Power: I did not say "Get up."

Mr. Goldberg: I must suggest to you there were three members of the Gardaí – yourself, Garda O'Connell, and Garda Kenny – after Garda O'Keeffe went to bed. I must suggest that 13 fractures involving nine ribs, which the deceased sustained, were sustained after Garda O'Keeffe had gone to bed and as a result of kicks?

Garda Power: You are saying that.

Mr. Goldberg: Yes.

Garda Power: No such thing could have happened. At no time could such a thing have happened.

At this point, the Coroner entered the cross-examination.

Coroner: You took it upon yourself that it wasn't necessary to call a doctor?

Garda Power: That's right.

Coroner: Do you not consider that you breached the regulations?

Garda Power: If the man was not able to wake, I would then have sent for a doctor.

The most important evidence was that of the Assistant State Pathologist, Dr. Raymond O'Neill. He noticed the abrasions to the cheeks which suggested O'Mahony's face had been rubbed on a hard gritty, dirty surface. There was a mark on the back of the scalp which was consistent with his head hitting something hard like a floor. There was discoloration on both sides of the chest and abdomen. The injuries were on both sides, ribs 6 to 10 being broken, resulting in bleeding into the chest cavity, and would have been the direct result of injury to the chest wall. The impact was more severe on the right side. The internal bleeding was directly related to the impact which caused the right rib injury. He considered that the fact that the deceased was inclined to roll off his bunk suggested great confusion and restlessness which were common symptoms of people who had internal bleeding which was not controlled.

Mr. Harvey: From the evidence you have heard, you are of the opinion that these injuries which caused this man's death were sustained before he arrived at the Bridewell at all?

Dr. O'Neill: I believe the symptoms as I heard them could be related to internal bleeding and traumatic shock.

Mr. Harvey: As he was brought in with two other men, all three of them being brought in for being under the influence of drink, do you think a member of the Gardaí could diagnose those injuries?

Dr. O'Neill: This is one of the pitfalls of diagnosis, even at medical level. It is a problem which is constantly arising. People go to hospital intoxicated and injured and to decide whether they are drunk or injured often poses great problems. They are not infrequently sent home, to be found dead later: they have been sent to police cells where they have been found dead or dying. So, I think it is difficult.

Mr. Harvey: You would not expect the average Garda to be able to diagnose his injuries as such?

Dr. O'Neill: No, unless this man was examined medically and he would have to be unclothed, I think.

Mr. Harvey: What effect would the alcohol have on any pain he may have sustained as a result of the injuries he suffered? Would the alcohol act as an anesthetic?

Dr. O'Neill: Well, alcohol in sufficient quantity acts the same as an anesthetic. It is not used as an anesthetic because it is too dangerous, but its effect is the same at a certain level.

Under cross-examination, Dr. O'Neill said the man's condition should have been evident to Gardaí in Winthrop Street, but it might not have been so in the cell because of poor lighting. Certainly, in the day room, they could have noticed his color and if he needed assistance. But he added that sometimes medical people who are skilled have missed this time and time again and would do so in the future. O'Mahony was likely to have been in control of his senses. The injuries may have been caused by falling off a bar stool in the Long Valley Bar. Dr. O'Neill did not think O'Mahony's collapse in Winthrop Street would have caused his injuries. Dr. O'Neill thought O'Mahony could only mount the steps to the Bridewell steps because he was intoxicated; otherwise, he would not have been able. Between 8.00 pm and 12.00 midnight, the effects of alcohol were wearing off. Both sides of the ribs were not fractured at the same time. They could have been caused by falling across a chair, or on rather hard objects on two occasions or in a car crash. He agreed they could have been caused by blows or a series of kicks. O'Mahony would have been conscious of being kicked on the floor of a cell. If he was conscious, he would have said so. To produce those injuries, one would have to stand back and kick with all one's might and fury. O'Mahony's breathing would have been limited and shallow. This might only be observed by someone who knew what he was looking for.

One witness was called for the next of kin: Surgeon Ian McKillop, who said he did not think the fall in the Long Valley Bar could have caused the injuries sustained. He agreed with Dr. O'Neill that the injuries were sustained in separate incidents, but did Dr. O'Neill think that, if the injuries had been sustained in the bar, the deceased could have travelled to the Bridewell, walked up the steps to the day room and the cell without showing signs of them? Surgeon McKillop also said that, having regard to the injuries, he was surprised the deceased could breathe at all. It should have been obvious to anyone looking at him.

Mr. Harvey: In these circumstances, would you think that an ordinary Garda in a barracks should be expected to differentiate between an alcoholic condition and injuries caused by fracture of the ribs?

Mr. McKillop: No.

Mr. Harvey: There was evidence that this man had fallen from a stool on two occasions. We don't know whether he came on top of the stool or the stool came away from him, but is it possible that these injuries could have been caused by these falls?

Mr. McKillop: I should say that a fall from a fair height on to a stool or a blunt object would cause these injuries.

That was the end of the evidence in the hearing. There was no official stenographer's report. Reliance has been placed on the news reports which are quite extensive, though not complete. This was a theme that Gerald referred to in his address to the jury. He asked how the Commissioner of the Gardaí or the Minister for Justice could be satisfied to make a proper assessment relying solely on newspapers.

The jury returned a verdict in accordance with the medical evidence. The Coroner said: "You have not said anything about how the injuries were received. They didn't just occur." The jury retired again and, when they returned, they had added the words: "We have insufficient evidence to say where and how the injuries were received."

In a final flourish after the Coroner thanked the jury for their care in their deliberations and the manner in which they examined the evidence, he said he expressed those views on behalf of himself, Mr. Harvey, and Mr. Goldberg.

Mr. Harvey: I think we both agree.

Gerald: I do not.

The Inquest: A Postscript

The Inquest into O'Mahony's death caused considerable disquiet throughout the country. It was discussed everywhere and there were articles in the newspapers, including, I believe, in the *Sunday Times*. These commentaries caused questions to be asked in Dáil Éireann, leading to calls for a Judicial Tribunal of Enquiry. The Minister for Justice, Brian Lenihan, was under much pressure which he initially rejected. The President and Secretary of the Irish Association for Civil Liberties wrote a letter to all newspapers, noting the unease in public opinion, and saying it was in the public interest, and the interest of the Gardaí, that no question should be left unanswered.

The Minister bowed to the pressure and set up a judicial enquiry to find the facts and circumstances surrounding the death in Garda custody, on May 30, 1967, of Liam O'Mahony. Three judges were appointed, one from each division: Mr. Justice William Fitzgerald, Chief Justice; Mr. Justice George Murnaghan, High Court; and Judge Charles Conroy, Circuit Court. They sat in Cork over 11 days in August 1967 and heard 77 witnesses. Before the Tribunal commenced, the Commissioner of An Garda Síochána had already issued new regulations for treatment of persons in custody, which was welcomed by the Tribunal.

The evidence was largely the same as at the Inquest, except that the State Pathologist offered a theory as to cause of death. He hypothesized that the deceased fractured his ribs and ruptured his mesentery by a fall onto a bar stool, which was lying on the ground. To support his theory, the witness told the Tribunal that he carried out an experiment by falling himself on a metal bar stool similar to the one in the Long Valley Bar. This resulted in bruising which he showed to the Tribunal. However, he did not sustain a crushing fracture to his ribs bi-laterally, nor any ruptures or hemothorax. However, a professor of surgery at UCC agreed with and supported this theory.

The Tribunal concluded that there was no case to answer. The judges were satisfied that O'Mahony sustained the injuries as a result of falling on a stool. They held that he did not suffer any of the injuries in the Bridewell Station. The Gardaí were not in breach of any regulations. O'Mahony would have died even if he had had medical attention, but that it would have saved a good deal of public disquiet if a doctor had been called to examine him. Regarding the lay witnesses, Coughlan and Hartnett (his fellow drinkers) and Patrick O'Mahony (brother-in-law), the Tribunal said they were unreliable and lacking credibility and rejected their evidence. All the Garda evidence was accepted as truthful and accurate. They had done nothing wrong.

Gerald was dismayed. He found the conclusion hard to accept, but he had to do so.

DPPV v Madden, Lynch and Others

The final case had three phases:
- Proceedings for contempt against Irish Press Ltd, Tim Pat Coogan, T.P. O'Mahony and Gerald himself, regarding an open letter Gerald wrote to the Minister for Justice relating to the case, and published in the *Irish Press*, before it came to trial.
- The trial was of four men – Madden, Lynch, O'Donnell and Doyle – in the Special Criminal Court for the murder of Laurence White. Gerald was retained by all four men for their defense. They were convicted by the non-jury court.
- An appeal against conviction, based on the manner in which the investigation was carried out, and statements taken.

The Case

At about midnight on June 10, 1975, in Cork City, a man named Laurence White was gunned down on his way home after visiting a pub with others. This was a carefully planned murder. A white Ford Cortina car was used, in which there were two men: one drove, while the other had a machine-gun. White was stopped, the gun-man got out, shot him, and re-entered the car which sped away up a hill. At the top of the hill, the men transferred to a waiting Volkswagen truck and drove away. When the car, which had been stolen in Co. Limerick on June 6, was found the next day, it was noted to have false plates and a supply of paper parking discs. At that time, Cork City required drivers to pay for parking using these discs which were sold widely for that purpose. These discs were punched to indicate place and time and could pay for between one and three hours. When the Gardaí found the car, there were two used discs, both with O'Donnell's fingerprints on them. Another, unused book of discs was found with Doyle's fingerprints.

The case against Madden relied solely on his statement made in custody. The case against Lynch was more circumstantial, relying partly on a statement and partly on his knowledge that the car was stolen: his defense was that that he had wanted to talk to O'Donnell. This linked him to the case by the finding of O'Donnell's fingerprints on the parking discs. The case against O'Donnell largely rested on his fingerprints. The case against Doyle rested also on his fingerprints found on the unused book of tickets.

There were allegations that these statements were involuntary, having been made under violence, threats of violence, and oppression and that the law regarding length of time in custody had been flouted. So it was that long before the criminal case ever came to trial, Gerald found himself again embroiled in a dispute with the State.

DPP v Irish Press Ltd, Tim Pat Coogan, T.P. O'Mahony and Gerald Y. Goldberg

On July 11, 1975, Gerald wrote an open letter to the Minister for Justice, Patrick Cooney (himself a solicitor), which he sent to the *Irish Press* office in Cork. It was received by a staff reporter, T.P. O'Mahony, who turned it into an article. The article was considered at an editorial meeting by Tim Pat Coogan, editor, and it was published headlined: "'Torture being used on suspects,' says lawyer. Letter to Cooney claims 'brutalities.'" The "open letter" to the Minister for Justice was published as part of the article on July 11, 1975.

A leading Cork solicitor called on the Minister for Justice, Mr. Cooney, to end "physical and psychological methods of torture" allegedly being used on some people held under the *Offences Against the State Act.*

In an open letter to Mr. Cooney, the solicitor, Mr. Gerald Goldberg, who is also a Fianna Fáil member of Cork Corporation, claims several examples of alleged brutalities and malpractices which infringe Constitutional rights.

These incidents were an affront to the dignity of man, to the institutions of the State, and the Rule of Law, he said, and were frightening and dangerous in their implications and possible consequences.

Denied
Mr. Goldberg claimed he had been denied the right in his professional capacity to interview some of his clients without let or hinderance, and of being present, if required by them, to advise and counsel them during interrogation.

This, he said, was particularly true in the case of Messrs. Lynch, O'Donnell, Doyle, and Madden, on whose behalf he had been retained and against whom very serious charges had been preferred.

Mr. Goldberg said he had requested an explanation from the Minister in view of the fact that, at no time, while any of his clients were under interrogation, was he permitted to attend, represent and advise them.

"In certain cases, statements have been taken. These statements were not voluntary. Surely as a solicitor, if I am to adequately represent a client, this right should have been afforded me?"

Refused
Mr. Goldberg has also asked the Minister to explain why he had been refused the right and privilege of interviewing his clients except "in the presence of a police officer who can overhear everything that is said."

As a result, he was limited in the interview to simple conversations and discussions of events already known to the Gardaí.

Even though he wrote for copies of statements made by his clients some time ago, he did not receive any until yesterday.

Mr. Goldberg also discussed the manner in which some other people have been treated. [He named them, but they did not feature in the trial.] Saying that he had very carefully interviewed the people named, Mr. Goldberg said he was convinced that "threats of dire happenings, assaults, beatings of the utmost severity and gravity have been committed by certain persons on the person of some of my clients or have been carried out with hands, fists, boots, pieces of timber, and other weapons."

Confused

He also believed that some, if not all, of his clients had been interrogated for excessive periods of time without adequate sleep so that they have become confused, disoriented and ultimately, unaware of that they were saying.

He believed that physical and psychological methods of torture had been used to "break" the refusal of his clients to make statements or admissions which they believed to be untrue.

They were in danger of being rearrested and subjected to the same or worse treatment in order to extract statements from them, he said.

Mr. Goldberg said that another person [named] was arrested in and interrogated in Limerick.

Having seen his arm on Tuesday, Mr. Goldberg said he could testify to the considerable and excessive bruising of it, which could, he believed, be established by medical evidence.

"I am instructed that the bruising which I saw was inflicted in the course of an interrogation which took place in a Limerick Garda barracks," he said.

The paper asked the Department of Justice to comment on this letter.

The reply of the Minister came in the form of an application to the High Court made by the Director of Public Prosecutions (DPP) to have the Irish Press Ltd, Tim Pat Coogan, T.P. O'Mahony, and Gerald Y. Goldberg committed for contempt. The heading in the *Evening Echo* said: "Solicitor, Editor Must Show Cause." Mr. Justice Finlay, President of the High Court, granted a conditional order against them. That meant that the respondents had to "show cause" why they should not be held in contempt.

The article was published at a time when the men were before the District Court. The DPP's application was made on the basis that the article could prejudice the trial later in the minds of the public before the trial took place.

Mr. Donal Barrington S.C. (later a Supreme Court judge) said that neither he nor the court were concerned with the various allegations, charges and counter-charges. The only issue was whether the article was intended to prejudice the trial. Gerald, in his replying affidavit, opened to the court, and said that he was careful to respect the *sub judice* rule. He was cautious and restrained in what he said in his letter, but he said he had a duty to express his concerns that his clients were undergoing prolonged interrogation from which he was excluded. He was also concerned that the Gardaí had not furnished copy statements which the men had made. He was satisfied there was nothing in his letter which could prejudice a fair trial and he wanted to ensure just that. He claimed that there was a failure on the part of the Minister, the Garda authorities, and the DPP to deal with his complaints and that if anyone was prejudiced by this it was the accused.

Tim Pat Coogan told the court that the letter was authentic, and they had considered whether to use it or not. It never occurred to anyone at the editorial conference that the letter could be a contempt of court. The article was vetted by two senior journalists for libel, but none was found. They said they never intended a contempt of court and that, if it had occurred, it was something they regretted. They were aware of the need for caution in what they printed.

Mr. Coogan said he was surprised when he learned that the letter had been written by Mr. Goldberg who was known the length and breadth of the country. Mr. Goldberg was not known as someone who dealt with republican or political people, nor was he anti-establishment.

Counsel for Gerald, John Lovatt-Dolan S.C., said the article was never contemplated by Gerald, he had no control over it, and he had no legal responsibility for it. Whilst he may have given the facts, he was not responsible for the form of the article. If the letter was published in full, he would have been liable for what it contained.

The President of the High Court, Mr. Justice Finlay, said that no comment likely to prejudice a trial should be made. He held that he would allow the cause shown by all the respondents and discharge the conditional order of attachment. He thought the publication of the letter was unwise. It was unwise for a solicitor and unwise for a newspaper, but a lack of wisdom did not constitute contempt. In those circumstances, he would discharge the conditional order.

The Trial

In the course of the trial, which took place in the Special [non-jury] Criminal Court in December 1975, Gerald gave evidence regarding alleged ill-treatment of the men by the Gardaí, and the intimidation to which he himself had been subjected (*Irish Press*, November 20, and December 4). Despite the defense making many submissions on legal issues on these allegations, the Special Criminal Court convicted all four men.

The Appeal

On appeal to the Court of Criminal Appeal (judgement, November 16, 1976), Madden's appeal was allowed. It was held that his statement had been taken after the time for detention had expired and the court could not stand over such a Constitutional breach. The statement, though voluntary, was not taken in accordance with law and should not have been admitted.

Lynch had made verbal admissions to the effect that he had known of the stolen car and was anxious to talk to O'Donnell, whose fingerprints were on the parking discs. It could be inferred that Lynch had known the car was stolen and was going to be used in the murder, but as there was no evidence that he had been involved in the preparation or commission of the crime, his appeal was allowed.

In respect of David O'Donnell, the court held that at the time he parked the car he was aware of the general nature for which it was intended to be used. The finding of his fingerprints on the two parking tickets was also strong evidence of his knowledge of the murder. The court dismissed his appeal.

In Doyle's case there was his statement, and his fingerprints on the unused book of tickets. He complained that the statement was taken as a result of violence, inducement, and oppression which rendered it involuntary. He claimed also that he was denied legal representation, but the Court of Appeal held that it could not interfere with the trial court's finding of no breach of constitutional rights. The Court held that he had taken active steps in the crime and had admitted this in his statement.

In that period of time, prior to the *Criminal Justice Act of 1984*, there was some unlawful activity in Garda stations. There were some notorious cases, which went all the way to the Supreme Court where convictions were overturned. Perhaps Gerald in some way contributed to exposing this regime through his fearless pursuit of justice.

Postscript

These cases show the variety of work Gerald undertook, how conscientious he was, how he cared about the letter of the law, how he put himself on the line. His clients were ordinary men and women, mostly from working class backgrounds and he fought for their rights fiercely.

Gerald spent many years fighting cases against the State Solicitor for Cork City, Martin A. Harvey, and Cork, East County, Michael J. Dempsey. They went at each other hammer and tongs before District Justice Denis O'Donovan. Gerald made the Justice listen to law, even though the District Court is not a court in which law is usually opened. He and Martin sparred day after day. Gerald admired and respected him greatly.

Martin Harvey told his son, also, Martin, a story about Gerald representing a well-known criminal character called "Whacker" Keenan. Apparently, Gerald represented him many times, including a trial for manslaughter. But on this occasion, Gerald, when taking instructions from Whacker, told him he should "Leave the hatchet outside the court room."

Chapter 12

LIFE IN BEN-TRUDA

A house is made of walls and beams;
A home is built of love and dreams.

Ralph Waldo Emerson

There were many circumstances, influences and events that impacted his life and which went into shaping Gerald's personality, including his father and the events in Limerick described earlier – but the most powerful influence was Cork.

Gerald knew and loved Cork. He knew its streets and the history of its houses. He often walked the city with me, pointing out the Elizabethan buildings around the Coal Quay, Kyrl's Quay, and Bachelor's Walk. He expressed this sense of identity in an interview with Vincent Power in the *Evening Echo* in 1993.

> Of course, I felt that I was a rarity. Of course, I have felt that I am an exception. Of course, I have to face the accusation that, having been born into a Zionist family associated with the foundation of a Jewish home in Israel, I should be in Israel. The answer is that I should. I was asked twice by the Government of Israel to go there. I could have been a member of the Supreme Court in the State of Israel rather than a practicing solicitor in the city of Cork. But I am essentially an Irishman. I am essentially a Corkman. As a Jew who is both, I realized that I owe everything I am and what I have to the people of Cork. I have always acknowledged that. The financial matter doesn't really arise. I suppose I can say that financially I haven't done all that well. I must acknowledge with grateful thanks that I am comfortable and live comfortably. Money has never been my criterion. It has never been my reason for staying here. I have an affinity with the people of Cork. I love them dearly. I love their culture, their traditions and way of life. To live somewhere other than Cork would be my end, and I'm going to stay.

In that interview he acknowledges he was different from other Corkonians. He accepted and lived with it. He made everyone aware of his religion. He was, after all, living in a country which was 95% Catholic. The Jewish community of Ireland at its peak in the 1940s reached only approximately 5,000. During the first three-quarters of the 20th century, the Catholic Church had a strong hold over the country. Multi-culturalism, as it is defined today, did not exist. Certainly, he came across the power and influence of the Catholic Church in his practice and he took many difficult cases which no other solicitors would take.

Another element of the bond might have been our home, Ben-Truda. The house was their bastion: a warm, comfortable house.

Ben-Truda, from the back. (Photo: Goldberg Special Archive, UCC)

Gerald and Sheila, with Sheila's parents, Ben and Trudi, and Theo,
in Ben-Truda. (Photo: Debbie Levy Archive)

Sheila's parents, Ben and Trudi, gave Sheila and Gerald the house for their wedding present. Designed by John Wilkinson, of Chillingworth & Leavy, it was built by Patrick Coveney & Son, and cost £1,900. The site was one acre, which was purchased from the Sherrard family who occupied Maryborough House at the rear.

Ben-Truda was large, well-built and fairly standard for the time. Downstairs were the living-room, dining-room, breakfast-room and kitchen, which had a stove for heating water and a gas burner. There was also a back kitchen, outside toilet, coal hole, and garage. Upstairs were three bedrooms, a bathroom with separate toilet and a small room for a live-in assistant (in those days, called a maid). There were fireplaces in every room, and that was the only form of heat.

In the front and back of the house were large gardens. There was a vegetable garden in the front and a lawn on which were fruit trees. We played games there. In the back, there were fruit gardens behind some box hedges which separated them from the large lawn. Nearby, there were large fields with wonderful trees where we climbed and played with other children from the neighborhood. Especially great was a ring of six or seven trees with one in the middle. We climbed from one to the other. Now, these have been replaced by houses.

Ben-Truda was the name they gave the house, which became something of a lighthouse in Cork. Everyone knew of Ben-Truda. The name is a combination of both Ben and Trudi's names. Probably the house became a type of umbilical cord anchoring them to Cork, Belfast, and Ireland. They never cut it, and seemed unable to do so.

Over the years, as the family moved in and out, and other needs emerged, a number of extensions were added. The first was probably sometime in the late 1950s, when they pushed out the living room and incorporated the garage. This extension doubled the size of the living-room, and a new garage was built on the other side of the house.

Gerald commissioned the Cork sculptor Seamus Murphy to cut a stone with words of a prose poem by Seán Ó Faoláin for the outside wall. Gerald loved it. My brother, Theo, has it now.

The inscription is:

I looked at the climbing stairways of roofs upon roofs up to the great bell tower of Shandon. The clouds fell down into the water's stillness; the bells sank into the water and were drowned.

Sheila with her brothers, Stanley and Sidney.

Sheila, with Gerald's brother Yanks, arriving at Elaine and Bertie
Shillman's wedding, 1948.

Sheila phoned all her family regularly. Her brother Sidney was a painter, first in Belfast, and then in London. He had one daughter, Paula, who stayed with us on several occasions. Stanley was a radiologist in a London hospital. His daughters, Suzi and Debbie, came to visit Gerald and Sheila in 1955 before their sister Rachel was born. Remembering their visit in August 1955, both Suzi and Debbie recall how Sheila made an "amazing play area on the terrace at the back of Ben-Truda. It was a toy shop and play-house where we had hours of fun" (Debbie Levy, email to Paula Chabanais, April 11, 2021). Suzi remembers it was her sixth birthday. She writes: "There was a lot that made it memorable. Auntie Sheila gave me a little tiny wicker basket full of dolls clothes all knitted I think, and I also got a doll, and she was called Mary Jane." Debbie had a bad dose of chicken pox, and infected Suzi more mildly. She recalls: "Auntie Sheila played games with us endlessly, and I remember her setting up a shop in the garden with bottles of colored water – I think it was a chemist shop, and it felt like a magic summertime at Ben-Truda. Stanley had pneumonia while we were there, so all in all a tough time for Auntie Sheila but wonderful for us." Both Suzi and Debbie recall Gerald being much more serious and austere.

Ours was an English-speaking house. When our parents did not want us to understand their conversation, they spoke Yiddish. Sheila said that she learned Yiddish from Minnie, her aunt, with whom she spent much time. Sheila's Yiddish was very good, and she was always very critical of Gerald's. "You don't speak good Yiddish, " she would say, "I do. I learned from my aunt Minnie." And when Sheila told him this, he would be upset and purse his lips. I have always been puzzled why his Yiddish was poor. After all, his family also grew up speaking Yiddish. One explanation could be that, by the time he was born, the household might have adopted more English. Laban did speak, read and write English according to the census records. Rachel spoke Yiddish to the family, even when I was a child, but I never heard her sons speak Yiddish. I regret that, by ceasing to speak Yiddish, they deprived my generation of another and expressive language. Perhaps not speaking Yiddish was a mark of achievement, like Irish families stopped speaking Irish when they made progress in life. They didn't want to be reminded of the past, the life in *sheteleh*, in *der heim.* They had all moved on. Irish was lost in the same way. It reminded them all of hardship, which they wanted to forget.

Gerald and Sheila, c. 1940s. (Photo: Irish Jewish Museum, Dublin)

Attending the Blue & White Ball, Dublin, c. 1950. (Photo: Debbie Levy Archive)

Sheila and Gerald in the 1960s. (Photo: Debbie Levy Archive)

Art and Music

There was always art in Ben-Truda: many of Sidney's paintings – for example, a cornfield with cottages in France, a very good piece. Another was of the village of Dundrum, where he painted with the Belfast artist, Tom Carr. Sidney also painted a portrait of Sheila in a big red hat, and later, on a visit, he painted one of Gerald, who also commissioned him to paint two of the bridges on the river. Sheila and Gerald knew Victor Waddington, who then had a successful gallery in Dublin, and was the dealer for the Irish artist, Jack B. Yeats. In the 1940s, Victor offered them a painting by Yeats for £100 and told them they could pay whenever they had the money. The offer was declined; £100 was a huge sum of money then, and they never thought they could repay it. "Vhat the bleddy hell do you vant it for?" might have echoed in Sheila's head! It was an opportunity Gerald always regretted. He was usually adventurous and unafraid to spend money, even when he didn't have it.

One time, when the artists' agent Robert Jackson came to live in Cork, he rented Blackrock Castle as his home; the space was perfect for exhibiting paintings and sculpture. Jackson was Jacob Epstein's agent, and Gerald bought six pieces from him including a large-scale maquette of the heads of the Madonna and Child.

Sheila had an extremely good eye and she hung paintings very carefully. Often, she would decide just before going to bed at about 11.00 pm to move a painting. "I just think that is in the wrong place," she would say. Taking it off the wall, she would wonder where she could place it instead. That entailed taking down several other pictures and moving them all around. By about 3.00 am, she might have settled on a complete rehang. "We'll leave it and see what it looks like in the morning. Good night!"

When the living-room was extended, it incorporated two new bookcases, but those spaces did not stay empty for long. We quickly ran out of bookshelves and hanging space. Many years later, the kitchen was extended and also doubled in size. For a long time, Sean and Minnie Gill, who lived in Monkstown, had been very close friends. Sean was an engineer, and he did the build. The breakfast-room had become obsolete when the kitchen was extended, and let out onto a porch which was never used because the weather was seldom good enough to sit there. So, the porch was incorporated into another room, a study for Gerald to fill with more books and writing. As soon as the study was lined with bookshelves, they were filled immediately. Then he got trays from somewhere and these too were filled, sometimes stacked one on top of the other. A table was put in the room for Gerald to work on, but soon it was covered in books and papers, so a small desk was put in a corner. And despite all that, there was really nothing to read! Sheila cringed many times when he came home with cart loads of books. Collections were assembled, as Ben would put it: "In a part of a second!" Boxes arrived from English bookshops when he was researching Swift; and from America when he was researching Joyce. There were times when he had to get John to put books into his school bag to smuggle them into the house. Sometimes they were planted in the garage for a period before being moved into the house. "Where did these come from?" Sheila would ask. "Oh, darling, haven't you seen them? They've been there a long time." She would roll her eyes, and move on.

From the beginning, there was always music. Those were the days of 78s and a wind-up gramophone with a reproduction head and a needle that had to be changed about every third disc. These recordings were made on a material called shellac and the first ones had sound on one side only. They were brittle and easily broken when dropped. Many were! Gerald was never a safe pair of hands! The first records came from Percy Diamond's shop on Grand Parade. Percy, a member of the Cork Jewish community, was a very good tenor, and had sung with D'Oyly Carte. There was a big built-in bookcase on the gable wall of the living-room. It was divided: on top were books, and below were records. All the great recordings were there: Nellie Melba, Galli-Curci, Peter Dawson, Enzio Pinza, Paul Robson, Schnabel, Heifitz, Kreisler, Cortot, Busch Quartet, Solomon, Kathleen Ferrier, Toscanini, and Gigli among others. Then, when LPs came out, he bought them all again. Sometimes, he bought as many as five different versions of the same pieces; he liked to hear and compare the different interpretations.

Most evenings, music was playing while they read. Mahler became a great favorite, especially *Das Lied von der Erde* in the Bruno Walter version with Ferrier and Patzak. I think I was brought up on a diet of milk and Mahler! But not in a bookshelf! And certainly not on a Bible, as Gerald said he was! Sheila, too, was a great lover of music. She had learned the piano and sometimes she played part of the *Beethoven Pathetique* and some bagatelles, as well as Chopin. But she didn't take her playing very seriously, just played for enjoyment.

Gerald liked to go to music festivals, and so we all went to Edinburgh in 1950 and 1953. On one visit of those visits, the three of us boys were in the toilet when Sir Thomas Beecham came in. As we all stood in a line, he looked down at us and said: "What are you young squits doing here?" Gerald also bought many operas. He loved the music of Wagner but hated his virulent antisemitism.

I remember many times when Gerald held court in the living room. He stood with his back to the fire and declaimed to his loyal and devoted audience in mellifluent terms. He began by telling them about his most recent research project. They hung on his every word, as he was very engaging. Then he would remember a volume that was relevant, and he would bound to the bookcase at the other end of the room. He knew exactly where the book was on the shelf, and he also knew the page he wanted to open. He held books in his hand as if he was holding Meissen porcelain; in fact, he was more likely to drop a piece of porcelain than a book. They were his mistresses, they spoke to him gently, and he caressed them lovingly. Books never raised their voices, or answered back. They were all fountains of knowledge, and in our house they all played like the fountains of the Villa d'Este. When he held a book, it gave him confidence and authority. When he was well briefed and in full flow, he was unstoppable. From his books, he learned the great art form of oratory, at which he excelled. He serenaded and his words danced. His reading was eclectic, and from it he learned another dimension: how to see, though Sheila was better visually. He spent his life in front of his collections of paintings and sculpture. They were "sacred" objects about which he was quite jealous, often saying to himself that his collection was as good as several others which he named. These fireside lectures were quite frequent. People came often on Sunday morning, and some came during week-day nights.

There is no doubt that Gerald was a very complex person; he was a loner, independent and believed in his own abilities and judgment. I can remember when I was very young that he was part of a poker school. He liked to play cards for money, and was very good at it. I recall one night about 11.00 or 11.30 pm, there was a break in the game. I came downstairs for water, and Gerald was at the end of the hall with cash in his hand. He beamed at me, and said, "It's after supper that counts." Sheila left soup and sandwiches for them and, after the break, the game went on until 2.00 or 3.00 am. He was fearless, and bluffed, a tactic which he often used in negotiating case settlements in the High Court or any other. He often came home and said: "I horsed him."

There were days when he was easy to get on with: amusing, engaging, convivial, very caring and generous with his time and money. Other days his mood could be both dark and long-lasting, often for several days or weeks. Was it the black dog of depression on his shoulder? I think not: rather it seemed like unspoken rage. His face smoked with disdain. The corners of his mouth would turn down, and his eyes would narrow. There was no getting through for anyone other than Sheila, and there were times when even she knew it was best not to intervene. When the shutters were pulled down, sometimes in great haste, they remained down until the "perceived attack" was over. Yet, there were times when he was attacked, or at least he perceived he was being attacked, and the circumstances were such that he was unable to pull down the shutters at all.

(Photo: Irish Jewish Museum, Dublin)

Sheila was always there for him. She ensured he was well dressed and wore a Homburg hat. If she felt that he needed a new suit, she marched him into Patrick Street to Fitzgerald's Man's Shop. I can remember her saying to him: "Yaelie, that suit is *schmata* (rags). Come on, we'll go into Fitzes and get you a new suit." If it were not for her, it is possible that he would never have dressed well.

They also shared an innate sense of fairness and, in Gerald's case, justice. I understood how deeply affected they were by World War II, particularly the attempted destruction of the Jews. Like many families of the time, they refused for many years to buy anything German. Sheila would spit at such an idea. During the war, they were so concerned about the possibility of a Nazi invasion of Ireland that they arranged for the adoption of my brother John into a Quaker family, Knollys and Chris Stokes. Fortunately, the adoption was never necessary and the two families remained life-long friends.

Gerald also joined the Local Defense Force in Douglas, where he was instructed in the use of a rifle. He said: "It was just as well I didn't have to fire a bloody shot ..."

Gerald also had a unique way of saying that he did or didn't want to do something. He was a big tea drinker, and if he wanted a cup, but he didn't want to make it, he would ask: "Would you like me to make you a cup of tea?" The correct response to this was to reverse the question: "Would you like *me* to make *you* a cup of tea?" "Oh yes, please." But when I made tea, he would say that I didn't know how to make it, and I was not to do it again. He liked it very strong and with a biscuit or cake.

Dogs and Other Animals

Then there were the animals. I remember the arrival of Gin and Orange, two golden cocker spaniels who came from a client who was a breeder, in the early 1950s. I was deputed to look after them, so I changed the straw in the kennel and often sat in it with the dogs. They gamboled on the lawns, and would come into the house and go to sleep with their noses on the hearth where it was very hot; later in the night, they would get up and move to the end of the room to cool down.

But there was a terrible tragedy in 1957. The dogs were lured out the gate by locals and were so badly kicked and beaten that Gin died; Orange suffered injury to his spine and never ran properly again. Gerald believed this was an antisemitic attack and he became infuriated. He reported it to the Gardaí, but nothing came of it.

He wrote to the *Evening Echo* on December 21, 1957. He said had been made aware on 17th of Gin's whereabouts and that it had been suggested to him that Gin had been mauled by other dogs, which suggestion Gerald rejected. Gin's body was examined by a vet who established that the dog had been kicked or beaten with the heel or an instrument. The vet wasn't sure if Gin died as a result of these assaults or from being exposed to a very bad winter night.

Gerald continued: "I am concerned with the fact that a dumb animal who was gentle and loving was done to death by some person. I believe there are people who can provide information which will enable the Gardaí, to whom I have complained, find the guilty person." Gerald invited people to come forward and provide the information. He said: "I was not able to protect my dog from such cruelty. But I may be able to protect other witnesses and who knows other human beings from similar treatment."

Two kind people wrote supportive letters, but nothing came of them. Orange lived a long time but never ran again as he did before.

After Gin's demise, another client bred poodles, and there came a succession of them. They were Fitzpatrick, Patterson, Browne-Browne, and the Reverend. After poodles came dachshunds. These came from Sheila's sister-in-law, Litzi, who lived in London. I think there were only two who were called Siggy (after Freud) and Willy (after Willy Brandt). Gerald would sit in his chair reading with one draped around his neck and the other on his knees.

Gerald also had clients who bred goldfish and birds, so there came two tanks of fish and two cages of budgerigars. I think Gerald helped the client by buying the aviary. One bird was called Percy after Percy Diamond, and the other was called Scipio, after a Roman general. The fish did not last long. They were put in the garden one summer's day and a heron came and had a feed. The birds did not last very long either, but Gerald used to let them out of the cage to fly around the living room. They sang beautifully which he enjoyed, especially when one perched on him and sang.

Sheila, Gerald, Rachel Smith and a visitor, with David and Theo,
c. 1950. (Photo: Irish Jewish Museum, Dublin)

Always Lots of Visitors

Ben-Truda was full of fun, laughter, and happiness; it seemed as though there was always someone coming for tea or dinner.

It was not unusual for Americans staying in the Imperial Hotel, directly opposite Gerald's office on the top floor of Library House, Pembroke Street, to see the name on the windows as they looked across the street. They were not shy about dropping into the office to see and meet this strange creature, an Irish-Jew with the name of Goldberg. He had to be Jewish with a name like that, didn't he? When they called in, he might invite them home for dinner without telling Sheila. Though she would be furious that he didn't warn her, nonetheless, being an extremely good cook, she always managed something delicious.

In those early days, when the household was *kosher*, she cooked typical Jewish food. There was a minister, Reverend Bernard Kirsch, and he was a *shochet* (a person officially certified as competent to kill cattle and poultry in the manner prescribed by Jewish law). In the mid-1950s, everything began to ease after the war. Rationing was over, produce became more widely available, except for *kosher* meats, because Rev. Kirsch left Cork and took a pulpit in the North of England. There was a lacuna until Reverend Barron came, but he only stayed a short time. After another interval, Reverend Baddiel came. He stayed for six years and prepared me for my *bar mitzvah* but, as the community was beginning to dwindle, he too decided to leave, which meant the community again had no *kosher* meat. Sheila had to order from Rubenstein butchers in Dublin, who were relaxed about what they sent down by train. Parcels of peculiar cuts arrived which Sheila neither ordered nor recognized. And she had many rows on the phone over their exorbitant bills. After several months of this carry-on, she resisted and kicked back. She said to Gerald, in a flood of tears, "I can't do with this any longer. I am not putting up with it. I will just buy meat in the butcher's here." She could no longer keep a *kosher* house. It was recognized that the Community did not have a future. People started to leave, and by the end of the 1950s, there was a slow but steady exodus.

Gerald and Sheila's best friends were Max and Frieda Elyan. Max was a cabinet-maker and had a furniture business. Sheila and Frieda went to each other's houses regularly, were on the phone daily, and cooked together for various occasions. They did our *bar mitzvahs* together, and some weddings. We shared the *Seder* for *Pesach* (Passover, reading of the *Haggadah*). This is a home ceremony when there is a reading, then a dinner, then more readings and songs at the end. When we were very young, we always observed the two nights: one in our house, and one in Elyans'. The tables were laid with white cloths. Glasses for wine; four glasses have to be drunk, and when the wine is a rather unpleasant *kosher* number called *Palwin No. 10,* you could get terribly drunk, and I did, at the age of four. I remember banging spoons together and shouting, "Crash bang W8." Well, that had me removed from the table pretty quickly, and packed off to my bed. Sometimes with a smack. Gerald could lose it quite quickly.

Long before the arrival of *Pesach,* Sheila started the preparations. Most festivals do not require much preparation, if any, but *Pesach* is different because it is a festival of unleavening. This means that there cannot be any *hametz* in a house. *Hametz* (unleavened agents) derives from five grains: wheat, spelt, barley, oats and rye. This results in a vigorous spring clean when the housewives search for *hametz* with a feather and candle. I remember well that Sheila made all the preparations by changing all the tableware from the everyday to a set used only at *Pesach.* Cutlery was also changed.

In our house, when they first did *Sederim,* Gerald and Max sat at the top of the table together. They started the readings at very high speed without explanations. After many years of this, one evening Sheila stopped them and insisted that they slow down and do much more in English and *explain.* Then, after more years, it was a shared ceremony where everyone did some reading either in English or Hebrew. It is traditional to start the meal with a bowl of hard-boiled eggs, and salt water, a memory of the tears of the Israelites at the destruction of the Temple, but also a symbol of how hard life is, as if you need reminding. There was also a competition in the community, at least Gerald thought so, of how many hard-boiled eggs each person could eat. The other competition was who could finish their *Seder* first. It was always well before midnight when we finished. Gerald would get on the phone and call around people like the Jacksons to see how far they had got, and how many eggs they had eaten. Numbers were grotesque, but I cannot remember how many. It was all good fun for one night, but the second night was repetitious. So, Sheila declared, as she sometimes did, that she was not doing two nights anymore. It would be one only, and that was the first night. No one complained.

Travel

In the 1950s, Gerald and Sheila began to travel to Europe. We had been down as far as San Sebastian, having driven through France. We had gone up to Denmark via the ship to Bremenhaven. We had been to Amsterdam for music, and had trips to the beach at Scheveningen.

*Gerald and Sheila, feeding the pigeons in Trafalgar Square, on a
trip to London in the 1950s. (Photo: Debbie Levy Archive)*

I cannot be sure if they had been to Italy yet, but travel there was a revelation to Sheila: it opened her eyes to Italian cooking and the use of spices, herbs, and garlic. As she ate at different restaurants, she would try to work out the ingredients, and if she couldn't, she was not shy about asking. From all of this, and Elizabeth David's cookery books, she greatly expanded her culinary expertise. She subscribed to the *Cordon Bleu* magazines, and she followed Robert Carrier in the Sunday papers. Her repertoire expanded from good Jewish cooking, to French, Italian and others. Her dinner parties were often sumptuous. In summer, Ben's bookkeeper, Mollie Greene, always had a salmon sent down, packed in green reeds tied tightly with string. Just a tag label with the name and address. Sheila marveled at this every time. The call was put though to Mollie and a long conversation and thanks ensued. Then Sheila with her fish kettle got to work cooking it. When it was done, she removed the skin, and dressed it in her own mayonnaise, and then decorated it with thinly sliced cucumbers. The fish did not last long.

Late in the 1950s, I think, they made a first visit to Israel. They adored it and enjoyed everything they saw. It was then a fledgling country, and maybe it was then they were invited to go and live there. I am not sure if they contemplated such a move seriously. They would have discussed it, and I think they must have come to the conclusion that they would stay in Cork. For all Gerald expressed himself as a Zionist, which he got from his Uncle Sol, he was still more a Corkman dressed in the blood and bandages of the Cork hurling team.

Mary

The house was quite big, and once Gerald had established his practice, there was more money so it was just before my birth (1945) that Sheila needed help to run the house. At that time, it was customary for country girls to go into domestic service, and live with the family. Sheila placed an advertisement in the local press which was answered by a young girl called Mary Lynch who came from Ovens to the west of the city, near Ballincollig, a small town some miles away. The only thing I knew about Ballincollig then was that it had an old fort and was all good farming country. Today, it is almost a city in its own right.

Mary was wonderful, and she became a much-loved part of our family, and of my life as a youngster. She had a fantastic relationship with Sheila. They talked and laughed, sometimes it seemed all day.

Mary, in her "favorite place" in the kitchen. (Photo: Harriet Long)

Mary, with John and Theo, c. 1945. (Photo: Harriet Long)

Mary, on the day of her marriage to Larry O'Sullivan, August 1, 1953.
(Photo: Harriet Long)

It is hard to imagine what life must have been like for Mary working in a Jewish house, to have explained to her all the rules of *Kashrut,* all the strange observances of an Orthodox home. Those trips to Synagogue, not only on Saturdays but all the Holydays, especially *Rosh Hashonna* and *Yom Kippur.* And then what about *Pesach* (Passover) which lasted for eight days, during which *matza* was substituted for bread?

Sheila taught Mary all the recipes, and when Sheila had to attend services on those days, Mary prepared the meals. When we all came home, everything was ready. She could turn out a very good *tsimmas* and *kenadle,* a great chopped liver, and chopped herring. She could make a good roast; chicken soup from a boiled fowl, as well as *Latkahs.* One dish of her own which she brought to the kitchen was her apple tarts: these were exceptional. She cooked them with a complete casing.

Mary's mother was also a good baker. Whenever we took Mary out to Ovens to visit her mother, she always seemed to be cooking a Bastable cake. These were white cakes with sultanas and a little sugar, salt, soda or baking powder. They were good and were Mary's mother's specialty. She lived in a small, typical country cottage: a kitchen with a big fireplace mounted with cranes for cooking over the open fire. The cake was cooked in a pot oven – a three-legged pot in which the dough is placed, and is surrounded by hot coals with some on top of the pot as well.

Mary looked after me, calling me "little Pip." She swung me on her hip and carried me around the house while she did the wiping and cleaning. Always, she had with her a large jug of tea. It was a jug used for flowers, so it was big. The tea went cold, but that didn't bother her. There was a radio, one of those which had about six valves that had to heat up before any sound came out of it. That was on in the morning, playing a BBC program *Music While You Work.* And there was another called *Uncle Max,* a program for children on Saturday.

When Sheila went home to Belfast to see her parents, Mary was more than capable of keeping house. She cleaned the fire in the living-room in the morning and lit the stubborn stove in the kitchen – that was a beast of a thing, never easy to light. Coal came from Sutton's Yard on horse and cart. Hot water bottles were filled every night for each bed. When I had a bad dream or fright, she would take me into her bed. She was my mother too.

What is it about childhood summers? They were always long and hot. At least that is how I remember them. In the late afternoons when the sun was still high, Mary, dressed for dinner in black dress, pinafore and lace cap, took me up to the fruit bushes. If the gooseberries were ripe, we had a feed. Oh, they were good! Then she'd say to me: "Pip, that's enough. You won't eat your dinner, and I'll get blamed, Pip. C'mon, let's go now, I have work to do." And then, in the evenings after dinner or sometimes in the early afternoons, she and I sat in the kitchen making butter balls. There were two butter bats with ridge marking on them. There was a pail of water, and a slab of butter. We took a little dab and rolled it between the bats and then dropped them into the dish. The bats were dipped in the water before making the next butter ball.

Several years after she came to Ben-Truda, Mary met a man named Larry O'Sullivan who worked in the Douglas Woolen Mills. He was keen on soccer and dogs. Sometimes I went to a football match with him in the back Douglas pitch. They married and went to live in the estate called Grange Park, which is located overlooking Douglas. They had a daughter, Harriet. By then, Mary had lived in Ben-Truda for 11 years. There was never a cross word, and there was great sorrow when she moved out. Even then, she continued to come down a few days a week. Neither Sheila nor Mary was able to break the connection. Their wonderful relationship lasted all their lives. Mary lived to be 96.

Sharing Food and Laughter

We had a wonderful gardener, Michael, who wore a waistcoat and soft brown hat. He cultivated the vegetables and fruits, as well as looking after the grass and shrubs. He would come into the kitchen with a trug full of vegetables. The house was well run and comfortable. There were always activities, games, neighbors' children, and events. Sheila was good at improvisation, and creating activities for kids. We often played in the garden, kicking a ball, or riding a bike. We had races around the back at the side of the lawn.

The house was well loved, not only by us, but by the many who passed through. I think Sheila's charm was so endearing that people loved to call. There was always some tea or coffee and a biscuit or cake which she baked. There were afternoons too when she had some of the ladies from the community for tea. Yes, life in Ben-Truda was warm and loving.

There always seemed to be guests for supper. Of course, there were days when there were none; those were the days when I could moan about the soup being too hot or too cold if I didn't like it. And there was barley soup which I particularly disliked, but we ate well. Sheila was really excellent, and with Mary putting her hand to the pot, the food was amazing.

I can remember Gerald's brother, Yanks, often coming for lunch. In those days, the main meal was in the middle of the day. Yanks was quiet and gentle. He liked sport: horses and soccer. I can remember him playing for the Cork Community against the Dublin Community. He didn't seem to do anything, and he was supported by Gerald. He died very young.

Ben and Trudi came to stay from time to time, and so did Sheila's brothers and their wives: Sidney and Grace, Stanley and Litzi. Trudi's sister, Eva, came from Dallas with her granddaughter, Elsa. She was taking Elsa on a grand European tour. Sheila had a very large extended family, almost all of whom lived in the United States. Sadie Isaacson lived in New York and visited. Another visitor was a close correspondent, her cousin, Fran Racussen, who was a psychiatrist living in Chicago.

Fr. Tom Hand, on a visit to Ben-Truda. (Photo: Goldberg Special Archive, UCC)

Interestingly, there was a priest from the Augustinian Order, Fr. Tom Hand, one of three brothers, all of whom were priests in different orders, who became a close friend and a regular guest. Perhaps the food in the Friary was not as good as Sheila's! He wrote books which he asked Gerald's secretaries to type for him and he took up painting by correspondence course, and spent ages in the back garden painting a picture of the house. Then he announced that the course required him to paint a nude. There were serious giggles and raised eyebrows. How was he going to do that? Would he paint in the life room? At that time, John and Nancy were living in Cork. They laughed and sniggered so much that Sheila asked quietly and politely if they would like to be excused. They departed upstairs and continued to laugh. Fr. Tom showed his work to Gerald and Sheila, but I cannot remember if I was there or not. I still wonder how he managed.

Then another time, Fr. Tom said he was dreading the coming week because he had to give a marriage counselling course. Sheila could be caustic at times, but always in a humorous or gentle way. "And pray, Fr. Tom," she asked, "and what would you be knowing about marriage?" There was much laughter and even Fr. Tom enjoyed it. I don't think the painting or marriage counselling lasted too long. This was an extraordinary friendship, reminiscent of Laban and Fr. Cregan in Limerick many years before.

Sundays were especially busy. You never knew who would drop by. Certainly Fr. Tom, but also often a member of Dáil Éireann for the Cork South West constituency, Sean Collins. Sean was a nephew of Michael Collins, the great Irish leader of independence in the 1920s whom Gerald so admired. Sean looked like his uncle, with a big blocky square head and a shock of white hair. At the time, he weighed in at 23 stone. As well as being a parliamentarian, he was also a practicing barrister. Gerald briefed him, although not many others did. Sean had been in the army and on Sunday mornings he went up to the army stores at Collins Barracks, where he bought a lot of Sweet Afton yellow pack cigarettes in 50s, or Afton Major in the green packs. He came round to the house with a bottle of brandy for Sheila. He always called her "Duchess." He would roar "DUCHESS" as he came in the door and marched down the hall to the kitchen. "How's the DUCHESS?" and "A drop of brandy for the coffee, Duchess?" His voice was as big as he was. His humor was bubbling. He sat at the kitchen table holding court and telling jokes. The brandy was poured into the coffee, and more than one cup was drunk. We loved Sean's visits and stories.

Sean introduced his nieces, Mary Banotti and Nora Owen. Mary was a M.E.P. and Presidential candidate, while Nora was a T.D. for a north Dublin constituency and a Minister for Justice in the Fine Gael Government. Mary was a regular visitor to Ben-Truda. Often, she stayed with Gerald and Sheila rather than return to Dublin. She always arrived off a plane, beaming and smiling, rushing in from Brussels, or Luxembourg, or Strasbourg.

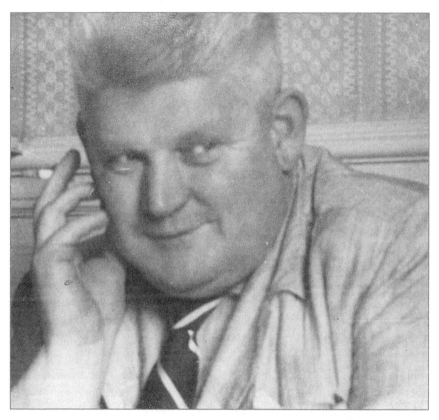

Sean Collins, a regular visitor to Ben-Truda. (Photo: Goldman Special Archive, UCC)

Another client who often arrived at the house was Melba Footte. Melba was very artistic. She could paint, sew, and make costumes and props, which she did for the Cork Ballet Company. She enjoyed good stories and jokes, and the food, of course. She was also a secretary of the Cork Orchestral Society and a keen fan of hurling. When I was very young and went to hurling matches with Gerald, we followed the Cork team everywhere. In the summertime, expeditions were arranged to hurling matches in Limerick (Ennis Road) and Clare (Semple Stadium). Sean and Melba came with boxes of food. Several cars went down in convoy. These often included senior members of the Gardaí, all of whom would have encountered Gerald in court. Sometimes Sean's cousin, Major-General Collins-Powell, joined us. I can remember, many times, being squeezed between two very large detectives in the back seat, my flag, the blood and bandages of Cork, rolled up in the back. Melba made the flag. We would get to the ground well before the first match began, which was always a Minor game. Sean would open his biscuit tin full of chicken drumsticks and consume quite a few.

Gerald loved both opera and sport. One time, there was a production at the Opera House. It was a Welsh production and two of the male lead singers were Welsh tenors. The performance took place during a weekend when Ireland was playing Wales in rugby. This was the early 1950s before television. Bill Twomey commentated for Radio Éireann and the tenors were invited to come to listen to the match. Ireland had a great number 9 and 10, John O'Meara and Jack Kyle. Wales had the great Cliff Morgan at number 10. Of course, Wales were beating Ireland pretty badly, and every time they scored Gerald handed two bottles of beer to the singers.

Gerald was also very keen on boxing. Frequently there were fights at the City Hall and he went to these either alone or with one of us.

Hycie, Gerald's sister, married Ike Lentin from Limerick and their first child Louis was born there. Louis used to come to Cork as often as he could because he didn't like his mother's cooking. "Ma can't cook," he used to say, but he was spoiled by Sheila. His father made him read medicine in Trinity College, but he loathed it. He joined the Trinity Players and became a theatre director, and then joined RTÉ when it started in 1961. He often rang up and asked if he could come down. He drove a small sports car. Sheila would always say "Yes," as they enjoyed his company. She would ask him when he would arrive, and Louis would give her a time, but then the time would come and go and no sign of Louis. Oh yes, he always turned up, but late, and Sheila called him "the late Louis Lentin." Once he was doing a production in Cork, and he phoned and asked if he could bring the cast out. Of course, they all came, and Sheila managed to rustle up some sandwiches and tea for them. She was always prepared for the unexpected because she knew it would happen.

Gerald acted for the writer, artist and founder of the Golden Cockrel Press, Robert Gibbings, who had a long, wispy, white beard and was one of the biggest men I ever saw. I was very young then. While he was at dinner with us, he sat on a chair in the living room and also a dining chair. As he sat down, I could hear a 'ping' in both chairs as he broke the springs.

Sheila with Gerald's mother, Rachel, c. 1955.
(Photo: Goldberg Special Archive, UCC)

One day, on a train to Dublin for a meeting, Sheila sat opposite a small lady
with ginger hair. They got talking. The lady was Elizabeth Friedlander who
was living in Summercove, Kinsale, and had a partner Alessandro Magri
McMahon (known as Sandi or Sandro). They had their own houses, very close,
but spent the days together. They became very regular visitors for lunch, and
Gerald and Sheila often went down to Elizabeth's cottage. Elizabeth was a good

cook and baker. When she came to Ben-Truda, she brought gifts like German cookies, or *Kugel*. She made her living by making crafts: pampooties, bookmarks, and other leather products with Celtic designs.

Both Elizabeth and Sandi had very interesting and eventful lives. Elizabeth (born on October 10, 1903, in Berlin) was from a Jewish family. She went to the Berlin Academy to study book and typography design. In the 1920s, she produced work mentored by her teacher Ernest Weiss. She was commissioned by the Frankfurt-based Bauer Type Foundry in 1927, becoming the first woman to design a typeface, and particularly one of such exhaustive variation. Completed in a variety of point sizes in roman letter and cursive and detailed in bold and swash characters, it took until 1939 for Elizabeth-Antiqua[1] and Elizabeth-Kursiv to be cut, three years after Elizabeth Friedlander had been forced to leave Germany. She fled Germany in 1936 and went to Milan where she worked for the Mondadori publishing company. In 1939, the upsurge in antisemitism in Italy forced her to move again. Her attempt to get to America failed. Instead, she went to London on a Domestic Service permit, which meant she could only do domestic work. She had brought with her a violin made by Klotz in 1702 which had belonged to her mother. I think Elizabeth played: she was very musical. She also had a spinet which Sheila later acquired. Elizabeth had had to learn Italian and then English. Luckily, she met Francis Meynell (a printer at the Nonesuch Press), who got her some commissions. She also worked for the Ministry of Information in 1942, in the black propaganda unit led by Ellic Howe. She produced forged Wehrmacht and Nazi rubber stamps, as well as fake ration books. By the end of World War II, she had made many friends and contacts, so she remained in England and took out naturalization. One of her great accomplishments was to design paper patterns for the Curwen Press and Penguin Books under Jan Tschichold. Later, she had the honor of designing the roundel for the company's 25th anniversary. Many publishers commissioned her talent – for example, Victor Gallantz and Chatto & Windus.

While she lived in London, Elizabeth met Alessandro Magri MacMahon who was born in Crema, Lombardy, in 1895. As the family name suggests, there was Irish blood. His mother was the MacMahon, and was the daughter of a Major General. She married Magri and he changed the name in the 1920s. Sandi, or Sandro as he was also known, went to England in

---

[1]   *Editor's note:* The typeface used for the headings in this book is Elizabeth ND, the digitised version of Elizabeth Friedlander's Elizabeth-Antiqua.

1927 and stayed there. He taught at the City Literary Institute and during the war he worked for the BBC Italian service. Later he taught at Morley and Bedford Colleges. He wrote two books: one on Italian history, and the other on fishing called *Fishlore* (1946). He founded the British Italian Society and was its Vice President. In 1958, he left London and went to Summercove, Kinsale. It seems that Elizabeth and Sandro did not come to Summercove together.

Elizabeth's lettering was beautiful, and Gerald commissioned her to inscribe a family motto on parchment.

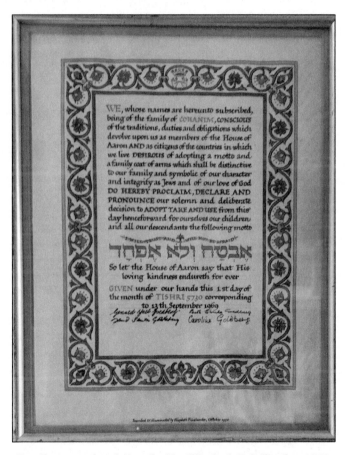

Family motto, hand-inscribed by Elizabeth Friedlander, 1969.

She gave them two other parchment inscriptions for Pesach 1973 and 1975. The first was just the words *Mazel Tov* (Good luck) and the second was a transcription of a prayer *Haskivenu adenoi elohan*. (Grant eternal God, that we may lie down in peace, and let us rise up to life renewed.) The coat of arms was the hands of the Cohanim forming the Shin, ש.

Elizabeth Friedlander's 1975 Pesach *gift to Gerald and Sheila.*

When she died, Elizabeth left all her portfolios to Sheila and Gerald, and she left Sheila a share in her cottage in Summercove, as well as her violin which Sheila donated to the Cork School of Music for use by students. It has been loaned to many.

For Better, For Worse

In the television interview with Tom Savage (RTÉ, 1977), Gerald was asked how his children felt about the way he brought them up. His reply revealed much of who he was.

He said that they had found him "... hard to communicate with ... that he was living within himself ... that we told him: 'when you talk, it's as if you're dictating into your Dictaphone. You say: "Dear Sir or Madam, please – stop, semi-colon, comma, inverted commas." He often worked at home in the morning and we said he had no time for us, that he was immersed in books, in study, so we could not reach him.

(Photo: Debbie Levy Archive)

Tom Savage asked how he felt about this, and he replied: "I felt very sad because I believed I had communicated. I'd played with my children. I took them to synagogue on Saturday morning, and I played games with them. I took them away to the continent, to music festivals. I talked to them. These comments were possibly one of the most stunning blows that I received."

Sheila was asked if she agreed with what we had said. She was more revealing: "He doesn't respond well; you just have to draw everything out of him. I think it's a legal thing. You ask a question and you expect someone to answer. But he doesn't talk about it. He gives you the answer. He asks: 'What's your problem?' and you tell him the problem and he says, 'Well, here are two things you can do about it. You can either do A or B,' giving you the two alternatives that he thinks are right – and there it is. Conversation finished at that point."

On this same occasion, Gerald recalled something which I had quite forgotten. When we were young, if there were disputes, they were resolved at the dining table with Gerald as judge, and he heard the "cases" and delivered his decisions. He said to Tom Savage there were "no rows nor disputes in our house," because we decided them in these courts. His decisions were final, with no appeal.

Indeed, I can recall that it was not possible to argue with him at any time. For example, he and I used to play Scrabble when I was a young kid, which he liked because he was good with words. Once I beat him, and he was so furious that he wouldn't talk to me for days.

I do know that Gerald always acted for an audience, and by all accounts was a good performer in court, although I never heard him. He told the writer, Mary Leland, that every lawyer had to be a good actor. So, in this television interview, as in all his interviews, I believe he performed for an audience, but Sheila did not. She was herself.

Gerald was asked about finding a wife, and he talked about "looking for a Lithuanian girl." Sheila said she didn't think either of them had been looking for anything. She said when they first met (in 1928) she was 12 and he was 17. (There was only four years between them.)

Sheila went on to say that Gerald was cautious about the letters he wrote to her. She put it that he always wrote with a mental "Without Prejudice" on the top of the letter, though he didn't actually write the words. Gerald said he didn't want to be caught before he was ready, so he admitted he was "cautious." They didn't meet again until he qualified in 1934. He said she was always "terribly understanding and advising."

Sheila was asked if she were more liberal than Gerald. She said: "I am – and always have been. That wouldn't be difficult, because Gerald isn't very liberal in his outlook. He is a very conservative Jew. A very orthodox Jew, very conservative and hasn't changed much in the years. I have. Things which were important to me when I was young are no longer important to me."

When he was asked about other things, such as if he minded driving on the Sabbath or striking a match, he replied that he accepted them, but he did mind. He was conscious of it all the time because it was not done when he was a boy in his father's house. However, like many in the community, he did drive on Saturday. Not only that, but I remember his demand to the three of us, John and Theo and me, that we were to go to synagogue and he would come and see us there. In the meantime, he went to his office to deal with the post, which in those days was delivered on Saturday. Many times, he did not appear at the service at all, and we had to go over to the office to collect him. Then we went to Miss Barry's small shop in Oliver Plunkett Street to buy the papers. He bought a stack: *The Irish Times, Cork Examiner, Times Literary Supplement, The Listener, Illustrated London News,* and comics for us. There may also have been a *Daily Telegraph.* The magazines were bound every year until the house was so full that Sheila said he had to get rid of them. But he only moved them into his office. Such was the man.

Postscript

I can only give details of a few of the people who came to Ben-Truda, but there were many more and many who were fun, or important, or clients, or politicians, or religious, or journalists, or people from TV, radio or the newspapers, artists, writers, poets and more. They left many memories.

Gerald and Sheila with John, his wife Nancy, and their children, Abigail, Micala, and Jacob. Gerald took them all to visit the Lord Mayor of the day and this photograph was taken in the Lord Mayor's parlor.
(Photo: Irish Jewish Museum, Dublin)

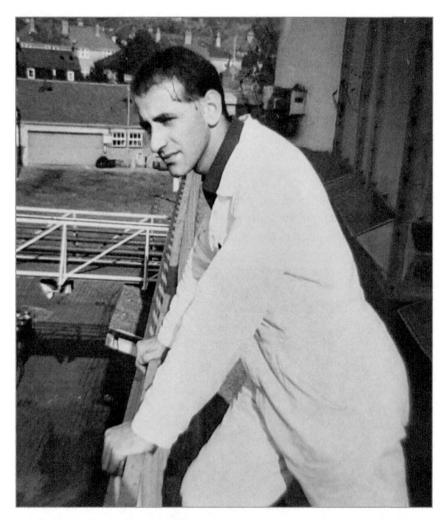

Theo, in the mid-1960s.

I cannot exclude family as often there were some of us visiting. On one visit Sheila, John, Nancy, Val, Theo and some of their children went to Youghal for the day. For some reason they could not find anywhere for lunch. John was appointed the scout. He went off but couldn't find anywhere. Then he noticed a stall selling fresh fish and chips from their own boats. He bought enough for everyone and brought back the bags which he distributed. Sometimes Sheila looked on things with disdain and she often muttered words under her breath in Yiddish, followed by something like *"Echt!"*. On this occasion she said, "I couldn't eat that," looking a bit disgusted, as Val recalled. The others shrugged their shoulders and continued to eat. Sheila gazed at the bag and picked up a chip which she put in her mouth, and then another, and another until she finished them all.

John then produced a bag of Mars bars. This delighted the children, but Sheila formed a picture on her face of utter horror. "I am not eating that," she said as she threw the bar back in the bag. Several minutes later she grunted. Then she proclaimed she had not eaten a Mars bar since before the war, and that she had to try it just to see if it had changed. When Val next looked, she noticed the Mars bar was finished.

Chapter 13

MUSIC, ALWAYS MUSIC

If music be the food of love, play on ...

William Shakespeare, *Twelfth Night*

From an early age, we were taken to concerts in the City Hall. These were promoted by the Cork Orchestral Society (COS), which was founded around 1938 by the Professor of Music at University College Cork (UCC), Aloys Fleischmann. He was the only child of Aloys and Tilly Fleischmann, and was born in Munich, but was brought up in Oileán Rua (the Red Island, also known as Hop Island) in Rochestown, not far from Ben-Truda. This house, which I loved to visit, was where I first took painting lessons with Maud Bennett, who bought it from the Fleischmanns. It has had a profound effect on me all my life. Aloys had also formed the Cork Symphony Orchestra which gave concerts once or twice a year, and accompanied the Cork Ballet Company. These were all events to which we were taken.

In June 1954, Sheila discussed with Gerald the idea of joining the committee of the COS, and he encouraged her. Quite soon after (in 1957-1958, I think), she became Secretary and a life-long friendship began with the Fleischmann family. Indeed, I often wondered what might have been if Aloys had done law, and Gerald had done music? I think the results would not have been too different. Gerald and Aloys were big men, with huge energy and enthusiasm for what they did. They took their work extremely seriously, and drove their projects like dynamos. They combined their wits and skills to achieve their ends. They were successful. Sheila had equally focused energies and goals. She diverted her resources into the COS and later into various charitable projects, while still supporting music and ballet in Cork. They were both aware of the importance of art in human development: how it could build bridges, and enlighten lives.

Aloys had been studying in Munich when the Nazis came to power. He left to continue his career in Cork. He was the youngest-appointed and longest-serving professor at UCC, completing 46 years. He had two students when he started, and a large faculty when he retired. His special interest was Irish traditional music; he collected, arranged and indexed many pieces. In all, he worked on 86 research projects. He was instrumental in the creation of the Cork Ballet Company and supported it for years. Like Gerald, he lived through and witnessed the Black and Tans and the republican movement. When he was young, he learned to speak Irish fluently.

Unlike Gerald, Aloys could take a position on an issue diametrically opposed to someone else, but was able to distinguish between issue and personality. So, although he engaged in many battles for the arts in Cork, and encountered much disappointment, it did not cause major rifts in personal communication. Ruth Fleischmann, in her book on Aloys (2000) illustrates this with the story of how, when the Arts Council withdrew funding from both the Cork Choral Festival and the Irish National Ballet, there were recriminations but afterwards Aloys and the Chairman of the Arts Council, Adrian Munnelly, continued to have "close personal contact, with friendly and personal relations." As Ruth points out: "He never discussed with the family what this cost him: we found awe-inspiring the strength of character which enabled him to stand above and disregard personal hurt in the service of the greater good." Sheila was like this too. If she disagreed with someone it did not cause a rift, but if it occurred between Gerald and another then it could lead to a total severance of contact.

In this, Sheila's ability was extraordinary; she rarely engaged in rows but was very capable of correcting people quite firmly, always with humor, a smile, and sufficient gentleness. Ruth Fleischmann says that Aloys never had notions of grandeur but saw himself as a servant of a cause, "not a prophet." His grandson, Max, writing in Ruth Fleischmann's book on the Cork International Choral Festival (2004), tells us that after lunch in Glen House where they lived, Aloys read the newspapers and then took a nap, as did Gerald.

Max tells many stories, the sort I like to hear because they make people come alive. He tells stories about Aloys' notoriously bad driving on his motorcycle and in his car. One story was how he gave a lift to a student on the back of his motorcycle, but she fell off and he didn't even notice. When he arrived at UCC without her, he was dismayed. She arrived later by bus.

A detail I remember is that for his own concerts, Aloys never had a bassoonist. He had to hire one from London and was horrified by how much it cost. It was about £50, but he couldn't do without one. When I was about 15, I was given a scholarship to study the bassoon, and so perhaps fill the need, but I was not destined to be a bassoonist.

Aloys was always formally correct. He always addressed everyone by their epithet: Miss A., or Mr. B., or even Master C. It went on for years, until one day Sheila said to him: "Please stop calling me Mrs. Goldberg. We have known each other long enough, so call me Sheila," which he did.

The Cork Orchestral Society

Prior to Sheila, there had been two joint Secretaries of the COS: Nancy McCarthy and Noreen O'Sullivan. Nancy had a bad stutter and ran a chemist shop in Douglas. Noreen had a café/restaurant in Academy Street, off Patrick Street, called The Green Door. Sheila combined and undertook the work of the two previous secretaries and worked by herself into the 1960s, when she was joined by Bridget Doolan, a pianist from Waterford, who took a position as a piano teacher in the Cork School of Music. After the retirement of Bernard Curtis, she was appointed principal of the School. Sheila and Bridget became great friends, and worked well together. Bridget often came to Ben-Truda, and they shared many fun moments. They arranged the Radio Éireann concerts in Cork each year and formed the Friends of the COS.

Sheila remained Secretary up to about 1970, and was then elevated to President in 1971 for a three-year period. She was President again from 1984 to 1986. As secretary, Sheila had several functions: organizing concerts from visiting orchestras, recitals, the Radio Éireann Symphony Orchestra, and schools concerts. She had to print tickets and posters and distribute them where she could, arrange advertising and any other publicity. She collected the visiting conductors and soloists from the airport and often brought them to Ben-Truda, and then for a look round some of the environs of Cork.

They were exciting times. There were always receptions for visiting orchestras after concerts. The members of the COS prepared plates of sandwiches and cakes, tea and coffee. It was at one of those receptions that I noticed Charles Lynch, the pianist, standing with a plate of cakes and a glass of milk by himself before he kindly came over and spent a long time talking to me.

A committee member, Barbro McCutcheon, originally from Sweden, had married and come to live in Cork where she taught French and German at a school. She told me the story that one evening at a committee meeting, Sheila announced that after the next concert there were going to be more people at the reception than usual. They would need extra sandwiches; so, she asked the members if they could make up two loaves instead of one. Someone piped up: "Oh, Mrs. Goldberg, I don't know I would have the time to do that." Sheila had a way of putting people down very politely and firmly but in such a way that they were never offended by her. "Well," she said, "if you could just get up one hour earlier, then you could do it." And so it was done.

The story of how Barbro became involved in the COS is quite extraordinary. A Norwegian sailor was on his first voyage out of Norway. He arrived in Cork and was drinking in a pub near the quays. A fight broke out with an Irish sailor over a girl. The Norwegian kicked the Irishman at the quayside and he fell into the water. Since he could not swim, the

Irishman drowned. The Norwegian was taken to Union Quay Garda Station where he was detained and questioned. The Gardaí phoned Gerald and called him in to represent the sailor. They also called Barbro to come in and interpret. Her language was Swedish, but there is a close relationship between Swedish and Norwegian and Barbro was the nearest they could find. She went in and assisted. The sailor was returned for trial to the Central Criminal Court, Dublin, on a charge of murder. I was a student at King's Inns at the time, and attended court every day. During the trial, Gerald had called in someone from the Norwegian Embassy who sent down an interpreter. But, apparently, the official interpreter couldn't understand the sailor, so Barbro then took over the interpretation for the trial. When it was over – the sailor was convicted of manslaughter – and they were going home on the train, Barbro told Gerald she was very interested in music and in fact, played the sousaphone (of the tuba family). He told her she should join the COS and that is what she did. One Christmas time, Barbro was playing in Douglas Shopping Centre with a brass band. Sheila was shopping and saw her. Sheila asked her, "Are you playing in a brass band? You should be playing in a symphony orchestra," said Sheila. "It is only one size smaller than a tuba. You would only have a few bars to play. In a band, you have to play all the time."

Sheila, like Gerald, was an early riser. She loved the early mornings in spring and summer. There was a blackbird who sang outside her bedroom window, and she loved it. Often she went out early and got things done. She was coming home when others were going out. That is the kind of person she was. When I asked another surviving member of the COS committee, Allan Navratil, a farmer in Cork, he said that she was: "Gracious, wonderful, and diligent. If it was to be done, then it was done on time. Her letters and circulars were flawless."

One time, she went to a meeting in East Cork in the home of a Colonel Ffrench. After the meeting, Sheila got into her car to drive home, but it would not start. The Colonel said to her she must take his car. She got into it and asked him to show her the gears. He showed her all the forward gears, and when Sheila mentioned reverse, he said: "Don't bother with it, old gal, it's damn tricky."

Music never stopped, I am glad to say. There were meetings at night, phone calls during the day, and various arrangements. Radio Éireann used to phone about promotions for the Symphony Concerts on the radio. They called these promotions "bulletins after the News." Usually, concerts were full. The City Hall has very good acoustics, and musicians loved to play there. There was not a comparable venue in Dublin until the Concert Hall was eventually developed, but it does not have as good a sound as in Cork.

Many orchestras played in Cork. The world's leading conductors and soloists came. In 1955, Sir Adrian Boult came with the London Philharmonic. Sir Adrian was a very tall man, with a bald head and a great moustache. I remember him standing in the bay window of the living room in Ben-Truda, looking out at the garden. He stood still, tall, like a ramrod, or a regimental sergeant major. In my great ignorance, I addressed him as "Sir Boult." Perhaps he didn't notice.

One of Sheila's strangest experiences was entertaining Benjamin Britten and Peter Pears. After tea, she took them to Cobh, an interesting town with the deep-water port where Atlantic liners sailed to and from New York. She said that Britten was slightly odd because he remembered two things: one was being born, and the other was the sinking of the Titanic which occurred two years before he was born. They gave a recital of Britten's songs from the Thomas Hardy Wessex poems.

On another occasion, when Nancy was in Cork with my brother John, Sheila went to collect the pianist John Ogdon. Ogdon was a very big man, with curly hair and thick glasses. Sheila drove a small car. She told Ogdon that he would have to sit in the back seat because Nancy was pregnant. He had an enormous suitcase, so Sheila had to drive with the boot open. Ogdon somehow folded himself into the back seat. As Nancy said: "Sheila was gracious and never awed by anyone's position." Ogdon had won the Tchaikovsky Competition in Moscow. Once when he was playing in the Concert Hall in Dublin with the RTÉSO under Bryden (Jack) Thomson, he lost his way and Thomson had to whistle the intro to him. Later that evening, I met him on the stairs of the Concert Hall looking very lost and disoriented.

Saving the COS

The COS was 21 years old in 1956, when the opportunity arose to bring the Vienna Philharmonic Orchestra to Cork. A unique experience, but it had to be funded. Bringing an entire orchestra was expensive; even funding from just London to Cork required a lot of money, not something the COS had. On this occasion, Gerald and Sheila stepped up to the mark and launched a fund-raising campaign. A report from the *Cork Examiner* of April 24, 1956, said that it was intended to pay down the debts of the COS and put it on a sound footing. Gerald wrote to the members:

Dear Friend,

For 21 years the Cork Orchestral Society has, nobly and unselfishly, served the cause of music and music lovers in Southern Ireland and, this year, on the occasion of its coming of age, is responsible for the first visit to Ireland of the world-famous Vienna Philharmonic Orchestra. Many members and friends have expressed the hope and wish that a suitable gesture should be made to the Society, in keeping with the two-fold event, and I have asked for, and received, the privilege of being responsible for the organization of your expression of appreciation.

I have learned, with regret, which I know you will share, that the burden of bringing a visiting orchestra to Cork has been heavier than the funds of the Society has been able to afford and has resulted in the accumulation of heavy debt. It has occurred to me, and I have been encouraged by consultation with many individual members, that the best appreciation which we can show for the wonderful work of the Society during the last 21 years, would be the discharge of the debt incurred, and also the placing of the Society on a sound footing for, at least, some time to come. With this in view, I would respectfully ask your co-operation in a scheme which will, whilst paying tribute to the Society and achieving the desired result, also reflect credit on its Members. This scheme is, simply, nothing more or less than the adoption, by individual Members (or groups of Members) of an instrument in the Cork Symphony Orchestra.

The following are the best-known instruments in the Orchestra: First Violins, Second Violins, Violas, Violincello, Double Basses, Flute, Piccolos, Oboes, Cor Anglais, Clarinets, Bassoon, Horns, Trumpets, Trombones, Tuba, Tympany, Percussion and Harp.

First Violins may be adopted by Members (or groups of Members) at the subscription rate of £10.10.0 each. All other instruments may be adopted at the subscription rate of £5.5.0. Those who would like to do so may pay special tribute to the Conductor of the Orchestra, who may be adopted (as often as desired) for £52.10.0.

I am enclosing a stamped address envelope for the favor of your reply. All those subscribing will receive special mention in the records of the Society, as "Sponsors of the Cork Orchestral Society 1955/56" and it is intended to include their names in the special Souvenir Program of the Vienna Philharmonic Orchestra's performance in Cork.

I shall also be glad to call on any Member who would like me to do so. Sincerely yours, Gerald Y. Goldberg

The *Examiner* report shows there was another aspect to this fund-raising exercise. In relation to the proposal to "adopt the conductor," the report says: "The Jewish Community have paid a remarkable tribute to Professor Aloys Fleischmann, the conductor of the orchestra." It tells us that, at the beginning of World War II, a petition was presented to the professorial staff of UCC, protesting at the discrimination and persecution of the Jewish professors and students in European universities. The petition was prepared by Gerald and the dentist, Eric Scher (one of the family of very famous dentists in Cork) and Aloys Fleischmann was the first to sign it. He enthusiastically supported the cause and earned the gratitude of the Jewish community. This scheme to raise funds was seen by them as a unique way to pay tribute to Aloys Fleischmann. The adoption of the conductor was substantially over-subscribed within a few hours. The overall response was excellent. I can recall this as being a great concert. No soloist, just the mellow, round sound of the Vienna Philharmonic. The conductor was Andre Cluytens and the concert included Mozart's 40th and Beethoven's 7th symphonies.

Aloys wrote two letters to Gerald to express his deepest thanks. One was to Gerald as President of the Cork Hebrew Congregation which was on UCC faculty notepaper, and the other was personal, from his home address. He described the community's contribution as "… surely one of the most generous contributions ever made in Cork to any cultural cause." In his personal letter, he said, "it must be first time in Cork's history that a single individual made such a big-hearted contribution to the artistic effort in the city." He observed that people generally were not used to making a financial sacrifice except for charitable or religious circumstances. He thought this was a reason why there was such a low response to the arts generally. He likened it to the days of the d'Estes and Medicis.

Gerald and Sheila made several donations of paintings and sculpture to the Crawford Art Gallery and other institutions. Gerald was very philanthropic and enjoyed giving away his art as much as he enjoyed hanging it at home. In later life, he made a large donation of books and papers to UCC.

Lunchtime Concerts

Towards the end of 1962 or perhaps at the beginning of 1963, Gerald and Sheila went on a trip somewhere, I really cannot remember where; it might have been London. They returned having been to a lunchtime concert. The

BBC used to do one every week at St. John's, Smith Square. For them, the experience was novel; they really were taken by the idea that they could listen to some classical music at lunchtime. They talked about the idea of doing a series in Cork and, together, worked out a plan. Gerald said he thought the Crawford Gallery in Emmet Place would be an excellent venue. I recall him saying to Sheila: "I'll go over and ask Der if he would let us use the Gallery." Der Donovan, the curator, was a quiet cultured man, easy to get on with. When Gerald went to see him, Der said he would like to host the concerts. The Gallery was under the control of the Vocational Education Committee, run by Mr. Parfrey. They also got his approval easily.

And so, the Lunchtime Concerts were born. Sheila used her amazing organizational skills to form a committee of women who would make sandwiches, tea and coffee. She decided that patrons should also get a piece of fruit and that the lunch would run from 12.50 pm to 1.10 pm, and the concert from 1.10 pm to 1.50 pm. The concerts would be held on each Thursday during May and June of that year. The event required some advertising in the local newspapers. As neither Sheila nor Gerald was competent to engage the musicians, they entrusted this to Bernard Curtis, Principal of the Cork School of Music. He was a most pleasant and erudite man and there was never any difficulty retaining players. The event also became a showcase for young musicians, many of whom gave their first recital there. The idea of a lunchtime concert is to provide an excellent opportunity to relax for an hour in the wonderful world of great sound, and superb surroundings. It gave people in business, trade and the professions a moment to get away from the harassment of commerce; a haven in the center of the city and lunch as well, all for the price of £1.

Gerald decided that the first concert on May 16, 1963, would be a milestone occasion and he wrote a letter to Aloys and Tilly Fleischmann, parents of Professor Aloys:

Dear Herr and Frau Fleischmann,

You are, no doubt, aware that on Thursday May 16, 1963, I am sponsoring a series of nine Summer Lunchtime Concerts, which will take place every Thursday from that date, at Cork School of Art. This is the first occasion on which such a series of concerts will have been held in Cork. I would like, if I may, to dedicate and offer the entire series of concerts to you both, in token of my sincere admiration and appreciation of all that you have done, throughout the years, for music and the Arts in Cork. May I please do so?

Gerald Y. Goldberg

Ruth Fleischmann, their granddaughter, says: "Needless to say they were deeply moved at the quite unexpected honor." Why Herr Aloys and Frau Tilly? They were both German musicians of considerable repute in Germany, England and Ireland. Tilly was the pupil of Liszt's last student, Stavenhagen. Tilly's father was Herr Swartz and had the position of organist in Cork Cathedral. When he retired, Aloys and Tilly came back to Cork to live and Aloys took his father-in-law's position. Tilly gave recitals twice yearly in Cork, and also in Dublin and London. The end of an article in the *Evening Echo,* May 21, 1963, stated: "Herr Aloys and Frau Tilly Fleischmann have always been known in Cork, not only for their fine musical gifts and artistry, but also for their own personal attributes. Thus, the lunchtime concerts come as a welcome opportunity for the citizens of Cork to show their real appreciation and affection for this couple, who have done so much for our city."

Gerald produced the program on his office Gestetner machine. The first recital was by the renowned and local pianist Charles Lynch. He was to do many more. A short article in the *Evening Echo* (May 14, 1963) said:

> When Charles Lynch opens the first of nine lunchtime concerts at Cork School of Art on Thursday next, a new era in the musical life of the City of Cork will have been inaugurated. Conceived as an experiment in worker-culture relationships, the concerts by their very scope and format present an opportunity to every worker, clerk, secretary, or assistant in the city to enjoy light classical music, view great works of art and eat a satisfying lunch on one day each week for the next nine weeks. The monotony and tedium of work or business will be relieved. The inspiration afforded by the combination of music and art may, in itself, make a contribution of an interesting nature to the everyday work and life of our city. All this may become a reality because of the ideals of a number of people who believe that something well worthwhile is being attempted...
>
> ... In the composition of programs every care has been taken to ensure than nothing which might regarded as "heavy" would be included, whilst at the same time regard has been had for the classical aspect.

The article went on to say that some thrilling programs had been planned. Indeed, no one stood by the piano with a list of forbidden works on the grounds of weight. Beethoven's *Appassionata Sonata* certainly got an airing, at least once, along with some string quartets by Bartok and Beethoven.

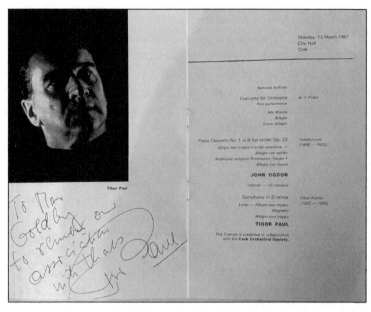

A concert program, March 13, 1967, featuring John Ogdon and Tibor Paul.
(Photo: Irish Jewish Museum)

Gerald and Sheila at a Lunchtime Concert at the Crawford Gallery, with Mr.
Parfrey, CEO, Cork Vocational Education Committee, Senator Jennie Dowdall
and Charles Lynch, pianist. (Photo: Irish Jewish Museum)

For many years the concerts took place each May and June. At some point, they were reduced to six per season. I think they are still at that number, but food is no longer served. The use of the word "era" in that article was prescient, as they continue to this day and are likely to go on and on.

The concerts were first held in the sculpture gallery which had a terrazzo floor, hard walls and ceiling. There were two jutting support walls which divided the gallery into two parts. The sound was better in the inner part, near the instruments, than the outer, nearer the door. The concerts remained there for many years, but ultimately, they were moved to the lecture theatre which has a lot of wood, so the sound was much better.

Gerald did not really have any input into the organization of these concerts, though he produced programs for a number of years. However, he couldn't pass up the opportunity for a speech before the concert on May 26, 1987, which was the jubilee year. He simply thanked so many people who "had inspired himself and Mrs. Goldberg to begin the series 25 years ago and those who had maintained their support of this important cultural event in the ensuing years."

The events became Sheila's domain. She ran the concerts with Bernard Curtis, and her crew of wonderful sandwich-makers. No doubt there was much laughter when the women were preparing lunch. There was always laughter when Sheila was around. Eventually, they got an Arts Council grant or a support against loss. But these concerts were immensely successful. They were full every week of the season.

Bridget Doolan must have been involved from very early on, if not the beginning. When Bernard Curtis retired from the School of Music and Bridget was appointed his successor, she was the person who arranged the players. There were always new names or rising stars, and there were regulars who came back year after year to swoon the audience with the most delicious music.

Some of the players who are now famous both within and outside Ireland are, in no particular order: John O'Connor, The Vanbrugh String Quartet, Radio Éireann String Quartet, Roger Raphael, Irene Russell, Miceál O'Rourke, Hilary O'Donovan, Bernard Geary, Jan Cap, Marianna Sirbu, Mary Beattie, Nicholas O'Halloran, Eibhlin Grant, Angela Climent, RTÉ Academica String Quartet, Jane O'Dea, Michael McNamara, Cork School of Music Orchestra, Mary McSweeney, Veronica McSweeney, Patricia Harrison, Therese Timoney, Gillian Smith, Eleanor Malone, Bebhinn Ní Mheara, Margaret McKenzie, Clare Carberry, Irene Gilmore, Iona Pectu-Colan, Michael Joyce, Eilish O'Sullivan, Darina and John Gibson, Leonie

Curtin, Maureen Elliman and Trudi Goldberg. These are just a few; there were more but I don't have a record of them.

Maureen Elliman is Gerald and Sheila's grand-niece. Her mother, Elaine, was the daughter of Gerald's sister Molly, who married Bernard Shillman. Maureen won a scholarship at the Feis Ceoil, Dublin to study for three years at the Royal College of Music, London. She played two lunchtime concerts and one at the School of Music which was a pre-début recital. She said: "A first leg on the ladder can bring so much more." When she played her second concert, a news report said: "Young star returns." My daughter, Trudi, played a concert in the 1992 season with Eleanor Malone, piano. Trudi played oboe then and had a beautiful tone.

Many of the concerts were reviewed by Geraldine Neeson who signed with her initials G.N. She was effusive in her support for young players. Writing about Clare Carberry, cello, and Irene Gilmore, piano, she wrote in the *Cork Examiner* (July 11, 1969):

> The sixth and last of the series of Lunchtime Concerts at the School of Art was given yesterday by two gifted young artists... It was an occasion to remember, for seldom has it been possible to hear this beautiful Sonata (Brahms Op.99 in F Major) played with professional ease, exactness of style and musical vision, and yet retaining the exuberance and freshness of youth.

Mrs. Neeson had heard this young artist the previous year when she thought she "gave every promise of becoming a cellist of stature. This year, all suggestion of patronage must be dismissed and she must be treated on a serious plane of professional level." Equal praise for Irene Gilmore. After that concert, Bernard Curtis paid tribute to the generosity and civic sprit of "the sponsors, Mr. and Mrs. Gerald Goldberg. Cork owes a large debt to the broad artistic vision of the Goldberg family, and indeed that debt is likely to increase as the years go by."

It is a remarkable testament to Sheila's organizational skills, as well as to her energy and enthusiasm for music, that these concerts are still continuing. On December 22, 2018, Thomas McCarthy wrote in Forum (*Irish Examiner*) :

> ... the intense atmosphere, the extreme heat of the packed auditorium in the Crawford, and all the while a sense of the absent presence of those Olympians of Cork life, Aloys Fleischmann and Sheila Goldberg.

At the opening of the 21st season on May 18, 1983, Charles Lynch was again the soloist, but as the report in the *Cork Examiner* said it was an emotional occasion "even before Charles Lynch struck a key." Lord Mayor Hugh Coveney attended and he was introduced by Sheila. He told the audience that it would be Sheila's last year of involvement. He reminded them that, when they started the concerts, Gerald was the guarantor before the Arts Council took it over. Presents, flowers and kisses were given to her with abandon.

Chapter 14

SHEILA'S PROJECTS

Her value in trade is better than silver,
Her yield greater than gold.
She is more precious than rubies;
All of her goods cannot equal her.
In her right hand is length of days;
In her left, riches and honor.
Her ways are pleasant ways,
And all her paths peaceful.
She is a tree of life to those who grasp her.
And whoever holds onto her is happy.

Proverbs, 3:14-18. (Translation in JPS, Philadelphia, 1999)

S heila loved her "projects." Through them, she found a voice for her own great energy. Whatever she did, she never neglected music. She always regretted that she never went to university, and she believed could have put her resources into business if she had wanted to. She often thought about it, but as was her wont, she rejected these ideas with a sort of snarl, something like "*Echt.*"

Meals on Wheels

In 1965, Sheila was one of the founders of the Meals on Wheels, a service organized by the Cork Senior Citizens Council. They were all lay volunteers who opened the first kitchen in the St. John's Ambulance Rooms in MacCurtain Street.

Sheila was instrumental in obtaining new premises at St. Vincent's Convent (Sisters of Charity), where they began by providing only six dinners per week. A year later, the organization had expanded to three kitchens, the other two being in the Lough and Bishopstown. The service expanded to 95 meals from one of the kitchens, 85 from another, and 25 from a third, working alternate days and producing 600 meals per week. Sheila wrote about this in the quarterly bulletin of the Red Cross in 1968. In it, she told of the likes and dislikes of the elderly. Acceptable were all stews, bacon, chicken, and corned beef. Unacceptable were mince, chops, tripe and sprouts. Oxtail soup was alright, but minestrone was not (although Sheila's minestrone really was marvelous).

I recall her telling the story of her first day in the kitchen with the other women. Sheila was the chef, and bacon was on the menu. She had never touched, eaten or cooked bacon. The smell of boiling bacon nauseated her, but she took on the task as a challenge. Cooking her first bacon! She put it on to boil, and probably added some spices (maybe cloves), but when she thought it was nearly ready, she said to the other women, "I can't touch this, so somebody will have to taste it and see if it is done." A slice was carved and the women put their forks into it, and gave it an immediate sign of approval. She had successfully cooked her first side of bacon!

Sheila went to different parts of the city talking to women about setting up kitchens, because there was a need. Long after Sheila's time, in the 1980s, the service moved to new premises in St. Patrick's Kitchen at the rear of the hospital on Wellington Road. By 1980, it provided a service three days a week. Recipients were asked to make a small subscription for the food so that they retained their sense of dignity and independence. And those who lived near a kitchen were asked to come and collect their meal, as this got them walking in some fresh air. Otherwise, the meals were delivered. By 1980, Meals on Wheels covered most of the city.

Financing the project was always a problem. Some funding was provided by the Cork Health Authority but it was not nearly enough. Sheila not only cooked, organized the various kitchens, the ladies and drivers, but she also fund-raised. "Fabulous Furs on Display" was a by-line in the *Cork Examiner* (June 21, 1966). She had persuaded the furrier Harry Barnardo, from Grafton Street, Dublin, to bring his winter collection to the Silver Springs Hotel in Cork for a fashion show. These furs were out of the reach of most women, but they duly paid their 10/- for a seat to admire them all. The event was sold out, and a substantial sum was raised for the raffle of a mink hat. The chairman of the Cork Senior Citizens Council paid special tribute to Sheila for her organizational skills and the work she had done. By then, more than 6,000 meals had been served. It is not surprising that she persuaded Harry Barnardo to return with another show in 1967 – although, it was said, by that time, the price of mink had fallen!

Abigail Goldberg. (Photo: Goldberg Special Archive, UCC)

By 1969, the name of the service had changed to "Abigail Meals on Wheels," after Sheila's first grandchild. A news report (*Cork Examiner*, March 17, 1969) said the name "Abigail Meals on Wheels" was chosen as a mark of respect to "Alderman and Mrs. Goldberg." On one occasion, when Abigail was very young, she went with her mother Nancy and Sheila to the kitchen, where she was introduced to the Mother Superior. Unable to get her tongue around Mother Superior, Abigail called her "Mrs. Shapiro" to everyone's amusement. The kitchen in Gurranabraher Parochial Hall opened in October 1969 and was sponsored by two local associations: Churchfield and Gurranabraher. These volunteers had been actively trying to help people who were unable to look after themselves, which led to the setting up of the kitchen. Meals were difficult to transport and this caused a problem. Initially, hot food was provided in the Hall. There were 12 meals provided on Tuesday, Thursday and Saturday; this quickly grew to 85 meals per week. Financial assistance mostly came from the local people and the volunteers. The Lord Mayor Alderman J. Bermingham, opening the new facility, said that the most heartening feature of the project was that so many people were involved, and it was gratifying to see such manifestation of community spirit. He continued: "With efforts such as this, the position should be reached in the not-too-distant future that no old person living alone in Cork should be left without the solace of communication and good meals." He congratulated Gerald and Sheila for their interest in the project and said it was a job well done. Fr. Walsh, the local priest, said that it was a wonderful idea "first conceived by Alderman Goldberg and taken up by the Development Association and it had succeeded. They all appreciated the invaluable practical help given by Mrs. Goldberg. The ladies working on this project were wonderful, giving as they did, so many hours each day, well into the evening." Gerald paid tribute to all the people of Gurranabraher who had come together to provide this wonderful service:

> In all Cork, a city with a population of 120,000, there are not more than 100 or so women doing such work and that is a very small proportion of the total population. Every credit is due to those involved in the kitchen, to Mr. Rogers, and the Development Association, and, above and beyond all, to Mrs. Hurley and Mrs. McCarthy and the ladies who helped them.

Since then, the service has continued to grow and now covers not only the entire city but the county as well. A report in the *Evening Echo* (December 20, 2019) said that 430,000 meals were served every year; of these 361,000 meals are delivered, and 69,000 are sit-down. Meals on Wheels is now in its 57th year and comprises 48 services in the City and County. Some volunteers have now been serving for 50 years.

Lavanagh and the Hydrotherapy Pool

Today, the hydrotherapy pool is run by Enable Ireland, which was once the National Association for Cerebral Palsy, and the history of which is well documented in a booklet, written by a volunteer, Phil O'Donovan. The booklet covers the period from 1954 to 2000 and has provided much of the background information in this section. Since 2000, the major change has been a new building, which is much larger and caters for more patients – all children and young adults who have physical and sensory disabilities.

In 1954, there were no such facilities. The Association began due to the vision and work of a few doctors who were looking for ways of treating children with physical disabilities. Dr. Robert Collis, or Bob as he was known by everyone, was a pioneer in developing treatments. Bob was born in Dublin in 1900, the son of a lawyer. He studied at Cambridge and Yale. Then he worked at King's College, London, and later in various parts of England. He did research at John Hopkins, Baltimore, and Great Ormond Street, London – and he also played rugby for Ireland.

When he returned to work in Ireland, he was unhappy with both the political division, after the civil war, and the social inequality. Medicine was fairly basic, so he set about organizing pediatrics and developed a neonatal clinic at the Rotunda Hospital, Dublin. He became Professor of Medicine at Trinity College.

During the war, disturbed by the Holocaust, he joined the Red Cross and in 1945 he went to Bergen Belsen where he was much needed. There, the first child he picked up said to him: "My father is dead. You are my father now." That child became the author, Zoltan Zinn. His father was killed in Ravensbruck, and the children with their mother were sent to Bergen Belsen, but on the day of liberation she died, and soon afterwards their brother died. Zoltan and his sister Edith survived. There were three other children there: Tibor (Terry) and Suzi Molnar from Debrecin, in Hungary, and another girl, Evelyn. When it was necessary to decide what to do with these children, Collis decided to bring them all back to Ireland. He adopted Zoltan and Edith, who took his name; Terry and Suzi were adopted by the Orthodox family of Samuels; Evelyn apparently went to Australia. I knew Terry. He was a good spin bowler, and I have met Suzi on a few occasions. She married a solicitor, Alec Diamond, who was the son of Percy Diamond, the tenor who took *Shabbat* services in *Shul* in Cork and had sold Gerald all his 78s.

Bob recognized the need to treat children with cerebral palsy. The National Association of Cerebral Palsy was formed in Dublin in 1951. Premises were found in 1953 in Sandymount, Dublin, where the headquarters of Enable Ireland are still located.

Between 1950 and 1954, there were no services for children with cerebral palsy in Cork. Dr. Richard Barry became Professor of Pediatrics at University College Cork, and wanted to do something for these children. Also, people in local government, including the Lord Mayor, Pat McGrath, were working quietly behind the scenes. However, there was some resistance from the Catholic Church: Bishop Lucey was reluctant to attend a meeting of interested people. He had reservations about State intervention in the provision of healthcare for children, and was concerned about the erosion of parental rights.

One of the first people to become involved in this project was a man who later became a Lord Mayor of Cork and a T.D. for the Fianna Fáil Party in Dáil Éireann: Gus Healy. He had a scoliotic deformity, which was quite pronounced. Cork wits, cruelly, called him "Humpy Healy." He did much work for the handicapped. He knew the importance of treatment for these children, and he became the first chairman of the first center.

Dr. Collis attended and addressed this meeting. Others who joined the committee were Dr. C.J. Saunders, Mrs. Norma Crosbie (the family were proprietors of the *Cork Examiner*), Mr. C.J.F. McCarthy, Mrs. Tom Barry, Mrs. Frost, Senator Jennie Dowdall (also a President of the Cork Orchestral Society), Mr. Tom Doyle (whose wife was also on the committee of the Cork Orchestral Society), Mr. Martin Harvey (Solicitor). Many businesses supported the effort with significant donations.

The first clinic was The Hall in Brown Street. The first physiotherapist was Mrs. Anne Maxwell, from Edinburgh, who was appointed the first superintendent and remained until her retirement in 1978. Fund-raising went on continuously. The clinic moved to Grattan Street in 1958. A residential unit was opened in Beech Hill, Montenotte. In 1964 a large house and gardens, Lavanagh House in Ballintemple, became available and was purchased for £8,000. During all these years it had been known as the Cork Spastic Clinic. However, the word "spastic" went out of use, and was excised.

Lavanagh House

Lavanagh House was built *circa* 1745, in what was then the countryside near Cork. A new clinic and school were built on this site: the house was retained for future use. The new building commenced in 1967 and was completed in 1969. Apartments were constructed and made available for overnight accommodation and a "drop-in" day center was built in the basement. Several organizations provided funding – in particular, the Variety Club of Ireland was always helpful. Landscaping was done on the old gardens. There was a grand opening by the Minister for Health, Erskine Childers, on October 22, 1971, followed by a dinner for special guests. In September 1972, Dr. Bob Collis visited the new clinic and praised it: "I was delighted with the efficiency of the whole scheme and the splendid clinic which has been provided which is as good as any we will find anywhere. The general running of the clinic is excellent." Two hundred children attended two or three times per week.

The Hydrotherapy Pool

In 1955, the first children attending all had cerebral palsy. Twenty years later, other conditions, including spina bifida and muscular dystrophy, were treated. Soon it became apparent that exercising in a hydrotherapy pool would offer great relief. However, to be effective, the water temperature must be kept at 19 degrees Fahrenheit, which is expensive. Municipal swimming pools had closed because local authorities could not manage the running costs. The board considered building a pool. The Variety Club offered to assist. Mrs. Maxwell persuaded the Southern Health Board to pay the running costs. A public appeal was launched in early 1979 to raise the sum of £80,000, then the current estimate, but in the end it cost £150,000.

The fund-raising was launched on March 8, 1979. Sheila said: "It would be of great benefit to handicapped children because swimming is one of the few sports that these children can participate in..." (*Cork Examiner*, March 9, 1979).

The Variety Club was the principal sponsor. Its chairman, Jim Clancy, organized a "Wheelathon" which was held in Musgrave Park, home of rugby in Cork, and raised £30,000. Many other businesses contributed generously and, within two years, the target sum of £100,000 was reached, according to Phil O'Donovan. This left a shortfall of £50,000 and I do not know how this was made up. I had thought Sheila had raised all the money necessary.

Sheila described to us her first visit to the clinic. Remember that, back in 1979, children and adults with handicaps were hidden away. It was thought to be shameful for the families and distressing for others to see them. While this attitude was slowly changing, it was still easy to be shocked at the sight of some of the disabled children. Sheila described how her initial recoil of pity was swept away: a child sat there with a runny nose, and no-one had noticed. "Haven't I wiped enough runny noses in my time?" she said to herself as she cleaned the child's nose.

Theresa Campagno, the Director of HR & Corporate Affairs, was most helpful in my research and, while she did not know Sheila, she knew of her. When we spoke, she thought there were very few people left who were involved with the fund-raising campaign, but she thought that Mrs. Peggy Cashman and possibly Mrs. Pauline Coveney might also have been involved. Shortly after I talked to Theresa, I got a call from Peggy Cashman. She remembered Sheila very well, but could not tell me much about the committee.

Peggy said that she learned a lot about how to raise funds from Sheila. She cited one occasion when she gave Sheila a £50 donation. Sheila explained that Peggy needed to make the money grow by adding value. Peggy described the example of an antique auction which raised a lot of money. She found a chair which was not in good condition and took it to a restorer who brought it back to life. The cost was £15 but the chair made £100 at the auction. This auction is referred to in Phil O'Donovan's booklet.

Peggy also told me about Sheila's sense of humor. She said to Peggy one day: "When I am 70, I will not be able to wear high heel shoes anymore." Peggy asked why, and Sheila replied: "Because they might be too dangerous, or they might pinch my feet, and if they did, it would show on my face."

ABODE: Doorway to Living

Accommodation for the Disabled in the Environment (ABODE, now known as Doorway to Living) was probably Sheila's greatest achievement. This was the last of the major projects she undertook, and the one which she not only enjoyed the most, but in which she took a *special* interest. Born out of the hydrotherapy pool she had just helped complete at Lavanagh, the concept came from two of the women who were involved in the care of the physically disabled: Mrs. Chris Roche, who had become the superintendent at Lavanagh, and a next-door neighbor, Anne Moloney, the resident psychologist at Lavanagh. With many others, they realized that, once the clients went home, there was often nowhere they could go to advance or progress their skills. So, the ladies created a committee to raise funds for another center which would accommodate people between the ages of 18 and 45 who needed a day and residential center from which they could go to university or do courses at other institutions. Sheila was invited by Chris Roche to join the fund-raising committee and she was appointed chairman. Until she retired recently, Claire Brazil was the only Chief Executive Officer of ABODE since its foundation and she told me the story of how it all came about.

Three different organizations that were involved in providing services for the physically handicapped amalgamated and these were: the Irish Wheelchair Association, the Cork Spastic Clinic and the Cork Spina Bifida and Hydrocephalus Association. The Southern Health Board (now the Health Service Executive) also became involved.

Frank Baily was the treasurer and later became finance director. Sheila and Frank joined the committee about the same time. He worked very closely with the project and remained on the Board for 20 years – until 2002. He found the work very rewarding.

Both Claire and Frank recall the beginning of the fund-raising. There was huge activity; up to £100,000 had been raised by Christmas 1983. They were then in a position to look for a site, because they felt secure that they would succeed in reaching the target they needed to build. Sheila and Frank discussed how and where they might locate a suitable site. They were agreed they would have to pay for it, but also, they required a long lease. Sheila arranged a meeting with Joe McHugh, the City Manager, with whom she worked when she was Lady Mayoress of Cork. She and Frank thought they could afford to pay £10,000 for a site and then there would be rent as well.

They decided, in advance of the meeting, that they would make Joe McHugh an initial offer of £5,000. Before they went in, Frank recalls that Sheila said to him: "Let me do the talking." He was delighted he wouldn't have to speak. Joe McHugh offered them a site. She was grateful for this generous offer, but explained the difficulty of raising money for rent, and the costs involved. Joe was a pipe smoker. He leaned back in his chair, looked at them as he puffed, and he said: "We are not going to charge you anything for all the great work you have done." That was a huge bonus. Frank said that Sheila had great energy for fund-raising. She charmed everyone.

As Claire put it: "When Sheila asked for something no one could refuse her. The site was then in Ballinure, later known as Mahon, next to a graveyard. The building was designed by Roddy Hogan, architect, but no one really knew what they were doing because there was no guidance. So long as a wheelchair could be turned in a room that was probably as much as anyone knew at the time. Sheila was always there. We'd see her driving up in the car and we'd say, 'We have to tidy up.' Everyone had enormous respect for her. She was so full of fun."

They had to negotiate with various Ministers and the Southern Health Board. A member of the Health Board, Harry Kemp, was also a Director of ABODE. He was very comfortable with the project. The Health Board never said "No" to Sheila, according to Frank Baily.

Claire Brazil began her tenure on August 11, 1986. What a great pleasure it was for me when I began researching to find she is still the CEO. But I also discovered on a Zoom call we did in June 2021, that there is another person still there from Sheila's time, Dermot O'Mahony, who started in 1988. This is the most direct connection I have had to any of the projects Sheila undertook.

Claire describes the interview for the job. She said: "Mrs. G. had her eye on me from the start. She sat back in the chair and she never spoke a word, she just looked and listened intensely." She said that Sheila had the ability to spot the potential in people. Claire recalls her first day at ABODE. Sheila was there to welcome her and make her feel at ease. There was no furniture in the place, and Sheila sat on a window sill waiting to reassure her. "She was hands on. If you had an issue or a problem, you could ring Mrs. G. We all knew her as Mrs. G. A fantastic lady. She was like a grandmother to us all. She was full of ideas. She would tell you to try this or that; do it this way or that way. Some would find it intrusive and annoying, but I didn't. I thought she was so wise."

How did Sheila raise the money and do it so quickly? Claire, Dermot, and Frank told me that she began by running Tea Dances in Jury's Hotel and, when it closed for renovation, she moved them to the Crawford Art Gallery. These dances raised more than £30,000. Another important event was the coffee mornings. Sheila was very well connected, and she asked her neighbors and many others around Cork to hold a coffee morning. Anne Moloney, next door, had one or more, and Eileen Sherrard, whose family owned the land on which all the houses on Rochestown Road were built, had one in Maryborough House, now a hotel. All of these raised considerable sums.

Sheila was friendly with Michael and Eileen O'Halloran, whom Claire described as "her partners in crime." Michael was a member of the Gardaí. He set up a lot of projects involving members of the Force. At that time, Claire was doing some voluntary work with the Irish Wheelchair Association. She drove the ambulance and the bus. She got a call to go to Youghal, about 30 miles from Cork, where the Gardaí were holding a cycle race from Cork to Youghal. Claire was to pick them up if they fell or got injured; Sheila was there to welcome the Garda cyclists and thank them. This event raised nearly IR£13,500. So many organizations and small groups raised money.

The amount of money required to build ABODE had risen to IR£450,000. Sheila raised that sum and a further IR£80,000 which was enough to run it for the year. Holiday breaks were arranged for people which were a great success. A bus took clients out for the day. A group from the Open Door, Bray, Co. Wicklow, came for a week or two every year.

An example of Sheila's determination is illustrated by this story. One of the groups she approached to assist her was the Spina Bifida Group who were partners in the amalgamated group. Sheila went and talked to the chairman asking him to permit her to make an address to the meeting. She was told firmly: "Mrs. Goldberg, you are not on the agenda." She replied equally firmly: "Well, there is something on the agenda called Any Other Business, AOB. I am any other business and I would like to speak." She waited until the agenda reached AOB and then she rose to make her pitch. "This is for your kids and for the future. It is vital and we need to build this."

Sheila was very involved in ABODE. She was there for a Christmas party in 1986. She had decided it should be in fancy dress, and it was wonderful according to Claire and Dermot. She came laden with boxes of mandarin oranges and plum puddings. The music was provided by the No 1 Army Band of the Southern Command. No one knows how she secured them. Sheila went into the kitchen with the Christmas pudding, stuck a holly on the top, and poured brandy over it. A little too much. The pudding was floating on the plate. She lit it and started to carry it out from the kitchen to the Day Room when the brandy spilled onto the carpet still alight. It spilled all along the floor. She blazed a trail – literally! Claire and Dermot were there quickly with fire extinguishers putting out the flaming floor. Having raised the funds to build ABODE, she nearly razed it to the ground.

She went on fund-raising and then set up the Friends of ABODE with Beth Sherrard, another board member. I can remember their being on the phone daily about things to do and how to do them. She devised a cookery book called *Food for Friends* which included recipes from not only all the well-known people in Cork, but in the rest of the country too. It was illustrated by Dermot O'Mahony. Dermot was first employed on a Social Employment scheme. They were fortunate to employ such good people.

When Gerald and Sheila went to America to visit my brother John in Philadelphia, she noticed "thrift" shops that sold various donated items. She thought that was a good idea. There were no such shops in Cork then. So, she discussed it at the Wednesday night meeting of the committee. The idea was approved. Someone was required to manage the shop. Anne Moloney prodded Angela Moore and suggested to her that she could do that. Angela said she had never worked in a shop in her life. Ann said: "Try it." Angela did, and ran the shops until about 2002. Sheila went back to Joe McHugh to find a suitable premises. He offered the old Gas Company building on the corner of Patrick Street and Merchant's Quay, beside the famous Mangan's clock. They moved in and got donations of clothes and other items. One evening, Angela told me, Anne Moloney came in to dress the window. "It was gorgeous," she said, but the next morning when she came in, everything was sodden. The building was full of leaks. It was not suitable because of these and other problems. Sheila rang Angela every night to see how it was progressing. Ann told her she was standing from morning to night, her back sore from hanging clothes up on the rails. "Will I ever get used to it?" she asked Sheila. And Sheila replied: "As my father used to say, you can get used to anything."

Angela said the shop moved seven times in 15 years. They always looked for rent-free premises. She recalled Sheila's great contacts, and also the refrain that no one could refuse her. From the Gas Company building, they moved down to Caroline Street, next to Roches Stores on Patrick Street. They were there a year when they had to move to Lavitt's Quay. There were leaks in Lavitt's Quay too. So, then they moved to North Main Street which was a big space. They moved again, and then to Adelaide Street. But this was not rent-free, and the shop was no longer viable.

Sheila prepared flyers which said the shop offered "Good Second-Hand Adults and Children's Clothes, Leather Jackets, Books, Household Items and Bric-a-brac at Real Bargain Prices." They also sold hand-made products such as stools and trays made by the clients in the ABODE day-care center and hostel.

Angela recalls one of the earliest fund-raising events which was a flag day in 1983. Sheila got a caravan from somewhere, and parked it in Patrick's

Street. She was there at 8.00 am, as was Angela. Sheila was out on the streets all day meeting people and quietly relieving them of their change. Angela does not remember her eating anything, but thinks she may have had a cup of coffee. Everyone stopped for lunch, but Sheila went on. Angela said to her that she couldn't go without eating, and Sheila replied: "Oh! I am used to that."

A few years ago, the original ABODE center was closed because Health Information and Quality Authority introduced new regulations which the building could not pass. They moved to a new site nearby. Claire wanted to preserve the old building as it still had great potential. The new building was given in exchange for the old one, like Aladdin's lamp. When Claire tried to get the old building back, the Cork Corporation told her that they had earmarked it as a library. She wanted it as a dedicated respite, or special training unit. She was told: "No, it was going to be a library." Nothing happened for some time, then one day she came to work and saw that the old building had been knocked down.

Claire recalls that Sheila wanted the clients to be independent. She didn't feel that their parents should be doing their laundry or cooking or shopping for them. She had a bed wheeled into the day center and she said to the clients, "Now make the bed and do it properly."

Sheila's great legacy lives on in the new, bigger and better facility. When they moved into it, they first hung her photograph and plaque in the main hall. Upstairs, they designated as "Sheila's Tea Rooms," after the tea dances. When they were moving into the new building, there were noises in the radiators. Sheila said it was rats or mice. Now, every time they hear a noise, they say: "That's only Sheila."

Person of the Year and Other Awards

The year was 1983. Sheila had completed the hydrotherapy pool, and had been invited to join ABODE. She was nominated for the Person of the Year Award. This annual event is sponsored by the Rehab Group and given to people who "bring joy and light to the lives of others or have supported others in their darkest hours." The award is not just given to one person; usually eight people are awarded. Sheila was among seven other recipients, amongst whom was her fellow collaborator and friend, Joan Denise Moriarty, who founded the Irish Ballet, National Ballet and Cork Ballet Companies.

The Rehab Group is a charity that assists people with disability. Their aims are like those of Lavanagh and ABODE; they all seek to change the lives of people by helping them to become more independent within the community. Rehab provides people with the skills and confidence to be active in the workforce and supports them to take charge of their own health and wellness (*Rehab.ie*).

Sheila was nominated by the Soroptimists Club (an international global volunteer movement) of which she was a member. The nomination said:

> For life-long works in the fields of charitable and social endeavor, for service to the poor, the needy and less favored citizens; for deep and abiding contributions to the cultural life of Cork over a period of nearly 40 years; and for significant contributions to the cause of peace and of unity among different sections of the Irish people at home and abroad; and for outstanding leadership and endeavor as the Lady Mayoress of the city of Cork.

Frank Baily was the treasurer of the ABODE Board, and when the Soroptimists nominated Sheila for Person of the Year, he wrote a letter of support on September 22, 1983, to Kit McCarthy, president of the club.

> Dear Madam President
>
> **WOMAN OF THE YEAR**
>
> I understand that Mrs. Sheila Goldberg has been nominated by your Club for the title Woman of the Year.
>
> Mrs. Goldberg joined the Committee of ABODE as our Chairman in May of this year. ABODE had been launched some 12 months or so previously and its primary objective was, and is, to build in Cork a Hostel and Day Care Centre for Physically Disabled young people in the counties of Cork and Kerry. Total Capital budget for the project is IR£250,000 approx.
>
> Up to the time that Mrs. Goldberg took over the direction of the Committee as our Chairman, total net funds raised for the project amounted to some IR£15,000. Since then, total funds raised and committed to the project exceed some IR£100,000 and as a result of this the Committee is now satisfied that its objectives can and will be achieved.
>
> Were it not for the dedication, energy and dynamism of our Chairman, it is doubtful that we would be in this very satisfactory situation. We regard your nomination of Mrs. Goldberg for the title of Woman of the Year as being most appropriate indeed.
>
> Yours sincerely, J.F. Baily, for the Committee of ABODE

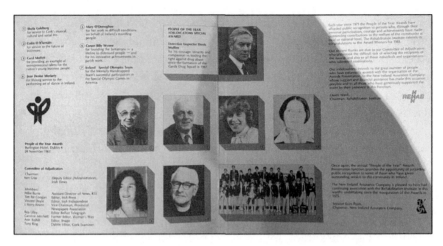

The program for the Rehab People of the Year awards, 1983.
(Photo: Irish Jewish Museum)

The nomination was successful. Gerald was delighted. It was a great honor and great recognition for Sheila's contributions to life in Cork. He wrote to Paula on November 14, 1983:

> ... Next let me tell you of some wonderful news. There is a most prestigious award in Ireland called "The Person of the Year Award." Eight people are selected by a panel of newspaper editors and public relations people, from among hundreds to receive the award of "Persons of the Year." The award is made for outstanding services to the nation. I am delighted to tell you that Sheila is one of the eight and on November 24, we will go to Dublin where in a televised presentation she will receive it from the Prime Minister. I do not have to tell you how proud and humble I feel for her and because of her. She is truly, a remarkable, noble, and wonderful person. For over 40 years, she had devoted herself to Cork and its people and hasn't spared herself...

Gerald said in the letter that Sheila's brother Stanley, his wife Litzi, my brother Theo and his wife, Valerie, Carla, Trudi and I would be there, as well as other family members and friends, but I do not remember everyone. The event was televised live and timed to go out on the 9.00 pm news bulletin. The compère for the night was a TV personality, Bunny Carr. He interviewed Sheila on the stage of the ballroom in the Burlington Hotel and asked her: "Mrs. Goldberg, to what do you attribute your success?" Sheila looked him in the eye and then straight at the camera. "Bunny," she said, "I never miss an opportunity, and I'm not going to miss this one either." Then she launched into a pitch to raise funds for ABODE. This was one of her most memorable and classic moments.

Sometime later, she also received the Paul Harris Fellowship from Rotary Ireland.

Co-Operation North

Brendan O'Regan (1917-2008) was a superb businessman. He was born in Co. Clare and studied hotel management in Switzerland. He came back to Ireland and ultimately became Chairman of Bord Fáilte (Tourist Board) and of the Shannon Free Airport Development Company.

In 1950, he set up a duty-free sales operation in a shed in Shannon Airport. Whiskey for $1, no tax. It took a lot of persuasion to convince the government and Revenue that duty free sales would be good for the economy, but Shannon Airport quickly became the largest duty-free shop in the world. Then he developed an international mail order business which sold luxury items.

In 1951, he created the Shannon College of Hotel Management, and was involved with the development of the now famous Bunratty Castle where they hold banquets.

O'Regan was a leader and innovator. Once he had a project up and running, he moved on to the next idea. In 1959, he started the Shannon Free Zone – a free trade zone – where corporation tax was only 10%. Shannon town also became the European manufacturing base for US companies, a development which created many jobs for the 10,000 residents.

O'Regan was very determined and knew how to short circuit Government and by-pass civil servants. His initials "BOR" were often translated as "Bash on Regardless."

By 1979, the turmoil in the North of Ireland had been raging for 10 years. O'Regan looked at developing peace in Northern Ireland and founded Co-Operation North whose aim was to improve cooperation between Northern Ireland and the Republic of Ireland, and in particular their economic, social and cultural links. As usual, O'Regan moved quickly: following its foundation in 1979, Co-Operation Ireland, USA was set up in 1981, a Belfast office opened in 1982 and 15 cross-border projects were initiated in 1983. In 1984, he created the "Maracycle": over three days, 1,500 cyclists competed in a return journey from Belfast to Dublin. And in 1986, crossborder youth and schools programs began.

A promotional booklet was published entitled *Co-Operation North: A Far, Far Better Way*, a title that originated from the editorial body of the *Belfast Newsletter* on October 8, 1979. The members of the board were invited by O'Regan and included captains of industry, banking, teaching, and trade unions. Sheila was invited to become a board member as the former Lady Mayoress of Cork. Perhaps this and the fact that she was a staunch social activist with proven organizational skills, and was originally from Belfast, were her credentials. The revised booklet says that it was a lack of communication and understanding between the North and South that created mistrust and suspicion which contributed to violence; because being sorry was not enough, people needed to build mutual respect and trust through practical co-operation without political involvement.

On October 6, 1979, O'Regan delivered a paper on behalf of the Council of Co-Operation North at the Annual Conference of the Irish Association of Larne and then to the Rotary Club of Belfast, explaining and outlining the aims of Co-Operation North and South. This was well received. The paper outlined a program to break the cycle of violence and unemployment. One aim was to restore confidence in Ireland, and bring about increased investment and employment, both north and south.

The name Co-Operation North continued in use until the Good Friday Agreement in 1998, when the name was changed to Co-Operation Ireland. The body continues and flourishes.

Because it is now over 40 years since its inception, no one is still there who knew or worked with Sheila or the other initial board members. Gerilyn Fadden is the longest serving member now, and she started in the 1990s. So, it is difficult to obtain information on Sheila's role, but I do know a little.

I know that she ran concerts in Cork, at one of which Una Hunt gave a piano recital. Sheila also proposed that £1,000 be contributed by the organization towards the expenses of the UCC Orchestra travelling to Belfast (Minutes, October 30, 1980). It was acknowledged that, prior to 1970, there had been much closer musical ties between Belfast and Cork and the board felt that this would be a good opportunity to re-open those ties. The grant was agreed. She also took the orchestra to Queen's University, Belfast for a concert (Minutes, May 21, 1981) but the attendance was very disappointing.

She did much more than music promotion. She went to Belfast and spoke to groups there. I think she also went to England for the same reason. And in the *Evening Echo* of August 18, 1982, there is a photograph of Sheila and Gerald with Mayor Erastus Corning, Albany, New York, where she spoke to a conference about North-South Co-operation. She was the special guest of Mr. and Mrs. Paul Grossinger during the convention. There were 900 mayors and their wives from New York State present, and she spoke to various groups on the work of Co-Operation North and its endeavor to improve north-south relations (*Soroptimists nomination, Person of the Year*).

Postscript

In unearthing all this information about my mother and her many achievements, I was profoundly struck by her commitment and energy, both of which seemed boundless. I realized how difficult it would be to acknowledge, in detail, the enormity and scope of her undertakings and their lasting benefit to Cork and its residents. One of my regrets is that I could not find more detail on her specific roles, which might well have dictated another book! But in writing what I could about her just draws me closer to her. I admire so much the way she went about her work, passing effortlessly from one project to another.

Mary Leland put it nicely in the *Sunday Independent* (date unknown). She was reviewing the book, already referred to, called *Food for Thought*, and expressed the view that when the roll call of the great and the good of Cork is taken:

> ... the name of Sheila Goldberg... will lead all the rest. The founding fathers never seem to give way to the founding mothers, and Sheila Goldberg's contribution to the life of Cork and its citizens is something everyone recognizes, but no one talks about much. Like so many other good things here it is taken for granted.

Mary Leland referred to strong men quailing, breaking down in tears, and scrawling their signature on a respectable-sized cheque at the rumor that Sheila was in the front office. Her lasting memorial will probably be ABODE, though she also brought the orchestras, conductors and soloists of the world to Cork advancing the great love of music and what it brings to each person.

There are two short stories which further illustrate Sheila's colorful approach. She was at a dinner in a leading hotel and ordered salmon. The waiter came with a very large platter covered by a very large dome. He removed the dome, Sheila looked at the plate, raised her head to the waiter and said: "I think on this occasion John West took the best."

On another occasion she arranged to meet two friends for coffee at the Crawford Gallery. It was very busy and on this day there was a queue going down a deep corridor outside and down the railings. Sheila marched in and went straight to the top of the queue and enquired if she could have a table for three. "Have you booked, Mrs. Goldberg?" asked the waitress. "Booked, no," said Sheila with great surprise and even slight hint of indignation. "Oh, I'm so sorry, we are full at the moment," uttered the waitress nervously. Sheila pointed to a table and enquired about it. "That is reserved, Mrs. Goldberg. I am so sorry." Sheila looked around and spotted something: "Well," she said, "what about that one there?" The waitress looked and said: "I am sorry, that is only for two." "Well," Sheila replied, "you could put another chair there and we will be fine." It was done.

Chapter 15

TALKING & POLITICS

The object of oratory alone is not truth, but persuasion.

Thomas Babington Macaulay

Nothing is so unbelievable that oratory cannot make it acceptable.

Cicero

W hen Gerald and Sheila made their visit to South Africa in 1987, they were greeted in Cape Town by Leonard and Sandy Hotz (*née* Weinronk). The Weinronks and Goldbergs are cousins from Lithuania and then Limerick. After drinks outside, dinner was served and, as Sandy said, it was piping hot, but Gerald felt that he needed to make a short speech. Everyone was in the dining room. Sheila looked at him, rolled her eyes to heaven and asked: "Is this going to be a short long speech, or a long short speech." Sandy thinks that three quarters of an hour later Gerald sat down. Robert Lentin, another cousin, doesn't remember the length of the speech but recalls that Gerald left everyone with a good impression. The food wasn't quite as hot as it had been, but that seemed not to affect anyone, as they were all charmed. It was what he was good at. Speaking.

Talking and Speaking

I suppose there is not much difference between talking and speaking. Gerald didn't really talk: he spoke. He had loved to speak since he was a student in UCC at the debating societies. He stood up to speak. He said that he practiced before a mirror, and advised young students to do the same. I can see him pacing from his room in the office and along the short corridor to the reception station and back, up and down, trying to tease out a legal problem – maybe an argument or speech to a jury or a tactical problem. There were many evenings when he paced up and down the back lawn of Ben-Truda, a large space, talking or arguing with himself. Sometimes, his finger pointed or wagged.

When people came to Ben-Truda, he entertained them by speaking to them about his latest research project. There were many. What he didn't really do was sit and have a conversation with someone, as one might in the pub or the hairdressers. He either listened or he spoke. But he spoke in paragraphs, as though he were writing a history with lectures illustrated by slides.

The Cork Literary and Scientific Society was organized by a lady named Cynthia Treston. She was flamboyant and vivacious, tended to wear colorful floral dresses and wonderful hats pitched at an angle on her head, had grey hair, glasses, and was always very well dressed. She dripped with large pieces of jewelry. Just about every year, she invited Gerald to give a talk on his most recent travels with Sheila. They went to Italy a lot. To prepare for these talks, he read copiously and quickly. Morton on Rome was one, I recall. From this, he was able to include history and such anecdotes as he gleaned from his reading. He was entertaining.

However, his photography lacked composition and precision. Sheila's head – or her arm or hand – was often cut off. These photographs were diapositives made on glass which he managed to break often. The society got publicity for the season in the *Cork Examiner* (September 13, 1952). The program included the historian A.L. Rowse, actor Robert Speight, photographer G.A. Carter, Sir Conrad Carfield on India, Lt.-Col. J.H. Williams on elephant management, Walter Higham on birds, Major Leonard Handley on the chateaux of the Loire, as well as Sir Charles Petrie. Among the local people to entertain the society were Gerald, Fr. M. O'Dwyer, Stuart Bently, Alec Day, Mrs. Treston and "the good companions." The Society brought some very important speakers each season. In 1953, Ambassador William Taft, the American Ambassador, was a guest, as was W.H. Murray, deputy leader of the Everest Expedition. More was heard from the bird man, Mr. Higham. Caleb Webb, Director of Dublin Zoo, talked on his trip to Kenya. Gerald lectured on our visit to the Edinburgh Festival, illustrated with slides and records.

In December 1956, Gerald also lectured on "Towards an appreciation of Opera" at the UCC Art Society. In that lecture, he imparted quite "a wealth of information on its various aspects" (*Cork Examiner*, December 14, 1956). His talk was described as a "real treat." He used a wide range of excerpts on high fidelity equipment. Among the composers covered were Wagner, Bizet, and Puccini. There were also illustrations. The meeting was chaired by Aloys Fleischmann, and it is more than probable he would not have invited Gerald to do this unless he was confident that Gerald knew enough about opera. But Gerald was knowledgeable about a lot of things, because he was able to read copious amounts of material and remember it. His mind was like the sorting office of *An Post*: information went into different Dictaphone belts.

There wasn't a *bar mitzvah* or wedding at which he did not speak. Gerald and Sheila often went to Dublin for these *simchat* (parties). His speeches were amusing, although Sheila made sure he didn't speak for too long. She gave him feedback afterwards, and she was not shy about telling him if it was good, or not, too long, or not funny.

The President of the Dublin Hebrew Congregation for many years was another very well-established solicitor, Herman Good, who ended his career on the District Court bench. One day, Judge Good was dealing with the parking ticket list. The defendants came up one by one and he asked each one his occupation. He imposed a fine of £1 in each case until the person before him was a draper. "19s.11d," said Herman Good.

Herman was also an extremely good after-dinner speaker. At functions, it was usual for Gerald and Sheila to meet Herman and Sibyl. But the fun started when Herman spoke first. He was witty, and erudite, but he loved to have a go at Gerald, whom he called "that man from Cork." And when Gerald rose to reply, he had fun in responding to Herman that he would "pay the transfer fee to bring him to Cork."

This difference between talking and speaking is illustrated by how Gerald and Sheila related to people. At these functions, Sheila conversed; Gerald spoke. It was always like this. Sheila had chat and fun with guests in Ben-Truda. Gerald did too, but in a different way: it is not that he was stuffy or pompous, although he could be. It was that he never had the art of general conversation, or what is commonly called "small talk." Sheila would have friends in for tea and they chatted all afternoon, about anything and everything. Gerald had no gift for this sort of talk.

When I started in practice. Gerald used to call me on Friday night, not to wish me *gut Shabbos*, but to give me my instructions for Motions on Monday in the High Court. When he finished, he would say: "I will hand you to Mammy." He was gone, but she would talk for ages.

If Gerald was not an invited speaker at an event, he would speak from the floor. There was a weekend seminar in both the Aula Maxima, UCC, and the Imperial Hotel over December 9 to 11, 1967. I am not entirely clear what it was about. The meeting on Friday night was full to capacity. John Healy (*Western People*, December 9, 1967), said:

> It was a tremendous experience. It was marvelous to see those young lads like John Naughton being involved and trying to make things better. It was delightful to see young Naughton, who turned out to be a great little Chairman, being tested by an old-line performer like Gerald Goldberg, solicitor and lately politician, who challenged him from the floor and who was absolutely shredded by one cool remark from the Chair.
>
> Cllr. Goldberg questioned whether Ireland had cancer of the soul and argued that if it were so, cancer was incurable. Young Naughton, without getting up, remarked deadly evenly: "Cancer can be cured if we diagnose it early enough."
>
> No more was needed. The perfect answer.
>
> The house rose to him and Gerald Goldberg, who was one of the main figures in the Cork Tribunal, told me afterwards he had scored brilliantly.

When he was retired, Gerald was asked to lecture to the law students at the Faculty of Law, UCC. He did so, and no doubt he would have enjoyed it as well as imparting a lot of advice and practical knowledge. The UCC Law Society inaugurated a silver medal for debating and named it after Gerald.

The Importance of Books

Gerald always wore his Judaism on his sleeve. But religion alone was not Gerald's only distinguishing characteristic. He had a highly developed intellect; his enjoyments were principally found in books, music and art. Interestingly, Gerald also remembers that his father read to them in Russian and translated as he read. The writers he read from were, among others, Tolstoy and Pushkin. Gerald said he had read these writers in English by the age of 10. That might have been a daunting task at such a young age, but then he was not an ordinary child. Gerald bought books with such money as he saved. The first books were from the Tinkers Library series which cost 6d in the 1930s and 1940s, and included classics.

Gerald's bookplate, designed by Elizabeth Friedlander.

A trait which continued through his life was reading newspapers at the dinner table. It was always set with two jugs of water, one at each end. Gerald used one to prop up his folded papers as he read quickly through them. He scoured them for information: The *Cork Examiner* (as it then was), *The Irish Times*, and *Daily Telegraph*. He collected information like a detective, remembering where he found it. Sometimes Sheila got frustrated with this reading and she would say, "Yaelie, put your newspaper away and talk to us." Gerald would put the newspaper down, look down the table, and say, "What would you like me to talk about?" It killed any hope of a conversation. Sometimes, when he found an item which amused him, he would read it to us.

Not until later in life did he amass his art collection, though the acquisition of books and records was constant. Gerald played music all his days.

Writing

For all that he read and spoke, it seemed as if Gerald never found a voice in which he could write. He did try: he wrote one thesis for an M.A. on the subject of *Jonathan Swift and the City of Cork*. This related to a period of Swift's life where there were four months that could not be accounted for. Gerald, using his forensic skills, unearthed the story of those months.

He also tried to write stories about his past and his antecedents, but for all that, his writing always had to veer into literary history. Literary, historical, and biblical figures appear in some of these drafts. He calls himself Yoel. He did not write about what his books meant to him and what they told him. He did not find a door which opened into clear air, where he could see his path. It is as though he had a car full of materials, but he couldn't start it. He was elderly before he started trying to write; he was good at research, and could find the earth under enigmas and obscure matter. He did a good paper in 1982 on Joyce for *The Crane Bag*, where he worked out who the dog Garryown was.

However, Gerald did not take criticism. There was an occasion when he was staying in our house in Dublin. Carla and my daughter, Trudi, were there. I believe I was somewhere down in a country court. At the time, he was engaged in his second thesis. This was for a doctorate. He began by examining the Jewish influence in Shakespeare: an enormous task. To do this, he set out to read all of the plays in several different editions. Then he read many academic and critical texts. But after a number of years, he found that he had taken on too much, so he changed his focus to a discussion of *The Merchant of Venice*. Gerald's thesis was that Shakespeare was not antisemitic, arguing from a reading of Shylock's speech to Antonio after the request for a loan: Christians viewed Jews as stubborn and obstinate people who refused to accept something that didn't fit in with their preconceptions. They didn't accept Christianity because it didn't fit into how prophesies of the Messiah could be fulfilled, and the example given is Shylock's twice refusing the money for his bond. He was being stubborn, because he couldn't see what was in his best interest. So, he says: "Hath not a Jew eyes? ... If you prick us, do we not bleed? If you tickle us, do we not laugh? If you poison us, do we not die? And if you wrong us, shall we not revenge? If we are like you in the rest, we will resemble you in this...." (*Merchant of Venice*, Act III, Scene I). Trudi, then a young teenager, and studying the play at school, put it to Gerald that Shakespeare would have been as antisemitic as the rest of society at the time. Trudi's argument was that when Shylock asks these questions, Shakespeare's answer is "No." Gerald sat and listened, but he simply did not hear her words. There was no discussion. He really could not accept an alternate interpretation. *The Merchant of Venice is* an antisemitic play. The fact that it is described as comedy demonstrates this: the Jew gets his comeuppance. Yet, Gerald couldn't see it. This was as strange as a sailor being unable to read the sea.

It is clear that Gerald did not understand what formed the basis of a doctoral thesis. He needed a hypothesis, and yet he couldn't formulate one, despite all the promptings from his professor and the family. Though he applied his considerable skills, as though he was defending Shakespeare (no stranger to courts and law himself) before a jury, it was never really clear to Gerald what he was defending him *against*. The thesis was never finished. How far he got with it I do not know. In a letter to Paula, Sheila said it was finished except for the notes and references, yet there is no completed text, only copious pages of notes and drafts of references.

There are other instances where he failed to complete his research efforts. For example, Gerald discovered information about the Jewish Cemetery in Kemp Street, not far from the Synagogue in Cork. Knowing there had been one somewhere near there, he had been trying to research it for a long time without success. He wrote to all the solicitors in Cork, and asked them if they ever came across any reference to anything "Jew, Jewish, or Jewish burial ground" in a Title Deed, would they let him know. After about 10 years, he was contacted by a solicitor who had found such a reference. There is a paper in his own hand in the Goldberg Special Archive, UCC, in which he wrote up this history. There is a little reference to the research. He told us the story, and the way he told it was very exciting. Carla said he should write it up just as he told it, but Sheila responded: "He couldn't do that. It's not the way he thinks."

Politics

Sometimes Gerald had a head full of ideas. What he expected would result from these did not always happen. There were, sometimes, adverse results. I am thinking about 1962, when he had already taken an interest in the Southern Law Association. He was Vice-President, and it was automatic that he would be elevated to the Office of President, except in Gerald's case that did not happen. When he was proposed for President, someone else was also nominated, and when it went to election he was blackballed – in other words, defeated. There was a *putsch* against him which both angered and depressed him. He couldn't understand how this could happen in the 1960s. It caused him grief for a long time. He saw it as an antisemitic act, and it may have been one of the triggers which caused him to side-step the Southern Law Association. After that defeat, he disassociated from the solicitors and refused to have anything to do with them for many years. That was Gerald's way of dealing with problems or people whom he believed had betrayed him. "To hell with them," he would have said to himself or Sheila. It might have caused him to aim higher. Instead, Gerald ran for election to the Incorporated Law Society and was elected to the Council in 1965.

He made a number of very good friends there. When he was a student, he knew Ignatius Houlihan (see the *Jehovah Witnesses Case,* **Chapter 6**), whose son Michael took over his father's practice and built it up considerably. He became President of the Law Society in 1982/1983. Michael and Gerald were also very good friends, and Michael attempted to mend some fences with the Southern Law Association by having a Dinner for Gerald at the Law Society. Some members from the Southern Law Association attended, and it did ease relations.

In 1967, Gerald decided to enter local politics and to run for Cork Corporation, for the North West Ward: the area of Gurranabraher. Churchfield, and Mayfield. He had no experience in politics. His only previous campaign was for the Council of the Incorporated Law Society. Local politics was very different. His constituency was all of the eligible citizens of the Ward areas, amounting to several thousand voters. Because he was known as "GY" by many people, he decided he would use his initials in his campaign leaflets, **Gerald Y. G**oldberg, and Nancy, his daughter-in-law, provided the slogan: "Who speaks for you?" He placed advertisements in the local papers seeking volunteers to canvas support. A meeting was called in the Imperial Hotel, and he had a very big response.

Several people came on board, some taking positions of responsibility and others being foot soldiers. Every night the volunteers knocked on doors, engaging voters and handing out literature. Sheila had a big part to play in this. She was already a very experienced organizer in the Cork Orchestral Society, Meals on Wheels and Lunchtime Concerts. She put her mind to Gerald's campaign and sorted out all the details and made all the arrangements. Every night the volunteers pounded the pavements. It was a successful campaign, and Gerald was elected on the first count with the highest number of votes.

One of Gerald's election cards.

However, once elected as an Alderman, Gerald found he was one of only two Independents. They had no power and could not do anything. It was difficult to survive against the two big parties. Gerald sought to break the pact between the parties when he ran for the Mayoralty in 1970. He was proposed by another Independent who said in his nomination speech that Gerald had done great work for everyone since his election to the Corporation. "I hope and pray he will be elected tonight," he said, "but I know it will be a miracle if he is." Gerald seconded his own nomination and made a strong plea for the Councilors' votes. He told them that it was fortunate we lived in a democracy. Freedom was the watchword. He said the Mayoralty was in the gift of the big parties but said independents "had equal and inviolable rights." The office was not something to be bought or sold or bartered. "It is necessary," he said, "that the world in general and the North of Ireland in particular should be aware of the fact that it is possible in this proud city of Cork for an Alderman to be elected Lord Mayor of Cork without any regard to class, creed, or religion." He made a challenge to the Councilors to make history: "Tonight is the first time in the 1,000 years in which this city has existed that a member of the Jewish faith is offered to the people of Cork as its Lord Mayor. Is there a Councilor," he asked, "who will have the honor to say to the people: 'I will not accept my party whip this evening and I will vote as I think I should without regard for pact, barter or agreement.' The moment of truth has arrived." After the vote was called, the result was: Barry, 16; O'Se, 13; and Goldberg, 2. It had been expected that Alderman Peter Barry T.D. would be elected as the Fine Gael nominee. This demonstrated clearly to Gerald that an Independent could not achieve anything without a party machine behind him. He could not, therefore, achieve his goal unless he joined a party.

Dr. John O'Mahony (Fianna Fáil) was then the youngest Councilor on the Cork Corporation. He had read medicine in UCC but he also had a strong interest in law. He read for the Bar and when he qualified, he went to the District Court to listen to Gerald. They became friends and remained so until Gerald's death. John admired Gerald enormously and wrote a beautiful obituary. When they were Councilors, another Fianna Fáil man, Dave Buckley, who was a barber in Shandon Street, realized that Gerald had a great interest in the Lord Mayoralty. Not only that, but they knew he would be very good for Cork and Ireland. They set about bringing him into Fianna Fáil. In or about 1973, Gerald joined a Fianna Fáil branch (*cumann*) in South Douglas. This was probably his last chance, according to John O'Mahony, to become Lord Mayor. He became a Fianna Fáil councilor which enabled him to have a tilt at becoming Lord Mayor, but he had to wait a few years.

PART
THREE

Chapter 16

THE LORD MAYORALTY

But I being poor have only my dreams;
I have spread my dreams under your feet;
Tread softly because you tread on my dreams.
W.B. Yeats, *Aedh Wishes for the Cloths of Heaven*

I n 1977, when he was 65, Gerald put his name forward as the Fianna Fáil nominee for Lord Mayor of Cork and won the nomination. The election for Lord Mayor was held on June 27, 1977, and he was elected. As the *Cork Examiner* (June 28, 1977) put it, he had "fulfilled his life's ambition and dream." All the national papers reported that he was Cork's first Jewish Lord Mayor. He wanted to be the first citizen of the city and, by achieving that office, he was telling everyone he was *primus inter pares* (first among equals). He had seen the back of any personal antisemitism. People could no longer attempt to push him out; he was now in, and well in. It had been a long journey. The wars he had fought repeatedly, since his youth, since those his father first fought in the streets of Limerick, and those which Gerald fought again in 1965 and 1970 (*see* **Chapters 7** and **8**), were at last at an end. The possible bitterness he experienced as a student in college, and later with his colleagues, was now over.

In *For Better, For Worse* (RTÉ, 1977), Sheila was asked how important it was to her that Gerald had been elected Lord Mayor. She said he had wanted it for a very long time, it made him very happy, and so it made her very happy too. She added that it made her realize that now nobody could say there is bigotry or antisemitism or anything. "I think it is a very good thing for Cork in that sense." But Gerald tried to put forward a different perspective. He dismissed the idea of bigotry or antisemitism. Strangely, he said that neither had arisen *at any time*. It was a question of "colleagues in the Cork Corporation... selecting somebody... they felt merited and deserved it." But this is not in accord with his first failed attempt when he offered himself for election independently as the first Jew in 1,000 years to seek election. Then, he invited the Councilors to ignore their whips and vote for him because of who and what he was. In the end, the decision was purely political.

Gerald's life ambition was to wear the gold collar of St. Sulpicius, Bishop of Bourges (*circa* 624-647) and so he wore the Mayor's Chain of Office with pride. In fact, he was so proud that he researched and wrote a pamphlet, *Terence MacSwiney and Cork's Gold Collar of S.S.*, which he gave to visitors. The links of the chain are joined alternately by links of looped gold and enameled cinquefoils, 51 links in all, terminating in a portcullis. Attached to the chain is a medallion bearing on the obverse the City Arms and on the reverse the following inscription:

Cork, 9th June 1787. The Right Worshipful Samuel Rowland, Esq.,
Mayor, was publicly invested by the Common Speaker, on behalf
of the Commons, in open Court of D'Oyer Hundred with the Gold
Chain and immediately after the Mayor conferred the like
Honour on the High Sheriffs, and lastly the Ceremony of
investing the Mayor with this Pendant and Collar of S.S. was
performed by a Deputation from the Council.

In recent times, the goldsmiths of Cork also made a medallion for the Lady
Mayoress.

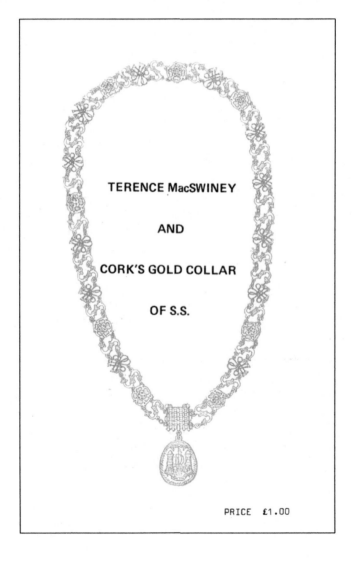

TERENCE MacSWINEY

AND

CORK'S GOLD COLLAR

OF S.S.

PRICE £1.00

Never one to miss an opportunity, in his first address to the Council, Gerald spoke in English, Irish and Hebrew. He recited the *Shehecheyanu* (a blessing which gives thanks for "being sustained and enabled to reach this day"). During his speech to the Council, Gerald said he was a Corkman, born and bred. He was proud of the city and its people. He said he would call on the Catholic and Church of Ireland Bishops and ask them to appoint chaplains to advise him. He emphasized that he wanted it to be known in Cork that it was a tolerant city. He spoke about love and referred especially to Northern Ireland.

He mentioned that one of his priorities was to ensure that Sheila had an office. She was equal in status and had the same rights as he had. A Lady Mayoress had never been involved in the work of the Mayoralty before, and no room existed for her, but one was provided by the city manager, Joe McHugh. Sheila was able to meet women's groups, initiate projects, and pursue her own objectives.

Gerald said that he would go out among the citizens and find out what sort of Lord Mayor and Lady Mayoress they wanted. He said: "I am interested in the weaker sections of the community, but I am not exclusively referring to the poor or less well off. I am concerned as much with youth as old age and as much with education as industry." He also said he was concerned with battered wives and women. Sheila said she intended to increase her involvement with voluntary organizations. She referred to the Cork branch of Meals on Wheels which she had founded.

Gerald also indicated that he was going to make the Lord Mayor's Parlor (the Lord Mayor's Chamber is called a parlor) available to local artists for exhibitions as he wanted to help them become better known. The Choral and Folk Dance Festival was something else he thought needed assistance; another task was to improve relations between the North and South.

After the public speeches, people were able to meet the new Lord Mayor and Lady Mayoress. The public gallery had been full. And later, there was one great event back in Ben-Truda, where the champagne and conversation flowed all night.

The next morning having taken calls from well-wishers, and attended to a large volume of work, he went to the District Court where he told the Justice that he was resigning from practice for the year (*Cork Evening Echo*, June 28, 1977).

Gerald Goldberg, Lord Mayor of Cork. (Photo: Irish Jewish Museum, Dublin)

Gerald was interviewed by several radio stations, including by Gay Byrne on RTÉ in his morning show. His election received coverage in all the Irish newspapers, but also in *Maariv, The Jerusalem Post*, both Israeli papers, and *The Jewish Chronicle*.

On a courtesy call to Bishop Con Lucey, with Joe McHugh, City Manager.
(Photo: Irish Jewish Museum, Dublin)

Gerald with Sean and Minnie Gill and their family.

Meeting Frank Daly, President, and members of the Southern Law Association.
(Photo: Irish Jewish Museum, Dublin)

Gerald officiating with Mairín Lynch, Aloys Fleischmann, An Taoiseach,
Jack Lynch, Sheila, Joan Denise Moriarty, Anne Fleischmann and
members of the Cork Ballet Company at a celebration to mark the 25th
anniversary of the establishment of the Company.
(Photo: Irish Jewish Museum, Dublin)

Sheila wrote to her brother Stanley and his wife Litzi (June 31, 1977), expressing her unbridled joy:

> *Seomra an Ard-Mhéara*, Lord Mayor's Room,
> *Halla na Cathrach*, City Hall,
> *Corcaigh*, Cork.
>
> Dearest Stanley, dearest Litzi,
>
> There is no way I can describe to you the greatest joy of the past few days. *Simcha* supreme. From the moment that Gerald was invested with his chain of office, looking superb and to the manor born, his recital in Hebrew of the *Shehecheyanu*, his wonderful speech and the applause of the people all standing and cheering and clapping and then my turn to receive the gold medallion and roses and roses and roses and roses from the many women's organizations that I have worked with over the years and from friends who wished us well. There was such a feeling of goodwill and happiness and I felt that for Gerald and me this was the crowning of all our work and endeavor and the washing away of the many frustrations and disappointments that came with the years. It was glorious in the true sense of the word and there was an elation and happiness that I experienced only once in my life on my wedding day. May this be as gratifying and bring as much to us as that day 40 years ago did. We had a wonderful party afterwards. I had asked some friends back for a drink. We got back to find the house bursting at the seams with people in every room and the kitchen and hall and at two in the morning and four cases of champagne later, the last one left! I thought of you all and mostly Ben and Trudi and I could almost hear Ben say, "What the hell do you want it for and are you mad?" and that's what he would have said but I know in his heart he and of course dearest Trudi would have been proud too.
>
> The next year will be a hard and demanding one. Already the next few weeks are pretty full, and I know they are only a sample of what is to come later. Whatever, I am going to enjoy it D.V. This is one year.
>
> Enclosing some press as promised.
>
> Glad Susan is making a good recovery. Send her my fond love and best wishes. This letter will have to suffice for all the family. Dearest and warmest love and love and love to you all.
>
> As always, your affec. (*sic*) sister, Sheila (The Rt. Hon. Lady Mayoress of Cork!)

*Maura Pyne, Aloys Fleischmann, Mairín Lynch, Gerald and
Sheila, and Jack Lynch.*

*Gerald presenting a painting by David Goldberg to Diarmuid Ó Donnabháin,
Curator of the Cork Municipal Art Gallery.*

Gerald and Sheila, with Val, Theo, Nancy, John, Litzi and Stanley Smith.
(Photo: Irish Jewish Museum)

By this time, Sheila had many of her projects well established or on the way to being so. Meals on Wheels, the Lunchtime Concerts, and the Cork Orchestral Society were still important to her. Meals on Wheels was close to her heart because she was concerned with the disadvantaged. As Ruth Fleischmann pointed out to me in conversation, "She lived in relative comfort, but gave a lot of thought to people without homes, or a breakfast in the morning: the destitute and deprived." That she took on their cause was a reflection of the connection which she and Gerald had for them. She had empathy: Gerald also served the poor of Cork in his practice. Their experiences fueled a desire to do something, and their understanding of the immigrant experience also helped them to enrich the lives of the people of Cork. They brought these insights to the Mayoralty. In particular, Sheila spent a lot of time trying to house people.

As Lord Mayor and Lady Mayoress, they received invitations every day to attend various and numerous functions. They opened exhibitions, ate Association dinners, attended Annual General meetings, received dignitaries, Cardinals and Bishops, Ambassadors, the Mayor of Limerick, the head of the Israeli Tourist Office, the victorious Cork Hurling team who won the Liam McCarthy Cup for the 23rd time, attended funerals and Masses, heard a lot of music, and much more.

Gerald opened a new foot bridge between Union Quay and Morrison's Island on October 14, 1977, very near the synagogue on South Terrace. It was called Trinity Bridge, but Cork humorists immediately dubbed it "the Passover" because Gerald opened it.

They presented endless trophies to students for excellence. They opened day centers for distressed women. Sheila ran fashion shows in aid of charities, and presented prizes for the tidiest district in the city. In September 1977, she began an anti-litter campaign and she continued to beat that drum on every suitable occasion for the rest of the year. In the same month, they had a Lord Mayor's reception in Fitzgerald's Park, in the Mardyke. The welcome sign was in Irish, Hebrew and English. There were concerts at the Cork School of Music in their honor, because of the significant role they played in the music and artistic life of Cork. For them, these were functions of the office – tiring but very exciting. They were out somewhere every day, including Saturdays and Sundays.

Trudi Goldberg, in the garden at Ben-Truda.

At the time of their election, my daughter Trudi was staying with Gerald and Sheila. When the journalist Maureen Fox went to visit and interview Sheila, she learned from Trudi, who was then four, that *Bubbe* and *Zeida* (Yiddish for grandmother and grandfather) were the new Lord Mayor and Lady Mayoress of Cork (*Cork Examiner*, June 29, 1977). Maureen went to do the interview because, in most Mayoralties, the Lady Mayoress does not have a role other than to turn up for functions. She asked the question: "What is Sheila really like behind the personality that is so much an integral part of her?" and spent the morning talking to Sheila "… in her elegant home, surrounded by the things she values most – a garden bubbling over with flowers, tame lawns and inside fascinating sculpture at every turn of the head." Through Trudi, Maureen glimpsed how much grandchildren meant to Sheila.

In the interview, Sheila also talked about her Judaism with which she was comfortable and happy. For her, Judaism was a way of life, not a dogma. She emphasized her home and family, and talked about the community and its decline since she arrived in Cork, 40 years earlier.

> Talking to Sheila Goldberg, one is immediately conscious of her serenity, she has a quiet and active sense of humor, but even this is gentle and subdued. She just doesn't lose her temper – even with a young grandchild competing for attention – but there is one topic on which she is particularly vocal.

This led into her campaign to clean up Cork. "If only we could clean up Cork," Sheila said. "I took Trudi to Fitzgerald's Park and the Lough the other day – beautiful places utterly spoiled by rusting Coke tins and crisp bags. The litter is sickening, and I feel so ashamed when visitors arrive. There is so little civic spirit here. It is unbelievable. You cannot expect the Corporation to do everything: it is up to the individual." Later in the interview she expressed her desire to return to Belfast with Gerald as Lord Mayor and Lady Mayoress of Cork: "That would be a wonderful experience," she smiled, "and of course it would illustrate that Cork people are not sectarian; after all we are Jews."

Maureen continued:

> Always content to remain in the background and help her husband unobtrusively, one immediately senses that Sheila is a tower of strength, an implacable comrade in good and bad times because she has an indefinable quality of caring that draws people to her. She is going to enjoy being Lady Mayoress, it will give her an opportunity to indulge in one of her favorite past-times: meeting people.

As Maureen Fox was leaving, they walked on the gravel in front of Ben-Truda, and Sheila said: "You know, Maureen, people are very important to me. Things are not."

Maureen ended the article saying:

> Cork is once again lucky to have a Lady Mayoress of whom it can
> be proud – I believe, in her quiet way, Sheila Goldberg will impart
> to this Office her own special brand of dignity and graciousness.

Indeed, she did, but it was done in both her quiet way and in her determined way.

When it came to litter, she really hit the high notes. Gerald took up the topic a few days after his election. He said that he would give the "anti-litter campaign, introduced in the Churchfield area by his predecessor Sean French, his fullest support, and that the Lady Mayoress was also engrossed in this problem" (*Evening Echo*, June 29, 1977). She was not only engrossed, but unwavering. The campaign went very well according to reports. By November, Litter Wardens had been employed, but it was not enough. At the end of the period of office (June 1978), Sheila made a speech in which she used her great sense of humor to drive home her point: "I'll be out of a job soon, and I'd really love to start work as a hygiene inspector in the city – I'd close the whole place down" (*Cork Examiner*, June 14, 1978). She regretted her failure to fulfil the pledge she had made to clean up the city. The report said: "It is fair comment to say that Mrs. Sheila Goldberg has been one of the most effective Lady Mayoresses this city has known. And she has worked hard!" When she went to schools, 58 of them, she talked to the students about litter. She wanted to impose substantial fines on adults for throwing away cigarette packets, and fines on children for throwing away lollipop papers.

She did not confine her remarks to Cork; she also gave both Dublin and Limerick a lash of her tongue. She wanted the people drawing social welfare to be equipped to clean the streets. Everything to do with hygiene was included: supermarkets and shops too. So, for all the effort she put into this campaign, it did not satisfy her. Sheila had a wonderful way of expressing her anger over such things privately. She would resort to Yiddish, which she spoke very well. She had a way of putting great expression into the use of the words like "*Gemuldich,*" or "*Schmutzich,*" or "*tzucht*" (words for "dirty").

A Visit to America

St. Patrick's Day on March 17 is a time when the country usually empties of politicians. Government Ministers disperse to different cities around the world, all with the objective to sell Ireland; the Taoiseach (the Irish Prime Minister) usually is invited to The White House in Washington for a St.

Patrick's Day celebration where he presents the President of the United States of America with a bowl of shamrock. These visits are all good for Ireland. Even Lords Mayor were invited to America, and Gerald was included. After consideration, he and Sheila decided that they did not want to desert the people of Cork or deprive them of their First Citizens on this important festive day. So, they decided they would stay home and have the celebrations here.

Gerald and Sheila, John, Nancy, Abigail, Jacob, Micala, Frank Rutzollo, Mayor of Philadelphia and Córas Tráchtála staff. (Photo: Debbie Levy Archive)

However, Córas Tráchtála (the Irish Export Board) was very anxious for Gerald and Sheila to do an American trip and to promote Ireland and Irish products. A visit to New York and other US cities was arranged for a few weeks before St. Patrick's Day. "Mayor to open huge US promotion" was the headline in the *Cork Examiner* of March 3, 1978. This promotion was the largest and most ambitious promotion of Irish food in the United States, the report said. Córas Tráchtála intended to promote £500,000 of food produce in more than 400 retail outlets. Gerald and Sheila flew out with the Chief of Córas Tráchtála from Shannon Airport on a Sunday. While on the plane, the Mayoral Chain was in its traditional locked wooden box to which a leather strap was attached. This was worn around Gerald's thigh. 18th century security!

In America, Gerald was to open branches of A & P Supermarkets, Sloan's Supermarkets, and Macy's. Gerald and Sheila paid a courtesy call on Mayor Ed Koch, also Jewish, in New York. There must have been a lot of fun at that meeting. Gerald would have charmed Mayor Koch with all sorts of stories. Gerald even said to him, as Koch was a bachelor, that he could offer to make him a match: "We have many beautiful girls in Ireland," he said. Gerald invited him to visit Cork "as early as possible." He might find a wife there. Gerald said: "Life could be heavenly in Ireland with a wife and 30 or 40 cows. I cannot think of any wife better than an Irish wife." He presented Mayor Koch with a silver tray bearing the coat of arms of Cork.

Gerald with Mayor of New York, Ed Koch, 1978. (Photo: Irish Jewish Museum)

The visit also included radio and television interviews. Gerald and Sheila were present at several meetings and functions where they met businessmen and tour operators. They also attended a fashion fair. These were the type of occasions at which both Gerald and Sheila excelled; they loved meeting and speaking to people. Gerald rose to these occasions with ease, and was eloquent and witty. They were both very good for Ireland.

However, one unpleasant incident did occur while they were in New York. Gerald and Sheila were invited to a dinner given by the Irish Northern Aid Committee (NORAID). A man got up to speak and began to collect money for the IRA. This was shortly after the bombing of the La Mon restaurant in Belfast on February 17, 1978, in which 12 people died and 30 were injured. Sheila was incensed and outraged. She said to Gerald they had to leave immediately, they could not stay and be party to this. Gerald tried to calm her, but she insisted. She got up and walked out. He had to follow and so too did the others with them. It was a brave act.

Whilst they were in America, a quiz appeared in a magazine. I don't know which one, but it went something like this: "This week, Mayor Koch was visited by Gerald Goldberg. Who is Gerald Goldberg? Mayor Koch's *Cheder* teacher? An Israeli diplomat? Lord Mayor of Cork?" This gave all of us a good laugh. He had finally made it big time!

After New York, the promotion moved to Philadelphia. Whilst in that city, Gerald managed to slip away to a library to do some research on William Penn. Penn was born in Cork and, when he went to America, he bought the land which is now called Pennsylvania. Gerald told the Philadelphians they should take a much greater interest in Penn as they owed him a great debt of gratitude.

Then they went on to Dallas, where Sheila had a lot of family.

On the tour, Sheila spoke to many women's organizations including Hadassa (an American Jewish women's volunteer organization), the School Teachers Association and the Irish Women's Society of New York. She spoke about Ireland, its contribution to world civilization and its search for peace. This contribution was recognized and acknowledged by Córas Tráchtála in the special album they produced (Soroptimists, 1983).

When they came back, it was almost St. Patrick's Day. There are always parades in the morning, and on the viewing stand were the Lord Mayor and Lady Mayoress. On this occasion, the Taoiseach, Jack Lynch (who stayed at home as well), was also on the stand. The Parade was dominated by 300 Bretons in traditional dress following six bands. There were also visiting groups from Seattle (*Irish Press*, March 18, 1978). In the evening, there was a Lord Mayor's reception at the Crawford Art Gallery. It must have been a very busy and tiring day.

Freeman of the City: Aloys Fleischmann

One of the honors which a Lord Mayor can confer is the Freedom of the City. Gerald decided he wanted to do this and the city manager, Joe McHugh, approved it. Gerald selected three people, one of whom was Aloys Fleischmann. Until that time, the people who had been given the freedom were mostly Princes of the Church (Bishops) and Captains of Industry, with some politicians or diplomats as well. Certainly, no artist was ever honored.

This event was scheduled for April 29, 1978, at a special sitting of the Corporation. There was a full house, with all the Councilors in robes. Also present were representatives of the churches, business, and the arts. The city manager read the resolution of Council conferring the freedom. Gerald said he was privileged, proud and honored on behalf of the people of Cork and the Corporation to confer upon one of the city's most distinguished musicians this highest honor – a rare and distinguished privilege:

> It marks the nobility, greatness and grandeur of one man singled out by his people for special recognition. Professor Fleischmann was born to be a teacher and composer. He inspired everybody with whom he worked. He had all the qualities which go to make a great man. He revitalized the life of music in the city of Cork and, not content with that, looked forward and appreciated the qualities of dance as an art form, collaborating with Miss Joan Denise Moriarty to form what has become Irish Ballet. When the Choral Festival was first mooted, the Professor threw himself into the work of organizing a Festival which is now unparalleled in the history of our country and after some years became its Director. No one can say enough of the new Freeman, all will feel in our hearts what he means to us. We are grateful to him for what he has done for us, and we will always honor and treasure his name in our city. (Maureen Fox, *Cork Examiner*, April 29, 1978)

Aloys then signed the Roll of Freemen of the City and was presented with a silver casket containing a scroll. In his response, Aloys said that his parents were established in Cork and his grandfather was organist in the Cathedral, so no one could accuse him of being a "blow-in." He said the honor was far too generous and out of all proportion with the little he had contributed.

Aloys spent some time bemoaning the lack of money being given to the arts. He compared it with the grants given in many other European countries and took the opportunity to make his plea for more funding. "It wasn't a question of money," he said, "it was a question of priority." He mused eloquently that £300 million was spent on drink annually and if only 1% was saved, we would have financial resources for an opera company. But he added: "It would be a brave person who would advocate that any person would give up a pint of local brew to contribute to opera – the shock would probably make them drink three additional pints." While he had a captive audience, he also harangued them about the Choral Festival, music in schools, and the proper use of leisure time. But he paid special tribute to

Gerald and Sheila for their hard work and their patronage of the arts which had considerably enriched the city.

Gerald and Aloys Fleischmann outside City Hall, following the conferring of the Freedom of the City on Prof. Fleischmann, 1978.

The *Cork Examiner* devoted an Editorial to the Conferring, in which it stated that Professor Fleischmann, despite his name, has as good a Cork accent as any other native-born son. He was most worthy. His parents had made their home in Cork, and he had made Cork a name in the musical world. Cork was the music capital of the country with the Choral Festival, the National Ballet Company, Orchestra, the Opera House, and the Professor was associated with every aspect of those. He had used his organizational skills on a huge scale – the armies of Napoleon were not more difficult to maneuver than the Choral Festival: 5,000 singers from all over Europe and schools throughout Munster. The honor conferred on him was much less than the good he had done for the city.

The Last Months

It was recognized throughout the city that Gerald and Sheila had both been splendid ambassadors and representatives. They had done the city proud, as they say in Cork. Gerald had the option of running again for a second term, but he was extremely tired, in fact exhausted. They had put everything they had into the roles. They declined the offer but there is no doubt that it moved them greatly. They continued with their engagements until the end of their term when a new Lord Mayor would be elected. Much of what they did comprised of the day-to-day engagements. I have not referred to the technical work on Traveler sites, taxi driver disputes at the airport, road design and construction, and many other issues. They would not really add anything to this memoir.

Gerald and Senator George Mitchell, US Special Envoy for Northern Ireland (1995 – 2001). (Photo: John Sheehan Photography, Cork)

Gerald's last official function was to open an exhibition of mine at the Lavit Gallery on June 26, 1978. It was a nice way to finish.

> I will have many proud and happy memories of a wonderful experience as Lord Mayor. But at the end of the day, my last act as Lord Mayor brings me great pride and happiness to open this exhibition which I believe will remain amongst my proudest memories that my son has come to Cork with his works on the last day of my mayoralty.

Postscript

Gerald continued on the Council of the Cork Corporation, and the Council of the Law Society at least up to 1983 and 1985. But, in 1985, he left Fianna Fáil and joined a new party, the Progressive Democrats, formed by Desmond O'Malley. I was never clear why Gerald left Fianna Fáil, but it did fit his character, because as mentioned earlier, he had a propensity to have rows with people and cut them out of his life thereafter.

I did not know, until I started researching, that Gerald made another attempt to become Mayor. In a letter to Paula on May 2, 1983, he wrote:

> ... there is a chance that I may be elected Mayor of Cork again. It's a good chance; but, then there's many a slip between cup and lip. I will know on May 30th when my party makes its nomination. There are four candidates seeking the party's nomination.

If he had succeeded, then he would have the nomination and certain re-election on June 29. In the nomination race, John Dennehy won, Gerald came second, and the other candidates were Chrissie Ahearne and Tom Brosnan.

Chapter 17

DER ABSCHIED

One leaf
webbed gold with fawn
fluttered to my feet
and fragile as a dead moth's wing
was shattered.

Marge Piercy, *Woman on the Edge of Time*

W e do not all age together in step, and often have to rely on one another in ways we could never have imagined, much less planned for: sadly, this is how Gerald and Sheila's endings unfolded. Carla and I became more involved in the minutiae of Gerald and Sheila's daily lives.

Gerald and Sheila at Lismore Castle, 1991. (Photo: Debbie Levy Archive)

In 1978 or 1979, Gerald developed heart problems. He had over-extended himself during the year as Lord Mayor and required a by-pass, which was done in the Mater Hospital, Dublin.

Sheila was as sick as he was, with the worry of it. John, Theo and I, together with Nancy, Val and Carla, marched her around Dublin while Gerald was on the operating table. She shrank visibly before my eyes. We did whatever we could to console and humor her. Her own great humor deserted her.

Then one day, in the late afternoon, we went to visit him. He was not in good humor. Next day, after visiting him, Sheila came out in a flood of tears. "He wants a divorce," she cried bitterly. I marched in and sat down. Taking his hand, I read him the riot act. "You will not divorce. Don't be stupid. You are full of gas, and it is making you say silly things. You love her deeply. She is irreplaceable. She loves you. Look what she has done for you for the last 40 years. Don't be ridiculous." He closed up and put his head back, shut his eyes. When he opened them again, Sheila was beside him and she took his hand too. He held it firmly, and that seemed to be the end of a rather farcical episode which was likely induced by anesthetic.

He was also visited in hospital by Lord Mayor of Cork Val Jacobs, and Chief Rabbi David Rosen.

After his operation and when he had returned home, their friend Sandy Hotz from South Africa came to visit. She had booked into a Bed & Breakfast so as not to burden Sheila and Gerald. She had flown in from New York and was very tired. Despite the fact that he was not supposed to drive, Gerald met her at the airport, though she had planned to take a taxi. They had supper in Ben-Truda which Sandy cooked, as Sheila was unwell. Sandy was given a tour of the garden which reminded her of gardens in Cape Town. After supper, Sandy wanted to go to bed and thought she would phone the Bed & Breakfast and tell them she was coming. Gerald asked her for the number and said he would phone. He went away and came back and told her that he had said to the lady at the Bed & Breakfast that they could "keep the deposit and we would keep the guest." She said he was like a naughty boy with his hand in the sweet jar.

Later, Gerald showed Sandy to her room. He said he would give her a night like no other man could give her! He then handed her the manuscript for *The Tailor and Ansty* by Eric Cross. Gerald told her it was given to him by Cross in lieu of fees. I do not know what case or work he did for Cross, who had been pilloried by the people of West Cork: three priests had gone to his cottage and made him bend on his knees in front of the fire and burn his book. That was about 1942.

Sandy told me the book was wonderful and she remembered holding something in her hands which was so precious. She wished she could have read it all, but was too tired.

Hospital stays clearly had a strange effect on Gerald, who on another occasion when he had to be hospitalized, brought with him not a novel or book of crosswords (which he never did) but the two-volume *Shorter Oxford Dictionary*. He sat in bed or on a chair reading pages of word meanings. He certainly loved words and understood them very well. Of course, they were the tools of his trade, but nonetheless this was an extraordinary thing to bring to hospital.

The Mists Rolled In

Sometimes, endings come slowly and painfully. The pain is as much that of the carer as it is of the patient. For all of us, the beginning of Sheila's illness was a great trauma. The weight of it caused Gerald to collapse. I was glad that I was there and able to do something for both of them. Unfortunately, I could not be there all the time. But there were others too who kept an eye on them. I am looking back at their ending and my beginning when I had to reflect on my parents and the totality of our relationship. Inevitably there were changes, and what I had to discover was what had changed in me. At first, I did not want to look in this mirror, and for the three years of writing and researching this memoir I tried to avoid it. But I was nudged very gently to stand in front of it and take a look. It is not until now that I can put down what change has occurred; it is quite substantial.

This journey began in 2020 when I was involved in the video about Jewish Cork which I referred to in the *Preface*. By "beginning" I mean the start of the discovery of self, my parents, and our interactions as I see them now in the summer of 2023. We continually create memories and so, when the mists rolled in and the diagnosis of Alzheimer's descended like a black cloud peeping over the purple mountain, it wiped everything away. Not all at once, but gradually, and painfully. What is there without memory? Much of our essence is built on memory and, without it, we are mute.

Symptoms of the illness came gradually: for instance, sometime in the late 1980s, Sheila was in town and when she went to drive home, she could not remember the way. She went into a shop and said: "I'm Mrs. Goldberg and I don't know where I live." On another occasion, after a meeting of ABODE in Blackrock, which is very near Ben-Truda, she was coming home and reached the roundabout at the Well Road and did not know which exit to take.

Alzheimer's took hold slowly but soon became extremely worrying, and she knew all was not well. This extract from a letter to Paula is from a time when Sheila was in the early stages.

> People think I'm eccentric. I think slightly senile is more like it. I'm still working very hard. The hostel for the handicapped young people is now a reality. It's a new concept in caring and there are problems to be ironed out, but no doubt with time it will come right and stop being the headache it presently is. I don't know why I keep doing things like this. Maybe it is essential. What would I do all day with nothing to worry about?

She wanted money in her purse. Gerald gave her too much and when they went shopping, she did not know how to count or provide the correct note. Fortunately, the shop assistants recognized her difficulty.

She became restless and would no longer walk in the lovely garden she had created. Many years ago, when we were young, she and I would walk up the lawn and look at the fruit bushes and canes, like I did with Mary, but no more.

In August 1994, when she was still in Ben-Truda, but clearly uncomfortable, Gerald replied to Paula, who had suggested that he could not handle everything himself:

> ... I accept and agree that I cannot handle everything myself and I would not wish to do so...

Sheila reverted to childhood and became obsessed with going to school and that her father was waiting for her. What would he say if she was late? What would the teacher say if she was late or hadn't done her homework? She could not remember what she did. But she did ask questions as Gerald explained to Paula in the same letter:

> I cannot bring you any good news. Things progress downwards, not upwards. What light there is, strangely, is in the past. Things of today do not even glimmer. Frequently, I am asked in the early morning hours, before daylight – "Must I go to school this morning?" – and I give my stock reply – "No, darling. I have sent an excuse to the teacher, and we are both excused."

How cruel was this? How did it happen to such an amazing woman? All that she had done she could not remember. What did she do to deserve it? Why does it happen to such good people? These are like the biblical curses. The disease took away all her interests; she could not tolerate any noise – radio and television were just noise. She could neither watch nor listen. Painfully, I watched her move knives and forks from a canteen of cutlery, which had been a wedding present, from the dining room to the kitchen and then back again.

Her sense of humor, as well as her sense of direction, vanished. For a woman who laughed and made others laugh so much, and travelled to so many places, she was now vacant as though she had gone somewhere and left those vital parts of herself in an inaccessible place. Now she had forgotten how to cook. What an outrage for a woman who loved to cook and who cooked so well. She could not remember: she could not read and follow recipes anymore. It was a bitter irony.

Again, in the same letter, Gerald wrote that he had got used to being alone:

> ... As Sheila walks along the road with me, she will look at the houses of neighbors and say, with a wave of her hand and some bitterness, "Not one of them will offer us a cup of tea." Then when motor cars pass at excessive speed, she says "Not one of them would give us the wave of a hand." I tell her that they are on her "hate" lists and it works a laugh. Age means one is alone in the world and that's hard to bear. I read voraciously, books, newspapers, legal journals. Also, Sheila goes to bed at any time between 5.30 pm and 7.00 pm and I am expected to follow. So, I lock up the house and casements and don't look out of the window in search of Jessica. [*This reference must be to his unfinished thesis on* The Merchant of Venice *in which Jessica plays a major part.*] Please don't think we don't enjoy life. Indeed, we do. For example, I scour the newspapers for stories both entertaining and otherwise and I will read them to Sheila with varying success. I enclose one from last week's London *Times*. I am called – for lunch. Are you keeping well? Please let me know. You know we think of you all the time and always with love.

All through 1994, while she was still in Ben-Truda, I grieved, trying to get used to the pain of this illness, this predatory thief that had entered her mind. Seeing her so helpless at home was excruciating, and Gerald, for all the great burdens he had carried, could not carry this one.

How did Gerald cope for the first time without his dearest wife? There is no one answer. On the one hand, he could be kind and patient and on the other his refusal to accept assistance, even when it was aimed at his well-being, was extremely frustrating. For example, Mary Walsh, who for years had been coming every day for five days a week and Saturday morning also, to tidy and clean, willingly prepared a lunch every day, and left something for the week-end. For some reason, Gerald took umbrage and dismissed her. Later on, during Sheila's illness, and in his weakened condition, this action caused unnecessary difficulty. His escape was to sit in his chair and read for hours. He had horrible outbursts, doubtless caused by deep frustration at his inability to care for her.

At that time, I was commuting from Dublin to Cork three or four days a week. Long gone was the time when Sheila and I sat in the kitchen and she would say to me: "Give me a bit of your craic, Davy." By then, Gerald found it difficult to manage her condition which had become ungovernable.

While doing criminal trials, I came to know a psychiatrist, Dr. David Dunne, a director at St. Stephen's Hospital in Sarsfield Court, Co. Cork. I talked to Gerald about how best to manage her illness, and suggested that I should go to see David Dunne. I thought that the time had come to think about moving Sheila into full-time care. After a long silence, Gerald agreed.

I visited Dr. Dunne, who talked for a long time as he told me stories and smoked his pipe. When we discussed Sheila, he said it would be better if she was in care, and he recommended a new nursing home, St. Luke's, on Blackrock Road very near Ben-Truda. I went to see the home. Gerald knew I was going. When I saw it, I was most impressed. I reported to Gerald and suggested that he should see it too. He was reluctant, but agreed, so we went together. The matron, Mrs. Hickey, showed us around the beautiful location, and convinced Gerald that moving Sheila was the right decision.

All the months of challenge and frustration probably spearheaded the resolution that it was necessary to move Sheila, much as we were loath to do so. There really was no option. And, in a way, I was slightly surprised when Gerald agreed to bring her to St. Luke's. The decision was good and right for both their sakes, and the home had the advantage of being nearby, and was very well run. There was great concern there, love and empathy. As much as one could ask for.

On April 21, 1995, Gerald wrote to Paula:

I was 83 years old on April 12.

On Friday last, April 21, I brought my beloved Sheila as a patient to St. Luke's Clinic... where she was admitted as an Alzheimer's patient in Unit D. This is one of four sections of varying nature, commencing with those retired or semi-retired and going downwards to Alzheimer's and others. I succeeded hospitalizing her on a diet of lies, assuring her that she is being treated for diverticulitis. This she no longer accepts. She constantly pleads to return home. I put her off. Since yesterday, she has been under sedation. There is no treatment. The clinic is only open since November last and is the brain-child of the Church of Ireland. It is built and designed with every modern convenience.

What can I say? I am shattered, broken-hearted. I live in a well of despair. My life is over. There can be none without Sheila. Excuse this maudlin display. David is here with me at the moment. The legal term has started again, and he will be here for a few days. Otherwise, I am alone. I can suffer that, but it is suffering. I visit all day long. She knows I am there and that is good. But how long, O Lord! How long?

I send you my love.

If you do write, do so cautiously. I will try to keep in touch with you. I say "try" because letters are pouring in, and it takes time to reply.

Ever yours, Gerald

Many people went to visit her. Barbro McCutcheon made many visits to St. Luke's. Gerald visited almost every day. One day, Sheila took off her shoes and socks. Gerald knelt down and said: "I am your Prince Charming, and I am putting on your shoes and socks." The stress on him was overwhelming.

In researching this memoir, I have, of course, consulted my family, all of whom remember her with love and delight, especially from their childhoods. She was a person who related so well to children, never talking down, always seeing the individual. Perhaps this piece by Paula best sums up what they all felt for her.

My Aunt

Paula Chabanais

Working with David on this book, so many memories emerge; some jointed, others not. As a small child, I spent quite a lot of time at Ben-Truda, watching Gerald in the morning with a strange, black leather box strapped to his head and arm as he intoned morning prayers, helping Sheila in the kitchen, teasing Mary, and crying when my plaits were tied to a small chair in the kitchen by my cousins! Theo, David and I all had our tonsils out at the same time, and we all recovered at Ben-Truda with bowls of ice cream, grapes and much love. The wonderful aromas from the kitchen; the old ice cream freezer in the garage from which all kinds of goodies emerged. Hours in the garden helping her pick flowers for the house. I never wanted to leave, my home seemed so unwelcoming and cold in comparison.

However, the later years are what I remember best. In the late 1960s Sara, my daughter, took her first faltering steps in Ben-Truda, pushing Sheila's trolley from the kitchen down the hall and into Gerald's waiting arms. Now, as I read of all her achievements, I ask how on earth did she find the time to give so much love to me, just one of many? Her affection, humor and gentle wisdom helped me navigate very stormy waters from childhood to motherhood. I was never turned away.

In 1976, my family moved to Canada after which there were only a few visits to Ben-Truda, but we kept a regular correspondence.

I can't say exactly when, but at some point I became aware that Gerald's letters were becoming more frequent and emotionally revealing as hers reduced both in number and content. Gradually, as Gerald started to refer to her "condition," it became clear that she was suffering from a frightening and debilitating disease, one that would eventually rob her of herself.

I went to Ben-Truda. Gerald, aged and stoic, was profoundly sad without his lifelong companion, but we spent many hours talking. By then, Sheila was in a new nursing home in lovely grounds. Gerald went to see her every day. When he entered the sitting room, his voice would boom out, "So where's my girl?" Without hesitation, Sheila got up and went to receive a bear hug. We all went to lunch in lovely surroundings, but watching my dearest aunt stirring her orange juice with a large soup spoon and trying to butter her bread with a fork, all while looking around with an expression of complete confusion, not knowing what was happening, was my tipping point. I broke and had to leave the table. As I walked an unfamiliar corridor, a kind nurse offered a tissue and sat me down to explain exactly what was happening to my aunt's brain.

Later, I found myself alone with Sheila on a veranda, where she was sitting with a multi-colored crochet rug round her lap, muttering to herself. I took her hand in mine and we just sat, I don't know for how long, when she suddenly turned to me and said, "I don't know who you are, but I think I'd like you." We hugged.

That was the last time I saw my beloved aunt; the woman who continues to be a shining inspiration in my life; a woman who could stand both for herself and others; a woman whose courage, hard work and common sense has quietly helped thousands; a woman who taught me the importance of family. I miss her humor and her guttural "Ach" that signified her impatient understanding of humanity's foibles.

Dearest Sheila, you are with me always.

After just around two years at St. Luke's, Sheila died on November 13, 1996, and the outpouring of grief and tributes was overwhelming. Here is an extract from just one (*The Irish Times*, December 9, 1996):

.... As her black coffin was being brought to the grave at Curraghkippane in Cork the sun, as it is wont to do, shone out suddenly in long bright beams across the valley below the cemetery. The Hebrew phrases were recited; we were reminded that she stretched out her hands to the poor, that in her tongue was the law of kindness, and that her own works praise her in the gates. The sun shone, the river glinted in the valley, family and friends clustered around Gerald's stoical figure. I thought of the verse from Tennyson's *Ulysses* chosen by Gerald for what was to be their last shared message at Christmas:

> *Tho much is taken, much abides, and tho / We are not now that strength which in old days / Moved earth and heaven, that which we are, we are, / One equal temper of heroic hearts, / Made weak by time and fate, but strong in will / To strive, to seek, to find, and not to yield.*

It only remains to say, inadequately: Dear Sheila – Thank You.
Mary Leland

Gerald's Final Years

As I write about their last years, it saddens me that the renowned name of Gerald Y. Goldberg is no more on a business nameplate in Cork. I have no doubt that had he been able to relax, delegate, share, expand, he would have become a much stronger person, and could have left a thriving practice, and perhaps his relationships would have been better, offering more geniality. Nonetheless, he was a good man who gave to, and supported, many. I am convinced that had he been able to put aside the traits and characteristics that had such a negative impact on his life and ours, he would have had even greater success. But it was not within his gift to do that.

Interestingly, Sheila's illness, if there is any benefit to be drawn from such a dread disease, resulted in a more inward-looking perspective. Buried deep in my father's spirit, somewhere behind that magnificent intellect, there was a well of emotion which, for me, emerged as I read the letters he wrote to my cousin, Paula, during this time.

On November 14, 1983, when he was 71 years old, he wrote:

> We are into November now. Here, in the space of two weeks the leaves on the trees turned into myriad colors of reddish brown, russet brown, golden brown and, then, sheer gold. Suddenly, they begin to fall. The base of the trees was carpeted to a depth of four to six inches. I walked out one morning in my bare feet just to feel myself sinking into the carpet itself. I never did that before. I liked it. What a pity I haven't done it before.

This is one of the most moving pieces he wrote, and it is beautiful. Time and time again, I come back to the word "pity." For me, the pity lies not only in his words but that he so seldom wrote, or felt, like that.

In that same letter, he wrote:

> Next again, let me say, as between ourselves, that I do not feel anything like I should. Perhaps it is my age (72) (*sic*). Perhaps it is my prostrate (*sic*) operation hasn't worked. Perhaps the damn thing does more to men than I know. "There are more things in heaven or hell that woth I with of Calpurnia" (*sic*). Anyhow, I have noticed a tendency on my part towards brooding and depression. I find my mind turning towards the calculation of time left for me in this world, and the consideration of what I can achieve before I die. I look at the thousands of sheets of paper on which I have written words over the years, and I ask myself what I have done with them. I know that sokem (*sic*) of the work which I have done in the field of literary and historical research is good. I know that I brought a lawyer's mind and training to the collection of facts and to setting them out in a reasonable manner. I also realize that the spark I am looking for is not there. In short, I am unable to bring my work to life. More than that I can write and approach a subject and write, as I do, several chapters on the same theme, but in different ways and, then, I do not know which I prefer. If I try to extract the best from what I have written, I find myself in a bog into which I tend to sink. So, I may be at a turning point in my life. The fortunate thing is that I possess a sense of humor and a realization that if I am to find myself face to face with a problem I must find a solution and I think I am strong enough to do that. There are no effects which cannot be overcome. Physically, I will have to put up with my declining strength. My memory is waning. I cannot remember names, nor can I remember the titles of books or sources as I did....

When Gerald reached 90, Carla and I hosted a lunch for him in Lovett's Restaurant, a small dining room with limited space. Family came from London, America, Canada, and South Africa. There wasn't room for everyone we wanted to invite. One special guest was the Lord Mayor, Councilor Tom O'Sullivan. He spoke movingly and told a story about when he was a student at Presentation Brothers College and Gerald, as Lord Mayor, addressed the students in assembly. Gerald told the students that he came from humble beginnings, but through hard work and focus he achieved his ambition to become Lord Mayor. He said if they did the same, they could be Lord Mayor one day too. Lord Mayor O'Sullivan told that story as one that caused him to form the ambition to be Lord Mayor.

As described throughout this book, Ben-Truda was Gerald and Sheila's hub. Twice they refused to move to Dublin: once when he was invited to amalgamate his practice with a Dublin firm, but he correctly assessed that that would not work; and later when they were both elderly, Carla and I suggested that we buy a two or three-family house together with separate spaces. Gerald said: "Mammy wouldn't like that." However, it became impossible for him to remain in the house alone, and he had to go into care, a move he fiercely, and understandably, resisted. During Sheila's illness and after her death, Gerald often tripped and occasionally fell. His latest fall resulted in a broken hip, and because of multiple health problems it was not possible to operate. He was in University Hospital, where Carla, I and Jake (John's son) spent every day with him, during which time I read him Shakespeare's *Sonnets*. He never opened his eyes, but I knew he was conscious, because a tear fell on his cheek. He could hear, but not respond. I was asked for and gave permission to move him to Marymount Hospice for palliative care. He wanted to go home to pass on there. When he was moved, perhaps he thought he was going home, and within an hour of being in Marymount he let go. He was 91.

Comparable to the tributes that followed my mother's death, Gerald was equally lauded. In an extract from one obituary (*The Irish Times*, January 10, 2004):

> The death of Gerald Goldberg on December 31, 2003, has deprived the small Jewish community in Ireland of one of its most illustrious members.
>
> ... Over a long lifetime of 91 years he was vigilant for the rights of his co-religionists, built up a successful legal practice, promoted the arts in his native Cork and became the city's first Jewish Lord Mayor.
>
> While priding himself on his Irishness and how he had fully integrated into the life of Cork, he was never afraid to speak out to defend Jewish interests or oppose prejudice. He believed that the government of the day and the administration had shamefully refused to help Jewish refugees from Nazi Germany in the 1930s. As an ardent Zionist, he was attracted at various times to the idea of settling in Israel but believed that he also "owed a debt" to Ireland and stayed...

Chapter 18

BEGINNING & ENDING

Ash on an old man's sleeve
Is all the ash the burnt roses leave.
Dust in the air suspended
Marks the place where a story ended.
Dust inbreathed was a house -
The walls, the wainscot and the mouse,
The death of hope and despair,
This is the death of air.

T.S. Eliot, *Little Gidding*

I n this reflection, I have concentrated on my parent's lives as best I could. I do not know if I have done them justice or been unkind. I do want to be honest, and that wish has caused me to touch upon some sensitive aspects of their lives, especially Gerald's. He was an all-consuming study; very dominant. At times, it was like being in a maze, taking many wrong paths leading to dead ends. Indeed, I wonder if I am still in it, or if I will find the exit. I have gone down cul-de-sacs, and left many unexplored. There is only so much I can do with what I could find. What is left now is for me to try and explain what I have discovered on my journey. Writing this book has been very painful, arduous, gratifying, and emotional. I recognize all that Sheila did and achieved and how, at the end of her life, she was robbed of her dignity and humor. All that she did was good, and all that she did lives on.

Gerald was an ailing 84-year-old man when she passed. He couldn't face the trials and tribulations of everyday life without her, despite the enormity of his strength and will. Autism is a genetic condition, which is neither a disease, nor is it malevolent. In fact, it can – and is often found to – make people brilliant. Gerald, his father Laban, his grandfather Shimon, and I all have it to some degree. In retrospect, we were cut from the same cloth which put us high on the spectrum. Perhaps this prevented Gerald from taking some practical steps to alleviate his difficulties. He reminded me of grandpa in Dylan Thomas' story, *Visit to Grandpa's*, in which a stubborn old man sets out to walk to a particular cemetery because the ground was more "comfy" there. At the end he was brought back home, and he stood looking stoically out to sea.

I am Gerald's son. I watched him struggle and succeed, struggle and fail. There were the days when he smiled, was warm and jovial. There were the days when he was dark and cold. I can remember Sheila asking him, when he came home for lunch, "How did you get on today?" If he won, he might say: "I wiped the floor with him," or "I left him for dead." One thing about Gerald was that he took no prisoners. As Sheila often said: "There's never a dull moment with you, Yaelie."

Gerald adored Sheila since they first met more than 60 years earlier. He did not fail during those 60 years, but when she was no longer at his side his great intellect was not there to make sensible rational decisions. He could not manage; yet he dismissed Mary from the house without any thought as to the consequences. The only way I can reconcile this is in the context of his autism. It was a time for practical solutions; instead, he sat in front of the fire all day reading, listening to music and depending on the generosity and charity of others to help him.

What I remember most about the time of Sheila's illness is not only how it wiped out her memory, but also mine of her. I could not see her. I did not – could not – know her. The person in front of me was not Sheila, not my mother, and I wondered what would happen to my lovely memories of our times together: when she nursed me with a broken leg, giving me many jigsaws to do; going to the Edinburgh Festivals; a long car journey to San Sebastian, and its conch beaches; many nights at the ballet, the concerts and receptions in City Hall. How was I going to see her again as I knew and loved her? The dreaded disease stole from both of us like a highway robber.

We rarely see women like Sheila, especially in those years when women were not as liberated. She was unique, ahead of and beyond her time: strong, full of energy, opinionated, but amazingly efficient; capable of getting things done her way, by using the art of gentle persuasion mixed with humor and determination. She was born to bring music to people, which she did for more than 30 years. She was born to help the impoverished with concern for where they lived, how they survived, their food and shelter. Whatever she took on, she made it work. My mother must have learned fund-raising on her feet because no one taught her. I heard her many times on the phone to committee members for hours on end. Always discussing, devising, scheming when one idea sparked another. In her lifetime, she raised thousands and thousands of pounds and brought all her major projects to completion. If she is anywhere now, if her spirit still moves among us, it is evidenced by all the projects she started, and which continue to flourish to this day. These are her monuments and her legacy.

She loved to live, and to give. Her arms could reach across the firmament and gather great clusters of people. The absence of her love was so agonizing. She who had always been available, amenable, inventive, and creative, was no longer. She was my mother, and I loved her dearly.

When I started this journey, I did not know what I was looking for or what I would find. It was a journey and voyage of discovery, and I cannot say whether it is over or not. There must be more for me to discover about myself, even though I am old now. I am in my late seventies and both Gerald and Sheila would be well in excess of the century. They live on. I am not sure yet whether they are inside or outside me. That is something yet to be revealed. I can only be very proud of all their remarkable achievements. I know them by the thousand. Now I know more about them both – and myself too. They were the yin and yang of marriage who moved around each other in perfect harmony. They adored each other, they were a special couple. A pair of perfect contrasts, the *animus* and *anima,* moving like moons around each other in that wonderful celestial dance of planets, coming together, never apart. She would be so pleased to see that all she did continues quietly; and perhaps no one knows that she was the one who started it.

When I started writing, I saw Gerald as being the more dominant, because that was how he seemed to me, but as I come to the end of their stories and look back, I am bound to say that Sheila was the genius of the family.

None of us knew anything about autism. Now that I do, it can be used and controlled. You know you have it and how to work with it to your advantage. Sheila knew how to get things done. She smiled, she laughed, she cajoled, and came away with a cheque. Gerald could never do that. For him, everything was a battle, which he was determined to win. Two determined people but with very different approaches. These configurations – moving stars in the firmament – release us from each other and bring us closer together.

Now I understand much more. Our lives are entangled forever in a celestial dance around the moon, one side of which is light and the other dark and unknown. Perhaps Gerald and I spent too much time on the dark side, which becomes a place of fear.

You consume and absorb me, not in a way that is always comfortable for both of us. We grieve together over what has been and what could have been. As a child, I remember waiting for you at the hall door when you drove the old V8 up the drive at 6.00 pm and scooped me up in your arms as you opened the door and dropped your briefcase. We journeyed together a long way over a long time. You were loving, generous, and yet I was never certain if *you* were there. There were always books, reading; music, listening; and art. What a great love of these you gave me. There were fabulous times and journeys. These memories are mingled with other different and more strained times. Your arms reached out to control things. It happens in brilliant people. We are one and the same, from the same Babushka doll, one inside the other. You achieved so much, climbing the mountains, and reaching the summit. I have been eclipsed by the shadow and achieved only a little of what you did. I shall not reach it now. I do not now have the strength to roll the stone up the hill. I watch and admire you as your star drifts out over the land like fireflies falling into the trees and going out. We worked together, doing many trials and cases, though we didn't always agree. Our differences paled into insignificance over time. Now, as I look back, I am greatly saddened that you didn't achieve the one thing you really wanted: a building that bore the name of Goldberg Solicitors.

Who remembers you and Sheila now? I hope this memoir will help people to remember who you were and the magnificent and splendid contribution that you made to Cork. I would like to have achieved what you both did. I understand so much more now than I did three years ago when I began this journey, and there may be many more miles to go before it is over. These last years have been a journey of a lifetime. In looking back over the period of research and writing, I have gleaned these insights and hopefully, I have now put them in perspective.

BIBLIOGRAPHY

Alter, Robert (2013). *Ancient Israel: The Former Prophets, Joshua, Judges, Samuel, and Kings*, W.W. Norton.

Benson, Asher (2005). Storm before the Storm, in Stuart Rosenblatt (*ed.*), *Irish Jewish Genealogy*, Vol. VII.

Cesarini, David (1996). Comparative Analysis of Emigrants from Southern and Eastern Europe from US Ship Passenger Lists, 1910, in Newman, Aubrey & Massil, Stephen (1996). *Patterns of Jewish Immigration*, Jewish Historical Society.

Chessman, Ralph (1967). *Lithuanian Jewry* (3 Vols.), Tel Aviv.

Citvarienė, Davia (2022). *The Jews of Kaunas*, VSJ Kaunas (illustrated by Darius Petreikis).

Diner, Hasia (2003). The Accidental Irish, in Marc Rodriguez & Anthony Grafton (*eds.*), *Migration in History: Human Migration in Contemporary Perspective 7*, University of Rochester Press.

Drury, Ian (1994). *The Russo-Turkish War, 1877*, Osprey Publishing.

Evans, Garry (2021), Kaplan webinar.

Feeley, Pat (1980). Rabbi Levin of Colooney Street, *Old Limerick Journal*, Vol. 2, March.

Fleischmann, Ruth (2000). *Aloys Fleischmann, 1910-1992*, Mercier Press: Cork.

Fleischmann, Ruth (2004). *Cork International Choral Festival, 1954-2004*, Glen House Press: Germany.

Gannon, Sean (2020). Revisiting the 'Limerick Pogrom' of 1904, *Irish History*.

Goldberg, Gerald (1982). Ireland is the Only Country…: Joyce and the Jewish Dimension, *The Crane Bag*, Vol. 6, No. 1.

Goldberg, Gerald (*n.d.*). *Notes towards an Autobiography*, unpublished, Goldberg Special Archive, UCC, Cork.

Jewish Publication Society (1917). *Tanakh (The Holy Scriptures)*.

Keogh, Dermot (1998). *Jews in 20ᵗʰ Century Ireland*, Cork University Press.

Keogh, Dermot & McCarthy, Andrew (2005). *The Limerick Boycott, 1904: Anti-Semitism in Ireland*, Mercier Press: Cork.

Keogh, Dermot & Whelan, Diarmuid (2008). *Gerald Goldberg: A Tribute*, Mercier Press: Cork.

Klier, John D. (2011). *Russian Jews and the Pogroms, 1881-1882*, Cambridge University Press.

Linn, Roger (2011). The Macaulay School: A Jewish School in Cuckfield, *Sussex Living*.

Marcus, Fanny (*n.d.*). *A Memoir*, unpublished, Goldberg Special Archive, UCC, Cork.

Ó Gráda, Cormac (2006). *Jewish Ireland in the Age of Joyce: A Socio-Economic History*, Princeton University Press.

Petrovsky-Shtern, Yohanan (2014). *Jews in the Russian Army*, Cambridge University Press.

Rosenblatt, Stuart (2014-2018). *Irish Jewish Genealogy* (18 Vols.), Rosenblatt.

RTÉ (1965). *The Jews in Ireland*, Discovery series documentary.

RTÉ (1977). *For Better, For Worse*, documentary.

RTÉ (1983). *An Irishman, a Corkman and a Jew*, documentary.

Ryan, Des (1984). The Jews of Limerick, *Old Limerick Journal*, Vols. 17 and 18, Winter.

Ryan, Des (2002). Fr. Creagh and the Mayor's Court of Conscience, *Old Limerick Journal*, Vol. 25, Summer.

Ryan, Des (2014). Jews of Limerick from 1790 to 1903, *Old Limerick Journal*, Vol. 48, Winter.

Sandefur, Timothy (2010). *The Right to Earn a Living: Economic Freedom and the Law*, Cato Institute.

Shillman, Bernard (*n.d.*). *A Limerick Incident*, unpublished, Goldberg Special Archive, UCC, Cork.

Sirutavičius, Vladas & Staliūnas, Darius (2010). Was Lithuania a Pogrom Free Zone? 1881-1940, in Jonathan Dekel-Chen (*ed.*), *Rethinking the Pogrom in Eastern European History*, , Indiana University Press.

Staliūnas, Darius (2015). *Enemies for a Day*, Central University Press.

Taylor, Rex (1958). *Michael Collins: The Big Fellow*, Hutchinson: London.

Ury, Scott (2019). Immigration as Redemption, *Jewish Culture & History*, Vol. 20 No. 1, 3-22.

Wynn, Natalie (2014). Irish-Jewish constructs of Tsarist Eastern Europe, in Aidan O'Malley & Eve Patten (*eds.*), *Ireland West to East*, , Peter Lang.

Wynn, Natalie (2018). An Accidental Galut: A critical appraisal of Irish-Jewish foundation myths, *Jewish Culture & History* (https://v/doi.org/10.1080/1462169X.2018.1478217).

Irish newspapers cited in the text are reproduced with the kind permission of National Irish Newspaper Archives.

Other Texts Consulted

Feeley, Pat (1983). Davitt and the Limerick Jews, *Old Limerick Journal*, Vol. 14, Spring.

Feeley, Pat (1992). Aspects of the 1904 Pogrom, *Old Limerick Journal*, Vol. 11, Summer.

Fleischmann, Ruth (1998). *Joan Denise Moriarty*, Mercier Press: Cork.

Gannon, Sean (2008). Ireland's questionable 'Pogrom,' *Magill*.

Gaughan, J. Anthony (1986). *Alf O'Rahilly*, Kingdom Press.

Haddick Flynn, Kevin (*n.d.*). *The Limerick Pogrom, 1904*
(https://www.historyireland.com/the-limerick-pogrom-1904/).

Lyons, F.S.L (1977). *Charles Stewart Parnell*, Gill & Macmillan.

McConvery, Brendan CSSR (2003), The Confraternity and the Jews,
Copwsa, Newsletter of the Redemptorists.

Newman, Aubrey & Massil, Stephen (1996). *Patterns of Jewish Immigration*,
Jewish Historical Society.

Ryan, Des (1989). The Visit of Fr. Raus, 1904, *Old Limerick Journal*, Vol. 25,
Summer.

Ryan, Des (2005). Fr. Creagh, Social Reformer, 1870-1947, *Old Limerick
Journal*, Vol. 41, Winter.

Sheehan, William (2017). *A Hard Local War*, The History Press.

Staliūnas, Darius (2004). Anti-Jewish disturbances in the NW Territories in
the early 1880s, *East European Jewish Affairs*
(doi:10.1080/1350167052000340913).

ABOUT THE
AUTHOR

(Photo above: Goldberg Special Archive, UCC).

Born in 1945, David Goldberg was educated at Christian Brothers College in Cork, Trinity College and the King's Inns, Dublin.

His love of painting was often at war with his profession as a barrister and he practiced both at different stages of his life. While he grew up in Cork, and lived mostly thereafter in Dublin, he travelled extensively in Europe and the USA and later in South Africa.

This book – a memoir and analysis of his parents – explores the inner workings of a man's life and how these affect the outer aspect of the man.

INDEX

Printed in Great Britain
by Amazon

40490235R00163